Learn to Program
with C

■■■

Noel Kalicharan

Apress®

Learn to Program with C

ISBN-13 (pbk): 978-1-4842-1372-8

ISBN-13 (electronic): 978-1-4842-1371-1

Managing Director: Welmoed Spahr
Lead Editor: Steve Anglin
Technical Reviewer: Rohan Walia
Editorial Board: Steve Anglin, Louise Corrigan, Jonathan Gennick, Robert Hutchinson,
    Michelle Lowman, James Markham, Susan McDermott, Matthew Moodie, Jeffrey Pepper,
    Douglas Pundick, Ben Renow-Clarke, Gwenan Spearing
Coordinating Editor: Mark Powers
Copy Editor: Karen Jameson
Compositor: SPi Global
Indexer: SPi Global
Artist: SPi Global

Distributed to the book trade worldwide by Springer Science+Business Media New York, 233 Spring Street, 6th Floor, New York, NY 10013. Phone 1-800-SPRINGER, fax (201) 348-4505, e-mail orders-ny@springer-sbm.com, or visit www.springeronline.com. Apress Media, LLC is a California LLC and the sole member (owner) is Springer Science + Business Media Finance Inc (SSBM Finance Inc). SSBM Finance Inc is a Delaware corporation.

For information on translations, please e-mail rights@apress.com, or visit www.apress.com.

Apress and friends of ED books may be purchased in bulk for academic, corporate, or promotional use. eBook versions and licenses are also available for most titles. For more information, reference our Special Bulk Sales–eBook Licensing web page at www.apress.com/bulk-sales.

Any source code or other supplementary materials referenced by the author in this text is available to readers at www.apress.com/9781484213728. For detailed information about how to locate your book's source code, go to www.apress.com/source-code/. Readers can also access source code at SpringerLink in the Supplementary Material section for each chapter.

To my daughters
Anushka Nikita
ııııı⌐
Saskia Anyara

Contents at a Glance

Contents

About the Author

Dr. Noel Kalicharan is a Senior Lecturer in Computer Science at the University of the West Indies, St. Augustine, Trinidad. For 40 years, he has taught programming courses to people at all levels. He has been teaching computer science at the University since 1976. In 1988, he developed and hosted a 26-programme television series entitled Computers - Bit by Bit. Among other things, this series taught programming to the general public. He is always looking for innovative ways to teach logical thinking skills which go hand in hand with programming skills. His efforts resulted in two games - BrainStorm! and Not Just Luck - which won him the Prime Minister's Award for Invention and Innovation in 2000 and 2002, respectively. He is a Computer Science author for Cambridge University Press which published his international successes, Introduction to Computer Studies and C By Example. The C book is ranked among the best in the world for learning the C programming language. It has received glowing reviews from readers as far away as Australia, Canada, India and Scotland. This book is written in a more leisurely style. Born in Lengua Village, Princes Town, Trinidad, he received his primary education at the Lengua Presbyterian School and his secondary education at Naparima College. He is a graduate of The University of the West Indies, Jamaica, the University of British Columbia, Canada and The University of the West Indies, Trinidad.

About the Technical Reviewer

Rohan Walia is a Senior Software Consultant with extensive experience in client-server, web-based, and enterprise application development. He is an Oracle Certified ADF Implementation Specialist and a Sun Certified Java Programmer. Rohan is responsible for designing and developing end-to-end applications consisting of various cutting-edge frameworks and utilities.
His areas of expertise are Oracle ADF, Oracle WebCenter, Fusion, Spring, Hibernate, and Java/J2EE. When not working, Rohan loves to play tennis, hike, and travel. Rohan would like to thank his wife, Deepika Walia, for using all her experience and expertise to review this book.

About the Technical Reviewer

Acknowledgements

I would like to express my deepest appreciation to Shellyann Sooklal for the time and care she took in reading the manuscript, oftentimes finding subtle errors that a less critical eye would have overlooked.

Preface

This book attempts to teach computer programming to the complete beginner using the C language. As such, it assumes you have no knowledge whatsoever about programming. And if you are worried that you are not good at high-school mathematics, don't be. It is a myth that you must be good at mathematics to learn programming. In this book, knowledge of primary school mathematics is all that is required—basic addition, subtraction, multiplication, division, finding the percentage of some quantity, finding an average or the larger of two quantities.

Some of our most outstanding students over the last thirty years have been people with little mathematics background from all walks of life—politicians, civil servants, sports people, housewives, secretaries, clerical assistants, artists, musicians and teachers. On the other hand, we've had mathematical folks who didn't do as well as might be expected.

What will be an asset is the ability to think logically or to follow a logical argument. If you are good at presenting convincing arguments, you will probably be a good programmer. Even if you aren't, programming is the perfect vehicle for teaching logical thinking skills. You should learn programming for these skills even if you never intend to become a serious programmer.

The main goal of this book is to teach fundamental programming principles using C, one of the most widely used programming languages in the world today. C is considered a 'modern' language even though its roots date back to the 1970s. Originally, C was designed for writing 'systems' programs—things like operating systems, editors, compilers, assemblers and input/output utility programs. But, today, C is used for writing all kinds of applications programs as well—word processing programs, spreadsheet programs, database management programs, accounting programs, games, educational software—the list is endless.

However, this book is more about teaching programming basics than it is about teaching C. We discuss only those features and statements in C that are necessary to achieve our goal. Once you learn the principles well, they can be applied to any language.

Chapter 1 gives an overview of the programming process. Chapter 2 describes the basic building blocks needed to write programs. Chapter 3 explains how to write programs with the simplest kind of logic—sequence logic. Chapter 4 shows how to write programs which can make decisions. Chapter 5 explains the notion of 'looping' and how to use this powerful programming idea to solve more interesting problems. Chapter 6 deals with the oft-neglected, but important, topic of working with characters. Chapter 7 introduces functions—the key concept needed for writing large programs. Chapter 8 tackles the nemesis of many would-be programmers—array processing. Chapter 9 explains how lists of items stored in arrays can be searched, sorted and merged. And Chapter 10 deals with structures—the collection of one or more items, possibly of different types, grouped together under a single name for convenient handling.

The first step in becoming a good programmer is learning the syntax rules of the programming language. This is the easy part and many people mistakenly believe that this makes them a programmer. They get carried away by the cosmetics—they learn the features of a language without learning how to use them to solve problems.

Of course, you must learn some features. But it is far better to learn a few features and be able to use them to solve many problems rather than learn many features but can't use them to solve anything. For this reason, this book introduces a feature (like an if statement, say) and then discusses many examples to illustrate how the feature can be used to solve different problems.

This book is intended for anyone who is learning programming for the first time, regardless of age or institution. The material has been taught successfully to students preparing for high-school examinations in Computer Studies or Information Technology, students at college, university and other tertiary-level institutions.

The presentation is based on the experience that many people have difficulty in learning programming. To try and overcome this, we use an approach which provides clear examples, detailed explanations of very basic concepts and numerous interesting problems (not just artificial exercises whose only use is to illustrate some language feature).

While computer programming is essentially a mental activity and you can learn a fair amount of programming from just reading the book, it is important that you "get your hands dirty" by writing and running programs. One of life's thrills is to write your first program and get it to run successfully on a computer. Don't miss out on it.

But do not stop there. The only way to learn programming well is to write programs to solve new problems. The end-of-chapter exercises are a very rich source of problems, a result of the author's forty-odd years in the teaching of programming.

Thank you for taking the time to read this book. I hope your venture into programming is a successful and enjoyable one.

—Noel Kalicharan

CHAPTER 1

■ ■ ■

Elementary Programming Concepts

In this chapter, we will explain the following:

- How a computer solves a problem
- The various stages in the development of a computer program: from problem definition to finished program
- How a computer executes a program
- What is a "data type" and its fundamental role in writing a program
- The role of characters—the basic building blocks of all programs
- The concepts of *constants* and *variables*
- The distinction between *syntax* and *logic* errors
- How to produce basic output in C using the `printf` statement
- What is an escape sequence
- How descriptive or explanatory comments can be included in your program
- What is an *assignment statement* and how to write one in C

1.1 Programs, Languages, and Compilers

We are all familiar with the computer's ability to perform a wide variety of tasks. For instance, we can use it to play games, write a letter or a book, perform accounting functions for a company, learn a foreign language, listen to music on a CD, send a fax, or search for information on the Internet. How is this possible, all on the same machine? The answer lies with programming—the creation of a sequence of instructions that the computer can perform (we say "execute") to accomplish each task. This sequence of instructions is called a *program*. Each task requires a different program:

- To play a game, we need a game-playing program.
- To write a letter or a book, we need a word processing program.

1

- To do accounts, we need an accounting program.

- To learn Spanish, we need a program that teaches Spanish.

- To listen to a CD, we need a music-playing program.

- To send a fax, we need a fax-sending program.

- To use the Internet, we need a program called a "Web browser."

For every task we want to perform, we need an appropriate program. And in order for the computer to run a program, the program must be stored (we sometimes say loaded) in the computer's memory.

But what is the nature of a program? First, we need to know that computers are built to execute instructions written in what is called *machine language*. In machine language, everything is expressed in terms of the binary number system—1s and 0s. Each computer has its own machine language and the computer can execute instructions written *in that language only*.

The instructions themselves are very simple: for example, add or subtract two numbers, compare one number with another, or copy a number from one place to another. How, then, can the computer perform such a wide variety of tasks, solving such a wide variety of problems, with such simple instructions?

The answer is that no matter how complex an activity may seem, it can usually be broken down into a series of simple steps. It is the ability to analyze a complex problem and express its solution in terms of simple computer instructions that is one of the hallmarks of a good programmer.

Machine language is considered a *low-level* programming language. In the early days of computing (1940s and '50s) programmers had to write programs in machine language, that is, express all their instructions using 1s and 0s.

To make life a little easier for them, *assembly language* was developed. This was closely related to machine language but it allowed the programmer to use mnemonic instruction codes (such as ADD and names for storage locations (such as sum) rather than strings of binary digits (bits). For instance, a programmer could refer to a number by sum rather than have to remember that the number was stored in memory location 1000011101101011.

A program called an *assembler* is used to convert an assembly language program into machine language. Still, programming this way had several drawbacks:

- It was very tedious and error prone.

- It forced the programmer to think in terms of the machine rather than in terms of his problem.

- A program written in the machine language of one computer could not be run on a computer with a different machine language. Changing your computer could mean having to rewrite all your programs.

To overcome these problems, *high-level* or *problem-oriented* languages were developed in the late 1950s and '60s. The most popular of these were FORTRAN (FORmula TRANslation) and COBOL (COmmon Business-Oriented Language). FORTRAN was designed for solving scientific and engineering problems that involved a great deal of numerical computation. COBOL was designed to solve the data-processing problems of the business community.

The idea was to allow the programmer to think about a problem in terms familiar to him and relevant to the problem rather than have to worry about the machine. So, for instance, if he wanted to know the larger of two quantities, A and B, he could write

```
IF A IS GREATER THAN B THEN BIGGER = A ELSE BIGGER = B
```

rather than have to fiddle with several machine or assembly language instructions to get the same result. Thus high-level languages enabled the programmer to concentrate on solving the problem at hand, without the added burden of worrying about the idiosyncrasies of a particular machine.

However, the computer *still* could only *execute* instructions written in machine language. A program called a *compiler* is used to translate a program written in a high-level language to machine language.

Thus we speak of a FORTRAN compiler or a COBOL compiler for translating FORTRAN and COBOL programs, respectively. But that's not the whole story. Since each computer has its own machine language, we must have, say, a FORTRAN compiler for a Lenovo ThinkPad computer and a FORTRAN compiler for a MacBook computer.

1.2 How a Computer Solves a Problem

Solving a problem on a computer involves the following activities:

1. Define the problem.
2. Analyze the problem.
3. Develop an algorithm (a method) for solving the problem.
4. Write the computer program that implements the algorithm.
5. Test and debug (find the errors in) the program.
6. Document the program. (Explain how the program works and how to use it.)
7. Maintain the program.

There is normally some overlap of these activities. For example, with a large program, a portion may be written and tested before another portion is written. Also, documentation should be done at the same time as all the other activities; each activity produces its own items of documentation that will be part of the final program documentation.

1.2.1 Define the Problem

Suppose we want to help a child work out the areas of squares. This defines a problem to be solved. However, a brief analysis reveals that the definition is not complete or specific enough to proceed with developing a program. Talking with the child might reveal that she needs a program that requests her to enter the length of a side of the square; the program then prints the area of the square.

1.2.2 Analyze the Problem

We further analyze the problem to

- Ensure that we have the clearest possible understanding of it.

- Determine general requirements such as the main inputs to the program and the main outputs from the program. For more complex programs, we would, for instance, also need to decide on the kinds of files that may be needed.

If there are several ways of solving the problem, we should consider the alternatives and choose the best or most appropriate one.

In this example, the input to the program is the length of one side of the square and the output is the area of the square. We only need to know how to calculate the area. If the side is s, then the area, a, is calculated by this:

```
a = s × s
```

1.2.3 Develop an Algorithm to Solve the Problem

An *algorithm* is a set of instructions that, if faithfully followed, will produce a solution to a given problem or perform some specified task. When an instruction is followed, we say it is *executed*. We can speak of an algorithm for finding a word in a dictionary, for changing a punctured tire, or for playing a video game.

For any problem, there will normally be more than one algorithm to solve it. Each algorithm will have its own advantages and disadvantages. When we are searching for a word in the dictionary, one method would be to start at the beginning and look at each word in turn. A second method would be to start at the end and search backwards. Here, an advantage of the first method is that it would find a word faster if it were at the beginning, while the second method would be faster if the word were toward the end.

Another method for searching for the word would be one that used the fact that the words in a dictionary are in alphabetical order—this is the method we all use when looking up a word in a dictionary. In any situation, a programmer would usually have a choice of algorithms, and it is one of her more important jobs to decide which algorithm is the best, and why this is so.

In our example, we must write the instructions in our algorithm in such a way that they can be easily converted into a form that the computer can follow. Computer instructions fall into three main categories:

1. *Input* instructions, used for supplying data from the "outside world" to a program; this is usually done via the keyboard or a file.

2. *Processing* instructions, used for manipulating data inside the computer. These instructions allow us to add, subtract, multiply, and divide; they also allow us to compare two values, and act according to the result of the comparison. Also, we can move data from one location in the computer's memory to another location.

3. *Output* instructions, used for getting information out of the computer to the outside world.

1.2.3.1 Data and Variables

All computer programs, except the most trivial ones, are written to operate on *data*. For example:

- The data for an action game might be keys pressed or the position of the cursor when the mouse is clicked.

- The data for a word processing program are the keys pressed while you are typing a letter.

- The data for an accounting program would include, among other things, expenses and income.

- The data for a program that teaches Spanish could be an English word that you type in response to a question.

Recall that a program must be stored in the computer's memory for it to be run. When data is supplied to a program, that data is also stored in memory. Thus we think of memory as a place for holding programs and data. One of the nice things about programming in a high-level language (as opposed to machine language) is that you don't have to worry about which memory locations are used to store your data. But how do we refer to an item of data, given that there may be many data items in memory?

Think of memory as a set of boxes (or storage locations). Each box can hold one item of data, for example, one number. We can give a name to a box, and we will be able to refer to that box by the given name. In our example, we will need two boxes: one to hold the side of the square and one to hold the area. We will call these boxes s and a, respectively.

If we wish, we can change the value in a box at any time; since the values can vary, s and a are called variable names, or simply *variables*. Thus a variable is a name associated with a particular memory location or, if you wish, it is a *label* for the memory location. We can speak of giving a variable a value, or setting a variable to a specific value such as 1. Important points to remember are:

- A box can hold only one value at a time; if we put in a new value, the old one is lost.

- We must not assume that a box contains any value unless we specifically store a value in the box. In particular, we must not assume that the box contains zero.

Variables are a common feature of computer programs. It is very difficult to imagine what programming would be like without them. In everyday life, we often use variables. For example, we speak of an "address." Here, "address" is a variable whose value depends on the person under consideration. Other common variables are telephone number, name of school, subject, size of population, type of car, television model, etc. (What are some possible values of these variables?)

1.2.3.2 Example—Develop the Algorithm

Using the notion of an algorithm and the concept of a variable, we develop the following algorithm for calculating the area of a square, given one side:

Algorithm for calculating area of square, given one side:

1. Ask the user for the length of a side.

2. Store the value in the box s.

3. Calculate the area of the square (s × s).

4. Store the area in the box a.

5. Print the value in box a, appropriately labeled.

6. Stop.

When an algorithm is developed, it must be checked to make sure that it is doing its intended job correctly. We can test an algorithm by "playing computer," that is, we execute the instructions by hand, using appropriate data values. This process is called *dry running* or *desk checking* the algorithm. It is used to pinpoint any errors in logic before the computer program is actually written. We should *never* start to write programming code unless we are confident that the algorithm is correct.

1.2.4 Write the Program for the Algorithm

We have specified the algorithm using English statements. However, these statements are sufficiently "computer-oriented" for a computer program to be written directly from them. Before we do this, let us see how we expect the program to work from the user's point of view.

First, the program will type the request for the length of a side; we say the program *prompts* the user to supply data. The screen display might look like this:

```
Enter length of side:
```

The computer will then wait for the user to type the length. Suppose the user types 12. The display will look like this:

```
Enter length of side: 12
```

The program will then accept (we say *read*) the number typed, calculate the area, and print the result. The display may look like this:

```
Enter length of side: 12

Area of square is 144
```

Here we have specified what the *output* of the program should look like. For instance, there is a blank line between the prompt line and the line that gives the answer; we have also specified the exact form of the answer. This is a simple example of output requirements. This is necessary since the programmer cannot write the program unless he knows the precise output required.

In order to write the computer program from the algorithm, a suitable *programming language* must be chosen. We can think of a *program* as a set of instructions, *written in a programming language,* which, when executed, will produce a solution to a given problem or perform some specified task.

The major difference between an algorithm and a program is that an algorithm can be written using informal language without having to follow any special rules (though some *conventions* are usually followed) whereas a program is written in a programming language and *must* follow all the rules (the *syntax* rules) of the language. (Similarly, if we wish to write correct English, we must follow the syntax rules of the English language.)

In this book, we will be showing you how to write programs in C, the programming language developed by Ken Thompson and Dennis Ritchie of Bell Laboratories, and one of the most popular and widely used today.

Program P1.1 is a C program that requests the user to enter the length of a side and prints the area of the square:

Program P1.1

```
#include <stdio.h>
int main() {
    int a, s;
    printf("Enter length of side: ");
    scanf("%d", &s); //store length in s
    a = s * s; //calculate area; store in a
    printf("\nArea of square is %d\n", a);
}
```

It is not too important that you understand anything about this program at this time. But you can observe that a C program has something (a function) called main followed by opening and closing brackets. Between the left brace { and the right brace } we have what is called the *body* of the function. The statement

```
int a, s;
```

is called a *declaration*. The parts after // are *comments* that help to explain the program but have no effect when the program is run. And * is used to denote multiplication.

All of these terms will be explained in detail in due course.

Finally, a program written in a high-level language is usually referred to as a *source program* or *source code*.

1.2.5 Test and Debug the Program

Having written the program, the next job is to *test* it to find out whether it is doing its intended job. Testing a program involves the following steps:

1. *Compile the program*: recall that a computer can execute a program written in *machine language only*. Before the computer can run our C program, the latter must be converted to machine language. We say that the *source code* must be converted to *object code* or *machine code*. The program that does this job is called a *compiler*. Appendix D tells you how you can acquire a C compiler for writing and running your programs.

2. Among other things, a compiler will check the source code for *syntax errors*—errors that arise from breaking the rules for writing statements in the language. For example, a common syntax error in writing C programs is to omit a semicolon or to put one where it is not required.

3. If the program contains syntax errors, these must be corrected before compiling it again. When the program is free from syntax errors, the compiler will convert it to machine language and we can go on to the next step.

4. *Run the program*: here we request the computer to execute the program and we supply data to the program *for which we know the answer*. Such data is called *test data*. Some values we can use for the length of a side are 3, 12, and 20.

5. If the program does not give us the answers 9, 144, and 400, respectively, then we know that the program contains at least one *logic* error. A logic error is one that causes a program to give incorrect results for valid data. A logic error may also cause a program to *crash* (come to an abrupt halt).

6. If a program contains logic errors, we must *debug* the program; we must find and correct any errors that are causing the program to produce wrong answers.

To illustrate, suppose the statement that calculates the area was written (incorrectly) as:

```
a = s + s;
```

and when the program is run, 10 is entered for the length. (Below, 10 is underlined to indicate it is typed by the user.) Assume we *know* that the area should be 100. But when the program is run, it prints this:

```
Enter length of side: 10

Area of square is 20
```

Since this is **not** the answer we expect, we know that there is an error (perhaps more than one) in the program. Since the area is wrong, the logical place to start looking for the error is in the statement that calculates the area. If we look closely, we should discover that + was typed instead of *. When this correction is made, the program works fine.

1.2.6 Document the Program

The final job is to complete the documentation of the program. So far, our documentation includes the following:

- The statement of the problem.
- The algorithm for solving the problem.
- The program listing.
- Test data and the results produced by the program.

These are some of the items that make up the *technical documentation* of the program. This is documentation that is useful to a programmer, perhaps for modifying the program at a later stage.

The other kind of documentation that must be written is *user documentation.* This enables a nontechnical person to use the program without needing to know about the internal workings of the program. Among other things, the user needs to know how to load the program in the computer and how to use the various features of the program. If appropriate, the user will also need to know how to handle unusual situations that may arise while the program is being used.

1.2.7 Maintain the Program

Except for things like class assignments, programs are normally meant to be used over a long period of time. During this time, errors may be discovered that previously went unnoticed. Errors may also surface because of conditions or data that never arose before. Whatever the reason, such errors must be corrected.

But a program may need to be modified for other reasons. Perhaps the assumptions made when the program was written have now changed due to changed company policy or even due to a change in government regulations (e.g., changes in income tax rates). Perhaps the company is changing its computer system and the program needs to be "migrated" to the new system. We say the program must be "maintained."

Whether or not this is easy to do depends a lot on how the original program was written. If it was well-designed and properly documented, then the job of the *maintenance programmer* would be made so much easier.

1.3 How a Computer Executes a Program

First, recall that a computer can execute a program written in machine language only. For the computer to execute the instructions of such a program, those instructions must be *loaded* into the computer's *memory* (also called *primary storage*), like this:

memory
instruction 1
instruction 2
instruction 3
etc.

You can think of memory as a series of storage locations, numbered consecutively starting at 0. Thus you can speak of memory location 27 or memory location 31548. The number associated with a memory location is called its *address*.

A computer *runs* a program by executing its first instruction, then the second, then the third, and so on. It is possible that one instruction might say to jump over several instructions to a particular one and continue executing from there. Another might say to go back to a previous instruction and execute it again.

No matter what the instructions are, the computer faithfully executes them exactly as specified. That is why it is so important that programs specify precisely and exactly what must be done. The computer cannot know what you *intend*, it can only execute what you *actually write*. If you give the computer the wrong instruction, it will blindly execute it just as you specify.

1.4 Data Types

Every day we meet names and numbers—at home, at work, at school, or at play. A person's name is a type of data; so is a number. We can thus speak of the two *data types* called "name" and "number." Consider the statement:

```
Caroline bought 3 dresses for $199.95
```

Here, we can find:

- An example of a name: `Caroline`.

- Two examples of numbers: 3 and `199.95`.

Usually, we find it convenient to divide numbers into two kinds:

1. Whole numbers, or *integers*.

2. Numbers with a decimal point, so-called *real* or *floating-point* numbers.

In the example, 3 is an integer and `199.95` is a real number.

EXERCISE: IDENTIFY THE DATA TYPES—NAMES, INTEGERS, AND REAL NUMBERS—IN THE FOLLOWING

---

1. Bill's batting average was `35.25` with a highest score of 99.

2. Abigail, who lives at 41 Third Avenue, worked 36 hours at `$11.50` per hour.

3. In his 8 subjects, Richard's average mark was `68.5`.

Generally speaking, programs are written to manipulate data of various types. We use the term *numeric* to refer to numbers (integer or floating-point). We use the term *string* to refer to non-numeric data such as a name, address, job description, title of a song, or vehicle number (which is not really a number as far as the computer is concerned—it usually contains letters, e.g., PAB6052).

Programming languages in general, and C in particular, precisely define the various types of data that can be manipulated by programs written in those languages. Integer, real (or floating-point), character (data consisting of a single character such as `'K'` or `'%'`), and string data types are the most common.

Each data type defines *constants* of that type. For example,

- Some integer constants are 7, -52, 0, and 9813.

- Some real (or floating-point) constants are 3.142, -5.0, 345.21, and 1.16.

- Some character constants are 't', '+', '8' and 'R'.

- Some string constants are "Hi there", "Wherefore art thou, Romeo?", and "C World".

Note that, in C, a *character* constant is delimited by *single* quotes and a *string* constant is delimited by *double* quotes.

When we use a variable in a program, we have to say what type of data (the kind of constants) we intend to store in that variable—we say we must *declare* the variable. It is usually an error if we declare a variable to be of one type and then attempt to store a different type of value in it. For example, it would be an error to attempt to store a *string* constant in an *integer* variable. C data types are discussed in detail in Chapter 2.

1.5 Characters

In computer terminology, we use the term *character* to refer to any one of the following:

- A digit from 0 to 9.

- An uppercase letter from A to Z.

- A lowercase letter from a to z.

- A special symbol such as (,), $, =, <, >, +, -, /, *, etc.

The following are commonly used terms:

- *letter* – one of a to z or A to Z

- *lowercase letter* – one of a to z

- *uppercase letter* – one of A to Z

- *digit* – one of 0, 1, 2, 3, 4, 5, 6, 7, 8, 9

- *special character* – any symbol except a letter or a digit e.g. +, <, $, &, *, /, =

- *alphabetic* – used to refer to a letter

- *numeric* – used to refer to a digit

- *alphanumeric* – used to refer to a letter or a digit

Characters are the basic building blocks used in writing programs.
We put characters together to form *variables* and *constants*.
We put variables, constants, and special characters to form *expressions* such as

```
(a + 2.5) * (b - c);
```

We add special words such as if, else and while to form *statements* such as

```
if (a > 0) b = a + 2; else b = a - 2;
```

And we put statements together to form *programs*.

1.6 Welcome to C Programming

We take a quick peek at the C programming language by writing a program to print the message

```
Welcome to Trinidad & Tobago
```

One solution is Program P1.2.

Program P1.2

```
#include <stdio.h>
int main() {
    printf("Welcome to Trinidad & Tobago");
}
```

The statement
```
#include <stdio.h>
```

is called a *compiler directive*. This simply means that it provides information the compiler needs to compile your program. In C, input/output instructions are provided by means of standard *functions* stored in a standard *library*. These functions use variable (and other) declarations stored in a special *header* file called stdio.h. *Any* program that uses an input/output instruction (such as printf) *must* inform the compiler to *include* the declarations in the file stdio.h with the program. If this is not done, the compiler will not know how to interpret the input/output statements used in the program.

A C program consists of one or more *functions* (or, *subprograms*), one of which must be called main. Our solution consists of just one function so it *must* be called main. The (round) brackets after main are necessary because, in C, a function name is followed by a list of *arguments*, enclosed in brackets. If there are no *arguments*, the brackets must still be present. Here, main has no arguments so the brackets alone are present. The word int before main indicate the type of value *returned* by main. We will explain this in more detail later.

Every function has a section called the *body* of the function. The body is where the work of the function is performed. The left and right braces, { and }, are used to define the start and end, respectively, of the body. In C, one or more statements enclosed by { and } is called a *block* or *compound statement*.

The body of main contains one statement:

```
printf("Welcome to Trinidad & Tobago");
```

printf is a standard output function that, in this example, takes one argument, a string constant "Welcome to Trinidad & Tobago". Note that, as with all functions, the argument is enclosed in round brackets. The semicolon is used to indicate the end of the statement. We say the semicolon *terminates* the statement. When executed, this statement will print

---

Welcome to Trinidad & Tobago

---

on the "standard output." For now, take this to mean the screen.

■ **Programming Note**   As mentioned in the Preface, one of life's thrills is to write your first program and get it to run successfully on a computer. Don't miss out on it. See Appendix D for instructions on how to get a C compiler.

1.6.1 Run the Program

Having written the program on paper, the next task is to get it running on a real computer. How this is done varies somewhat from one computer system to the next but, in general, the following steps must be performed:

1.   Type the program to a file. The file could be named welcome.c; it is good practice to use .c as the filename extension to those files that contain C source code.

2.   Invoke your C compiler to compile the program in the file welcome.c. For instance, you may have to start up your C compiler and open the file welcome.c from the File menu or you may simply have to double-click on the file welcome.c to start up the compiler.

3.   Once the file is open, typically there will be a menu command to Compile or Run the program. (Generally, Run implies Compile and Run). If any (syntax) errors are detected during the compile phase, you must correct these errors and try again.

4.   When all errors have been corrected and the program is Run, it will print

---

Welcome to Trinidad & Tobago

1.6.2 A Word on Program Layout

C does not require the program to be laid out as in the example. An equivalent program is

```
#include <stdio.h>
int main() { printf("Welcome to Trinidad & Tobago"); }
```

    or

```
#include <stdio.h>
int main()
{
printf("Welcome to Trinidad & Tobago");
}
```

For this small program, it probably does not matter which version we use. However, as program size increases, it becomes imperative that the *layout* of the program highlights the logical *structure* of the program.

This improves its readability, making it easier to understand. Indentation and clearly indicating which { matches which } can help in this regard. We will see the value of this principle as our programs become bigger.

1.7 Write Output with `printf`

Suppose we want to write a program to print the following lines from *The Gitanjali* by Rabindranath Tagore:

```
Where the mind is without fear
And the head is held high
```

Our initial attempt might be this:

```
#include <stdio.h>
int main() {
    printf("Where the mind is without fear");
    printf("And the head is held high");
}
```

However, when run, this program will print:

```
Where the mind is without fearAnd the head is held high
```

Note that the two strings are joined together (we say the strings are *concatenated*). This happens because `printf` does not place output on a *new* line, unless this is specified explicitly. Put another way, `printf` does not automatically supply a *newline* character after printing its argument(s). A newline character would cause subsequent output to begin at the left margin of the next line.

In the example, a newline character is *not* supplied after fear is printed so that And the head... is printed on the same line as fear and immediately after it.

1.7.1 The Newline Character, \n (backslash n)

To get the desired effect, we must tell printf to supply a newline character after printing ...without fear. We do this by using the character sequence \n (backslash n) as in Program P1.3.

Program P1.3

```
#include <stdio.h>
int main() {
    printf("Where the mind is without fear\n");
    printf("And the head is held high\n");
}
```

The first \n says to terminate the current output line; subsequent output will start at the left margin of the next line. Thus, And the... will be printed on a new line. The second \n has the effect of terminating the second line. If it were not present, the output will still come out right, but only because this is the last line of output.

A program prints all pending output just before it terminates. (This is also the reason why our first program worked without \n.)

As an embellishment, suppose we want to put a blank line between our two lines of output, like this:

```
Where the mind is without fear

And the head is held high
```

Each of the following sets of statements will accomplish this:

```
printf("Where the mind is without fear\n\n");
printf("And the head is held high\n");
```

```
printf("Where the mind is without fear\n");
printf("\nAnd the head is held high\n");
```

```
printf("Where the mind is without fear\n");
printf("\n");
printf("And the head is held high\n");
```

We just have to make sure we print two \n's between fear and And. The first \n ends the first line; the second ends the second line, in effect, printing a blank line. C gives us a lot of flexibility in how we write statements to produce a desired effect.

EXERCISE: WRITE A PROGRAM TO PRINT THE LYRICS OF YOUR FAVORITE SONG

1.7.2 Escape Sequences

Within the string argument to `printf`, the backslash (\) signals that a special effect is needed at this point. The character following the backslash specifies what to do. This combination (\ followed by another character) is referred to as an *escape sequence*. The following are some escape sequences you can use in a string in a `printf` statement:

```
\n    issue a newline character
\f    issue a new page (form feed) character
\t    issue a tab character
\"    print "
\\    print \
```

For example, using an escape sequence is the only way to print a double quote as part of your output. Suppose we want to print the line

```
Use " to begin and end a string
```

If we typed

```
printf("Use " to begin and end a string\n");
```

then C would assume that the double quote *after* Use ends the string (causing a subsequent error when it can't figure out what to do with to). Using the escape sequence \", we can correctly print the line with:

```
printf("Use \" to begin and end a string\n");
```

**EXERCISE: WRITE A STATEMENT TO PRINT THE LINE: AN ESCAPE SEQUENCE STARTS WITH **

1.7.3 Print the Value of a Variable

So far, we have used `printf` to print the *value* of a string constant (that is, the characters of the string excluding the quotes). We now show how we can print the *value* of a variable ignoring, for the moment, *how* the variable gets its value. (We will see how in Chapter 2.) Suppose the integer variable m has the value 52. The statement:

```
printf("The number of students = %d\n", m);
```

will print this:

The number of students = 52

This printf is a bit different from those we have seen so far. This one has *two* arguments—a string and a variable. The string, called the *format string*, contains a *format specification* %d. (In our previous examples, the format string contained no format specifications.) The effect, in this case, is that the format string is printed as before, except that the %d is replaced by the value of the second argument, m. Thus, %d is replaced by 52, giving this:

The number of students = 52

We will explain printf and format specifications in more detail in Chapter 2, but, for now, note that we use the specification %d if we want to print an integer value.

What if we want to print more than one value? This can be done provided that *each* value has a corresponding format specification. For example, suppose that a has the value 14 and b has the value 25. Consider the statement:

printf("The sum of %d and %d is %d\n", a, b, a + b);

This printf has *four* arguments—the format string and three values to be printed: a, b, and a+b. The format string *must* contain three format specifications: the first will correspond to a, the second to b, and the third to a+b. When the format string is printed, each %d will be replaced by the *value* of its corresponding argument, giving this:

The sum of 14 and 25 is 39

EXERCISE: WHAT IS PRINTED BY THE FOLLOWING STATEMENT?

printf("%d + %d = %d\n", a, b, a + b);

1.8 Comments

All programming languages let you include *comments* in your programs. Comments can be used to remind yourself (and others) of what processing is taking place or what a particular variable is being used for. They can be used to explain or clarify any aspect of a program that may be difficult to understand by just reading the programming statements. This is very important since the easier it is to understand a program, the more confidence you will have that it is correct. It is worth adding anything which makes a program easier to understand.

Remember that a comment (or lack of it) has absolutely no effect on how the program runs. If you remove all the comments from a program, it will run exactly the same way as with the comments.

Each language has its own way of specifying how a comment must be written. In C, we write a comment by enclosing it within /* and */, for example:

```
/* This program prints a greeting */
```

A comment extends from /* to the next */ and may span one or more lines. The following is a valid comment:

```
/* This program reads characters one at a time
and counts the number of letters found */
```

C also lets you use // to write one-line comments. The comment extends from // to the end of the line, for example:

```
a = s * s; //calculate area; store in a
```

In this book, we will use mainly one-line comments.

1.9 Programming with Variables

To reinforce the ideas discussed so far, let us write a program that adds the numbers 14 and 25 and prints the sum.

We would need storage locations for the two numbers and the sum. The values to be stored in these locations are *integer* values. To refer to these locations, we make up the names a, b, and sum, say. (Any other names would do. In C, as in all programming languages, there are rules to follow for making up variable names, for instance, a name must start with a letter and cannot contain spaces. We will see the C rules in the next chapter.)

One possible algorithm might look like this:

```
set a to 14
set b to 25
set sum to a + b
print sum
```

The algorithm consists of four statements. The following explains the meaning of each statement:

- set a to 14: store the number 14 in memory location a; this is an example of an *assignment statement*.

- set b to 25: store the number 25 in memory location b.

- set sum to a + b: add the numbers in memory locations a and b and store the sum in location sum. The result is that 39 is stored in sum.

- print sum: print (on the screen) the value in sum, i.e., 39.

Program P1.4 shows how we can write this algorithm as a C program.

Program P1.4

```
//This program prints the sum of 14 and 25. It shows how
//to declare variables in C and assign values to them.
#include <stdio.h>
int main() {
    int a, b, sum;
    a = 14;
    b = 25;
    sum = a + b;
    printf("%d + %d = %d\n", a, b, sum);
}
```

When run, this program will print the following:

```
14 + 25 = 39
```

In C, variables are declared as *integer* using the required word int. (In programming terminology, we say that int is a *reserved* word.) Thus, the statement

```
int a, b, sum;
```

declares that a, b, and sum are integer variables. In C, all variables must be declared before they are used in a program. Note that the variables are separated by commas, with a semicolon after the last one. If we need to declare just one variable (a, say), we will write

```
int a;
```

The statement

```
a = 14;
```

is C's way of writing the *assignment statement*

```
set a to 14
```

It is sometimes pronounced "a becomes 14." In C, an assignment statement consists of a variable (a in the example), followed by an equals sign (=), followed by the value to be assigned to the variable (14 in the example), followed by a semicolon. In general, the value can be a constant (like 14), a variable (like b), or an expression (like a + b). Thus,

```
set b to 25
```

is written as

```
b = 25;
```

and

```
set sum to a + b
```

is written as

```
sum = a + b;
```

One final point: you may have gathered from a previous exercise that, for this problem, the variable sum is not really necessary. We *could*, for instance, have omitted sum from the program altogether and used this:

```
int a, b;
a = 14;
b = 25;
printf("%d + %d = %d\n", a, b, a + b);
```

to give the same result since C lets us use an expression (e.g., a + b) as an argument to printf. However, if the program were longer and we needed to use the sum in other places, it would be wise to calculate and store the sum once (in sum, say). Whenever the sum is needed, we use sum rather than recalculate a + b each time.

Now that we have a general idea of what is involved in writing a program, we are ready to get down to the nitty-gritty of C programming.

EXERCISES 1

1. What makes it possible to do such a variety of things on a computer?

2. Computers can execute instructions written in what language?

3. Give two advantages of assembly language over machine language.

4. Give two advantages of a high-level language over assembly language.

5. Describe two main tasks performed by a compiler.

6. Describe the steps required to solve a problem on a computer.

7. Distinguish between an algorithm and a program.

8. Programming instructions fall into three main categories; what are they?

9. Distinguish between a syntax error and a logic error.

10. What is meant by "debugging a program"?

11. Name five data types commonly used in programming and give examples of constants of each type.

12. What are the different classes into which characters can be divided? Give examples in each class.

13. What is the purpose of comments in a program?

14. Write a program to print Welcome to C on the screen.

15. Write a program to print the following:

    ```
    There is a tide in the affairs of men
    Which, taken at the flood, leads on to fortune
    ```

16. Write a program to print any four lines of your favorite song or poem.

17. Same as exercise 16, but print a blank line after each line.

18. If a is 29 and b is 5, what is printed by each of the following statements?

    ```
    printf("The product of %d and %d is %d\n", a, b, a * b);
    printf("%d + %d = %d\n", a, b, a + b);
    printf("%d - %d = %d\n", a, b, a - b);
    printf("%d x %d = %d\n", a, b, a * b);
    ```

19. If a is 29 and b is 14, what is printed by the following statements?

    ```
    printf("%d + \n", a);
    printf("%d\n", b);
    printf("--\n");
    printf("%d\n", a + b);
    ```

20. If rate = 15, what is printed by

    ```
    (a) printf("rate\n")?
    (b) printf("%d\n", rate)?
    ```

▓▓ ▓▓ ▓░

CHAPTER 2

C – The Basics

In this chapter, we will explain the following:

- What is an alphabet, a character set, and a token

- What is a syntax rule and a syntax error

- What is a reserved word

- How to create identifiers in C

- What is a symbolic constant

- The C data types—int, float, and double

- How to write int and double expressions

- How to print an integer using a field width

- How to print a floating-point number to a required number of decimal places

- What happens when int and double values are mixed in the same expression

- What happens when we assign int to double and double to int

- How to declare a variable to hold a string

- How to assign a string value to a string variable

- Some problems to avoid when using the assignment statement

2.1 Introduction

In this chapter, we discuss some basic concepts you need to know in order to write programs in the C programming language.

A programming language is similar to speaking languages in many respects. It has an *alphabet* (more commonly referred to as a *character set*) from which everything in the language is constructed. It has rules for forming *words* (also called *tokens*), rules for forming statements, and rules for forming programs. These are called the *syntax rules* of the language and *must* be obeyed when writing programs. If you violate a rule, your program will contain a *syntax error*. When you attempt to compile the program, the compiler will inform you of the error. You must correct it and try again.

The first step to becoming a good programmer is learning the syntax rules of the programming language. This is the easy part, and many people mistakenly believe that this makes them a programmer. It is like saying that learning some rules of English grammar and being able to write some correctly formed sentences makes one a novelist. Novel-writing skills require much more than learning some rules of grammar. Among other things, it requires insight, creativity, and a knack for using the right words in a given situation.

In the same vein, a good programmer must be able to creatively use the features of the language to solve a wide variety of problems in an elegant and efficient manner. This is the difficult part and can be achieved only by long, hard study of problem-solving algorithms and writing programs to solve a wide range of problems. But we must start with baby steps.

2.2 The C Alphabet

In Section 1.4 we introduced the idea of a character. We can think of the C alphabet as consisting of all the characters one could type on a standard English keyboard: for example, the digits; uppercase and lowercase letters; and special characters such as +, =, <, >, &, and %.

More formally, C uses the ASCII (American Standard Code for Information Interchange, pronounced ass-key) character set. This is a character standard that includes the letters, digits, and special characters found on a standard keyboard. It also includes *control* characters such as backspace, tab, line feed, form feed, and carriage return. Each character is assigned a numeric code. The ASCII codes run from 0 to 127.

The programs in this book will be written using the ASCII character set. The characters in the ASCII character set are shown in Appendix B.

Character handling will be discussed in detail in Chapter 6.

2.3 C Tokens

The *tokens* of a language are the basic building blocks that can be put together to construct programs. A token can be a reserved word (such as int or while), an identifier (such as b or sum), a constant (such as 25 or "Alice in Wonderland"), a delimiter (such as } or ;) or an operator (such as + or =).

For example, consider the following portion of Program P1.4 given at the end of the last chapter:

```c
int main() {
    int a, b, sum;
    a = 14;
    b = 25;
    sum = a + b;
    printf("%d + %d = %d\n", a, b, sum);
}
```

Starting from the beginning, we can list the tokens in order:

token	type
int	reserved word
main	identifier
(	left bracket, delimiter
)	right bracket, delimiter
{	left brace, delimiter
int	reserved word
a	identifier
,	comma, delimiter
b	identifier
,	comma, delimiter
sum	identifier
;	semicolon, delimiter
a	identifier
=	equals sign, delimiter
14	constant
;	semicolon, delimiter

And so on. Therefore we can think of a program as a *stream of tokens*, which is precisely how the compiler views it. So that, as far as the compiler is concerned, the above could have been written like this:

```
int main() { int a, b, sum;
a = 14; b = 25; sum = a + b;
printf("%d + %d = %d\n", a, b, sum); }
```

The order of the tokens is exactly the same; to the compiler, it *is* the same program. To the computer, only the order of the tokens is important. However, layout and spacing are important to make the program more readable to human beings.

2.3.1 Spacing Within a Program

Generally speaking, C programs can be written using "free format." The language does not require us, for instance, to write one statement on a line. Even a simple statement like

```
a = 14;
```

can be written on four separate lines, like this:

```
a
=
14
;
```

Only the order of the tokens is important. However, since 14 is one token, the 1 cannot be separated from the 4. You are not even allowed to put a space between 1 and 4.

Except within a string or character constant, spaces are not significant in C. However, judicious use of spaces can dramatically improve the readability of your program. A general rule of thumb is that wherever you can put one space, you can put any number of spaces without affecting the meaning of your program. The statement

```
a = 14;
```

can be written as

```
a=14;
```

or

```
a = 14 ;
```

or

```
a= 14;
```

The statement

```
sum = a + b;
```

can be written as

```
sum=a+b;
```

or

```
sum= a + b ;
```

or

```
sum = a+b;
```

Note, of course, that you cannot have spaces *within* the variable sum. It would be wrong to write s um or su m. In general, all the characters of a token must stay together.

2.3.2 Reserved Words

The C language uses a number of keywords to have a special meaning in the context of a C program and can be used for that purpose only. For example, int can be used only in those places where we need to specify that the type of some item is *integer*. All keywords are written in *lowercase letters* only. Thus int is a keyword but Int and INT are not. Keywords are reserved, that is, you cannot use them as *your* identifiers. As such, they are usually called *reserved words*. A list of C keywords is given in Appendix A.

2.3.3 Identifiers

The C programmer needs to make up names for things such as variables, function names (Chapter 7), and symbolic constants (see next page). A name that he makes up is called a *user identifier*. There are a few simple rules to follow in naming an identifier:

- It must start with a letter or underscore.

- If other characters are required, they can be any combination of letters, digits, or underscore.

The length of an identifier cannot exceed 63 characters.
Examples of valid identifiers:

```
r
R
sumOfRoots1and2
_XYZ
maxThrowsPerTurn
TURNS_PER_GAME
R2D2
root1
```

Examples of invalid identifiers:

```
2hotToHandle    // does not start with a letter
Net Pay         // contains a space
ALPHA;BETA      // contains an invalid character ;
```

Important points to note:

- Spaces are not allowed in an identifier. If you need one that consists of two or more words, use a combination of uppercase and lowercase letters (as in numThrowsThisTurn) or use the underscore to separate the words (as in num_throws_this_turn). We prefer the uppercase/lowercase combination.

- In general, C is *case-sensitive* (an uppercase letter is considered different from the corresponding lowercase letter). Thus r is a different identifier from R. And sum is different from Sum is different from SUM is different from SuM.

- You cannot use a C reserved word as one of your identifiers.

2.3.4 Some Naming Conventions

Other than the rules for creating identifiers, C imposes no restriction on what names to use, or what format (uppercase or lowercase, for instance) to use. However, good programming practice dictates that some common-sense rules should be followed.

An identifier should be meaningful. For example, if it's a variable, it should reflect the value being stored in the variable; netPay is a much better variable than x for storing someone's net pay, even though both are valid. If it's a function (Chapter 7), it should give some indication of what the function is supposed to do; playGame is a better identifier than plg.

It is a good idea to use upper and lowercase combinations to indicate the kind of item named by the identifier. In this book, we use the following conventions:

- A *variable* is normally written in lowercase: for example, sum. If we need a variable consisting of two or more words, we start the second and subsequent words with an uppercase letter: for example, voteCount or sumOfSeries.

- A *symbolic* (or *named*) *constant* is an identifier that can be used in place of a constant such as 100. Suppose 100 represents the maximum number of items we wish to process in some program. We would probably need to use the number 100 in various places in the program. But suppose we change our mind and want to cater for 500 items. We would have to change all occurrences of 100 to 500. However, we would have to make sure that we do *not* change an occurrence of 100 used for some purpose other than the maximum number of items (in a calculation like principal*rate/100).

- To make it easy to change our mind, we can set the identifier MaxItems to 100 and use MaxItems whenever we need to refer to the maximum number of items. If we change our mind, we would only need to set MaxItems to the new value. We will begin a symbolic constant with an uppercase letter. If it consists of more than one word, we will begin each word with uppercase, as in MaxThrowsPerTurn.

- We will see how to use symbolic constants in Section 4.6.

2.4 Basic Data Types

In Section 1.4 we briefly touched on the concept of a data type. For most of this book, we will use the following data types:

```
int, double, and char
```

These, among others, are referred to as *primitive* data types.

Each data type defines *constants* of that type. When we declare a variable to be of a particular type, we are really saying what kind of constants (values) can be stored in that variable. For example, if we declare the variable num to be int, we are saying that the value of num at any time can be an integer constant such as 25, -369, or 1024.

2.5 Integer Numbers - int

An int variable is used to store an *integer* (whole number) value. An integer value is one of 0, ±1, ±2, ±3, ±4, etc. However, on a computer, the largest and smallest integers that can be stored are determined by the *number of bits* used to store an integer. Appendix C shows how integers can be represented on a computer.

Typically, an int variable occupies 16 bits (2 bytes) and can be used to store whole numbers in the range -32,768 to +32,767. Note, however, that on some machines, an int could occupy 32 bits, in which case it can store whole numbers from -2,147,483,648 to +2,147,483,647. In general, if n bits are used to store an int, the range of numbers that can be stored is -2^{n-1} to $+2^{n-1} - 1$.

As an exercise, find out the largest and smallest int values on your computer.

2.5.1 Declaring Variables

In C, a variable is declared by specifying a type name followed by the variable. For example,

```
int h;
```

declares h to be a variable of type int. The declaration *allocates space* for h but *does not initialize it* to any value. You must not assume that a variable contains any value unless you explicitly assign a value to it.

You can declare several variables *of the same type* in one statement as in:

```
int a, b, c; // declares 3 variables of type int
```

The variables are separated by commas, with a semicolon after the last one.

You can declare a variable *and* give it an initial value in one statement, as in:

```
int h = 14;
```

This declares h to be int *and* gives it a value of 14.

2.5.2 Integer Expressions

An integer constant is written in the manner we are all accustomed to: for example, 354, 639, -1, 30705, and -4812. Note that you can use only a possible sign followed by digits from 0 to 9. In particular, you *cannot* use commas as you might do to separate thousands; thus 32,732 is an *invalid* integer constant—you must write it as 32732.

An integer expression can be written using the following *arithmetic operators*:

+	add
–	subtract
*	multiply
/	divide
%	find remainder

For example, suppose we have the following declaration:

```
int a, b, c;
```

then the following are all valid expressions:

```
a + 39
a + b - c * 2
b % 10 //the remainder when b is divided by 10
c + (a * 2 + b * 2) / 2
```

The operators +, - and * all give the expected results. However, / performs *integer division*; if there is any remainder, it is thrown away. We say integer division *truncates*. Thus 19/5 gives the value 3; the remainder 4 is discarded.

But what is the value of -19/5? The answer here is −3. The rule is that, in C, integer division truncates *toward* zero. Since the exact value of −19 ÷ 5 is −3.8, truncating toward zero gives −3. (In the next section, we show how to get the precise value for the division of one integer by another.)

The % operator gives the remainder when one integer is divided by another. For example,

```
19 % 5 evaluates to 4;
h % 7 gives the remainder when h is divided by 7;
```

You can use it to test, for instance, if a number h is even or odd. If h % 2 is 0 then h is even; if h % 2 is 1, h is odd.

2.5.3 Precedence of Operators

C evaluates an expression based on the usual *precedence* of operators: multiplication and division are done *before* addition and subtraction. We say that multiplication and division have *higher precedence* than addition and subtraction. For example, the expression

```
5 + 3 * 4
```

is evaluated by *first* multiplying 3 by 4 (giving 12) and *then* adding 5 to 12, giving 17 as the value of the expression.

As usual, we can use brackets to force the evaluation of an expression in the order we want. For example,

```
(5 + 3) * 4
```

first adds 5 and 3 (giving 8), and then multiplies 8 by 4, giving 32.

When two operators that have the *same* precedence appear in an expression, they are evaluated *from left to right*, unless specified otherwise by brackets. For example,

```
24 / 4 * 2
```

is evaluated as

$(24 / 4) * 2$

(giving 12) and

12 - 7 + 3

is evaluated as

(12 - 7) + 3

giving 8. However,

24 / (4 * 2)

is evaluated as expected, giving 3, and

12 - (7 + 3)

is evaluated as expected, giving 2.

In C, the remainder operator % has the same precedence as multiplication (*) and division (/).

EXERCISE: WHAT IS PRINTED BY THE FOLLOWING PROGRAM? VERIFY YOUR ANSWER BY TYPING AND RUNNING THE PROGRAM

```
#include <stdio.h>
int main() {
    int a = 15;
    int b = 24;
    printf("%d %d\n", b - a + 7, b - (a + 7));
    printf("%d %d\n", b - a - 4, b - (a - 4));
    printf("%d %d\n", b % a / 2, b % (a / 2));
    printf("%d %d\n", b * a / 2, b * (a / 2));
    printf("%d %d\n", b / 2 * a, b / (2 * a));
}
```

2.5.4 Print an Integer Using a "Field Width"

We have seen that we can print an integer value by specifying the value (either by a variable or an expression) in a `printf` statement. When we do so, C prints the value using as many "print columns" as needed. For instance, if the value is 782, it is printed using 3 print columns since 782 has 3 digits. If the value is -2345, it is printed using 5 print columns (one for the minus sign).

While this is usually sufficient for most purposes, there are times when it is useful to be able to tell C how many print columns to use. For example, if we want to print the value of n in 5 print columns, we can do this by specifying a *field width* of 5, as in:

```
printf("%5d", n);
```

Instead of the specification %d, we now use %5d. The field width is placed between % and d. The value of n is printed "in a field width of 5".

Suppose n is 279; there are 3 digits to print so 3 print columns are needed. Since the field width is 5, the number 279 is printed with 2 spaces before it, thus: ◊◊279 (◊ denotes a space). We also say "printed with 2 leading blanks/spaces" and "printed padded on the left with 2 blanks/spaces."

A more technical way of saying this is "n is printed *right justified* in a field width of 5." "Right justify" means that the number is placed as far right as possible in the field and spaces added in *front* of it to make up the field width. If the number is placed as far *left* as possible and spaces are added *after* it to make up the field width, the number is *left justified*. For example, 279◊◊ is left justified in a field width of 5.

The minus sign can be used to specify *left justification*; %-wd will print a value left justified in a field width of w. For example, to print an integer value left justified in field width of 5, we use %-5d.

For another example, suppose n is -7 and the field width is 5. Printing n requires two print columns (one for - and one for 7); since the field width is 5, it is printed with 3 leading spaces, thus: ◊◊◊-7.

You may ask, what will happen if the field width is too small? Suppose the value to be printed is 23456 and the field width is 3. Printing this value requires 5 columns, which is greater than the field width 3. In this case, C ignores the field width and simply prints the value using as many columns as needed (5, in this example).

In general, suppose the integer value v is printed with the specification %wd where w is an integer, and suppose n columns are needed to print v. There are two cases to consider:

1. If n is less than w (the field width is bigger), the value is padded on the left with (w - n) spaces. For example, if w is 7 and v is -345 so that n is 4, the number is padded on the left with (7-4) = 3 spaces and printed as ◊◊◊-345.

2. If n is greater than or equal to w (field width is the same or smaller), the value is printed using n print columns. In this case, the field width is ignored.

A field width is useful when we want to line up numbers one below the other. Suppose we have three int variables a, b, and c with values 9876, -3, and 501, respectively. The statements

```
printf("%d\n", a);
printf("%d\n", b);
printf("%d\n", c);
```

will print

```
9876
-3
501
```

Each number is printed using just the number of columns required. Since this varies from one number to the next, they do not line up. If we want to, we could get the numbers lined up using a field width of 5, for example. The statements

```
printf("%5d\n", a);
printf("%5d\n", b);
printf("%5d\n", c);
```

will print (◊ denotes a space)

```
◊9876
◊◊◊-3
◊◊501
```

that will look like this (without ◊):

```
9876
  -3
 501
```

all nicely lined up.

As a matter of interest, we don't really need three printf statements. We can replace the last three printf statements with

```
printf("%5d\n%5d\n%5d\n", a, b, c);
```

Each \n forces the following output onto a new line.

2.6 Floating-Point Numbers – float and double

A floating-point number is one that may have a fractional part. A *floating-point constant* can be written in one of two ways:

- The normal way, with an optional sign, and including a decimal point; for example, -3.75, 0.537, 47.0.

- Using scientific notation, with an optional sign, including a decimal point and including an 'exponent' part; for example, -0.375E1, which means "-0.375 multiplied by 10 to the power 1", that is, -3.75. Similarly, 0.537 can be written as 5.37e-1, that is, 5.37 x 10-1. The exponent can be specified using either e or E.

- Note that there are several ways to write the same number. For example, the following all represent the same number 27.96:

  ```
  27.96E00 2.796E1 2.796E+1 2.796E+01 0.2796E+02 279.6E-1
  ```

In C, we can declare a floating-point variable using either float or double. A float value is normally stored as a 32-bit floating-point number, giving about 6 or 7 significant digits. A double value is stored as a 64-bit floating-point number, giving about 15 significant digits.

A floating-point constant is of type double unless it is followed by f or F, in which case it is of type float. Thus 3.75 is of type double but 3.75f or 3.75F is of type float. Most calculations are done using double precision. The type float is useful if you need to store lots of floating-point numbers and you wish to use as little storage as possible (and do not mind just 6 or 7 digits of precision).

In this book, we will mostly use double for working with floating-point numbers.

2.6.1 Print double and float Variables

We have been using the *format specification* %d in a printf statement to print the value of an integer variable. If we wish to print the value of a double or float variable, we can use %f. For example, consider the following:

```
double d = 987.654321;
printf("%f \n", d);
```

The value of d will be printed to a predefined number of decimal places (usually six, but could vary from one compiler to the next). In this case, the value printed will be 987.654321. However, if d were assigned 987.6543215, the value printed would be 987.654322 (rounded to six decimal places).

Similarly, if x is of type float, its value could be printed using:

```
printf("%f \n", x);
```

We just saw that the specification %f prints the number to a predefined number of decimal places. Most times, though, we want to say how many decimal places to print and, sometimes, how many columns to use. For example, if we want to print d, above, to 2 decimal places in a field width of 6, we can use:

```
printf("%6.2f \n", d);
```

Between % and f, we write 6.2, that is, the field width, followed by a . (point), followed by the number of decimal places. The value is *rounded* to the stated number of decimal places and then printed. Here, the value printed will be 987.65, which occupies exactly 6 print columns. If the field width were bigger, the number will be padded on the left with spaces. If the field width were smaller, it is ignored, and the number is printed using as many columns as necessary.

As another example, consider

```
b = 245.75;
printf("%6.1f \n", b);
```

In the specification %6.1f, 1 says to *round* the number to 1 decimal place; this gives 245.8, which requires 5 columns for printing.

6 says to print 245.8 in 6 columns; since only 5 columns are needed for printing the number, one space is added at the beginning to make up 6 columns, so the number is printed as ◊245.8 (◊ denotes a space)

Similarly,

```
printf("%6.0f \n", b);
```

will print b as ◊◊◊246 (rounded to 0 decimal places and printed in a field width of 6).

If the specification was %3.1f and the value to be printed is 245.8, it would be printed using 5 print columns, even though the field width is 3. Again, when the field width specified is *smaller* than the number of print columns required, C ignores the field width and prints the value using as many columns as needed.

We can sometimes use this to our advantage. If we do not know how big a value might be, we can deliberately use a small field width to ensure it is printed using the exact number of print columns required for printing the value.

In general, suppose the float or double value v is to be printed with the specification %w.df where w and d are integers. Firstly, the value v is *rounded* to d decimal places. Suppose the number of print columns required to print v, including a possible point (there will be no point if d = 0; the value is to be rounded to a whole number) and a possible sign, is n. There are two cases to consider:

1. If n is less than w (the field width is bigger), the value is padded on the left with (w - n) spaces. For example, suppose w is 7 and the value to be printed is -3.45 so that n is 5. The number is padded on the left with (7-5) = 2 spaces and printed as ◊◊-3.45.

2. If n is greater than or equal to w (field width is the same or smaller), the value is printed using n print columns. In this case, the field width is ignored.

As with integers, a field width is useful when we want to line up numbers one below the other. Assume we have three double variables a, b, and c with values 419.563, -8.7, and 3.25, respectively. Suppose we want to print the values to two decimal places, lined up on the decimal point, like this:

```
419.56
 -8.70
  3.25
```

Since the biggest number requires 6 print columns, we can line them up using a field width of at least 6. The following statements will line them up as above:

```
printf("%6.2f \n", a);
printf("%6.2f \n", b);
printf("%6.2f \n", c);
```

If we use a field width bigger than 6, the numbers will still line up but with leading spaces. For example, if we use a field width of 8, we will get (◊ denotes a space)

```
◊◊419.56
◊◊◊-8.70
◊◊◊◊3.25
```

Again, we can use one `printf` instead of three to achieve the same effect:

```
printf("%6.2f \n%6.2f \n%6.2f \n", a, b, c);
```

Each \n forces the following output onto a new line.

2.6.2 Assignment Between double and float

As expected, you can store a `float` value in a `float` variable and a `double` value in a `double` variable. Since `float` is smaller than `double`, C allows you to store a `float` value in a `double` variable without any problems. However, if you assign a `double` to a `float`, some precision may be lost. Consider the following:

```
double d = 987.654321;
float x = d;
printf("%f \n", x);
```

Since a `float` variable allows only about 7 digits of precision, we should expect that the value of d may not be assigned precisely to x. Indeed, when run using one compiler, the value `987.654297` was printed for x. When d was changed to `987654321.12345`, the value printed was `987654336.000000`. In both cases, about 6 or 7 digits of precision were retained.

As an exercise, see what values are printed using your compiler.

2.6.3 Floating-Point Expressions

Floating-point expressions can be written using the following operators:

+	addition
–	subtraction
*	multiplication
/	division

These operate as expected; in particular, division is performed in the usual way so that, for example, `19.0/5.0` gives the value `3.8`.

If op1 and op2 are the two operands of an operator, the following shows the type of calculation performed:

op1	op2	type of calculation
float	float	float
float	double	double
double	float	double
double	double	double

Thus float is performed only if both operands are float; otherwise double is performed.

2.6.4 Expressions with Integer and Floating-Point Values

It is quite common to use expressions involving both integer and floating-point values, for example,

```
a / 3 where a is float
n * 0.25 where n is int
```

In C, the rule for such expressions is this:

> *If either operand of an arithmetic operator is floating-point, the calculation is done in floating-point arithmetic. The calculation is done in float unless at least one operand is double, in which case the calculation is done in double.*

In the first example above, the integer 3 is converted to float and the calculation is done in float. In the second example, n is converted to double (since 0.25 is double) and the calculation is done in double.

How do we get the exact value of an integer division, 19/5, say? We can force a double precision calculation by writing one or both constants as double, thus: 19/5.0, 19.0/5, or 19.0/5.0. We can also use a *cast*, as in

```
(double) 19 / 5
```

A *cast* consists of a type name enclosed in brackets and allows us to force the conversion of one type to another. Here, 19 is cast to double, forcing 5 to be converted to double and a double precision division is performed.

However, we must be careful with a construct like

```
(double) (19 / 5)
```

This may not do what we think. This does NOT do a floating-point division. Since both constants are integer, the expression inside the brackets is evaluated as an integer division, giving 3; *this* value is converted to double, giving 3.0.

2.6.5 Assigning double/float to int

Consider:

```
double d = 987.654321;
int n = d;
printf("%d \n", n);
```

The value 987 is printed. When we assign a floating-point value to an int, the fractional part, if any, is dropped (not rounded) and the resulting integer value is assigned. It is up to us to ensure that the integer obtained is small enough to fit in an int. If not, the resulting value is unpredictable.

On one compiler, where the largest value of an int was 32767, when d was changed to 987654.321, the value printed was 4614, a far cry from what might be expected, seemingly unpredictable. (Not quite unpredictable; the value assigned is 987654 % 32768, which is 4614. In general, if big represents a value that is too big to be stored, the value actually stored is big % 32768 for integers stored in 16 bits.) This is because the truncated value of d is 987654, which is too big to fit in an int variable. As an exercise, see what value would be printed on your compiler.

If we want the *rounded* value of d stored in n, we could do this with

```
n = d + 0.5;
```

If the first digit after the point in d is 5 or more, adding 0.5 would add 1 to the whole number part. If the first digit after the point is less than 5, adding 0.5 would not change the whole number part.

For example, if d is 245.75, adding 0.5 would give 246.25 and 246 would be assigned to n. But if d were 245.49, adding 0.5 would give 245.99 and 245 would be assigned to n.

2.7 Strings

So far, we have seen several examples of string constants in printf statements.

A *string constant* is any sequence of characters enclosed in double quotes. Examples are:

```
"Once upon a time"
"645-2001"
"Are you OK?"
"c:\\data\\castle.in"
```

The opening and closing quotes *must* appear *on the same line*. In other words, C does not allow a string constant to continue on to another line. However, a long string can be broken up into pieces, with each piece on one line. When the program is compiled, C will join the pieces, making one string. For example,

```
printf("Place part of a long string on one line and "
"place the next part on the next line. The parts are "
"separated by whitespace, not comma or ; \n");
```

The *value* of a string constant is the sequence of characters without the beginning and ending quotes. Thus, the value of `"Are you OK?"` is Are you OK?.

If you want the double quote to be part of a string, you must write it using the escape sequence `\"`, as in

```
"\"Don't move!\", he commanded"
```

The value of this string is

```
"Don't move!", he commanded
```

Each `\"` is replaced by `"` and the beginning and ending quotes are dropped.

The C language does not have a predefined `string` type. This presents difficulties for the beginning programmer since he cannot work with string variables the way he can with numeric variables.

In C, a string is stored in an "array of characters." Since we discuss characters in Chapter 6 and arrays in Chapter 8, we *could* be patient and wait until then to understand what an array is, how strings are stored, and how we can use them to store a name, for instance. Or, we could accept a few things on faith and reap the benefit of being able to work with strings, in a limited way, much sooner than we normally would. We'll be impatient and choose the latter.

Suppose we wish to store a person's name in some variable name. We can declare name as follows:

```
char name[50];
```

This declares name to be a "character array" of size 50. As we will explain in Chapter 8, this allows us to store a maximum of 49 characters in name. If you find this is too much (or too little) for your purposes, you can use a different number.

If we want to, we can assign a string constant to name *in the declaration*, thus:

```
char name[50] = "Alice Wonder";
```

This stores the characters from A to r, including the space, in name. The quotes are *not* stored. Once this is done, we could print the value of name using the specification `%s` in `printf`, thus:

```
printf("Hello, %s\n", name);
```

This will print

```
Hello, Alice Wonder
```

The *value* of name replaces `%s`.

Unfortunately, we cannot assign a string constant to name, other than in the declaration of name. C does not permit us to write an assignment statement such as

```
name = "Alice in Wonderland"; // this is not valid
```

to assign a value to name. What we *can* do is use the standard function strcpy (for **string copy**), as in:

```
strcpy(name, "Alice in Wonderland"); // this is valid
```

But in order to use strcpy (and other string functions), we must precede our program with the directive:

```
#include <string.h>
```

We summarize all of this in Program P2.1.

Program P2.1

```
#include <stdio.h>  // needed for printf
#include <string.h> // needed for strcpy
int main() {
    char name[50];
    strcpy(name, "Alice in Wonderland");
    printf("Hello, %s\n", name);
}
```

When run, this program will print

```
Hello, Alice in Wonderland
```

In Sections 3.4 and 5.9, we will see how to read a string value into a variable.

Joining two strings is an operation we sometimes want to perform. We say we want to *concatenate* the two strings. We can do this with the standard string function strcat (**string concat**enation). For example, suppose we have:

```
char name[30] = "Alice";
char last[15] = "Wonderland";
```

The statement

```
strcat(name, last);
```

will *add* the string in last to the one in name. It is up to us to ensure that name is big enough to hold the joined strings. The result is that name will now hold AliceWonderland; the value in last does not change. The following statements will set name to Alice in Wonderland.

```
strcat(name, " in "); //one space before and after "in"
strcat(name, last);
```

2.8 The Assignment Statement

In Section 1.9, we introduced the *assignment statement*. Recall that an assignment statement consists of a *variable* followed by an equals sign (=) followed by the *value* to be assigned to the variable, followed by a semicolon. We could write this as:

```
<variable> = <value>;
```

`<value>` must be *compatible* with `<variable>` otherwise we will get an error. For example, if `<variable>` is int, we must be able to derive an integer from `<value>`. And if `<variable>` is double, we must be able to derive a floating-point value from `<value>`. If n is int and x is double, we cannot, for instance, write

```
n = "Hi there"; //cannot assign string to int
x = "Be nice";  //cannot assign string to double
```

It is useful to think of the assignment statement being executed as follows: the value on the right-hand side of = is evaluated. The value obtained is stored in the variable on the left-hand side. The old value of the variable, if any, is lost. For example, if score had the value 25, then after the statement

```
score = 84;
```

the value of score would be 84; the old value 25 is lost. We can picture this as:

```
score    25 84
```

A variable can take on any of several values, but *only one at a time*. As another example, consider this statement:

```
score = score + 5;
```

Suppose score has the value 84 before this statement is executed. What is the value after execution?

First, the right-hand side score + 5 is evaluated using the current value of score, 84. The calculation gives 89—this value is then stored in the variable on the left-hand side; it happens to be score. The end result is that the value of score is increased by 5 to 89. The old value 84 is lost.

It is possible that even though an assignment statement is *valid*, it could produce an error when the program is run. Consider the following (a, b, c, d, and e are int):

```
a = 12;
b = 5;
c = (a - b) * 2;
d = c + e;
```

Each of these is a correctly formed assignment statement. However, when these statements are executed, an error will result. Can you see how?

The first statement assigns 12 to a; the second assigns 5 to b; the third assigns 14 to c; no problem so far. However, when the computer attempts to execute the fourth statement, it runs into a problem. There is no value for e, so the expression c + e cannot be evaluated. We say that e is *undefined*—it has no value.

Before we can use any variable in an expression, it must have been assigned a value by some previous statement. If not, we will get an "undefined variable" error and our program will halt.

The moral of the story: a *valid* program is not necessarily a *correct* program.

EXERCISE: WHAT IS PRINTED BY THE FOLLOWING?

```
a = 13;
b = a + 12;
printf("%d %d\n", a, b);
c = a + b;
a = a + 11;
printf("a = %d b = %d c = %d\n", a, b, c);
```

2.9 printf

We have seen several examples of the printf statement. We have used it to print string constants, integer values, and floating-point values. And we have printed values with and without field widths. We have also seen how to use the escape sequence \n to force output onto a new line.

It is worth emphasizing that the characters in the format string are printed exactly as they appear except that a format specification is replaced by its corresponding value. For example, if a is 25 and b is 847, consider the statement

```
printf("%d%d\n", a, b);
```

This will print

```
25847
```

The numbers are stuck together and we cannot tell what is a and what is b! This is so because the specification %d%d says to print the numbers next to each other. If we want them separated by one space, say, we must put a space between %d and %d, like this:

```
printf("%d %d\n", a, b);
```

This will print

```
25 847
```

To get more spaces between the numbers, we simply put how many we want between %d and %d.

EXERCISE: WHAT IS PRINTED BY THE FOLLOWING?

```
printf("%d\n %d\n", a, b);
```

The following are some useful things to know about format specifications. Suppose num is int and its value is 75:

- The specification %d will print 75 using 2 print columns: **75**

- The specification %5d will print 75 with 3 leading spaces: **00075**

- The specification %-5d will print 75 with 3 trailing spaces: **75000**

- The specification %05d will print 75 with 3 leading zeroes: **00075**

For an example in which leading 0s might be useful, consider the statement

```
printf("Pay this amount: $%04d\n", num);
```

This will print

```
Pay this amount: $0075
```

This is better than printing

```
Pay this amount: $  75
```

since someone can insert numbers between $ and 7.

In general, the minus sign specifies left justification and a 0 in front of the field width specifies 0 (zero, rather than a space) as the padding character.

EXERCISES 2

1. In the ASCII character set, what is the range of codes for (a) the digits (b) the uppercase letters and (c) the lowercase letters?

2. What is a token? Give examples.

3. Spaces are normally not significant in a program. Give an example showing where spaces are significant.

4. What is a reserved word? Give examples.

5. Give the rules for making up an identifier.

6. What is a symbolic constant and why is it useful?

7. Give examples of integer constants, floating-point constants, and string constants.

8. Name five operators that can be used for writing integer expressions and give their precedence in relation to each other.

9. Give the value of (a) 39 % 7 (b) 88 % 4 (c) 100 % 11 (d) -25 % 9

10. Give the value of (a) 39 / 7 (b) 88 / 4 (c) 100 / 11 (d) -25 / 9

11. Write a statement that prints the value of the int variable sum, right justified in a field width of 6.

12. You are required to print the values of the int variables b, h, and n. Write a statement that prints b with its rightmost digit in column 10, h with its rightmost digit in column 20, and n with its rightmost digit in column 30.

13. Write statements that print the values of b, h, and n lined up one below the other with their rightmost digits in column 8.

14. Using scientific notation, write the number 345.72 in four different ways.

15. Write a statement that prints the value of the double variable total to 3 decimal places, right justified in a field width of 9.

16. You need to print the values of the float variables a, b, and c to 1 decimal place. Write a statement that prints a with its rightmost digit in column 12, b with its rightmost digit in column 20, and c with its rightmost digit in column 32.

17. What kind of variable would you use to store a telephone number? Explain.

18. Write statements to print the values of 3 double variables a, b, and c, to 2 decimal places, The values must be printed one below the other, with their rightmost digits in column 12.

19. How can you print the value of a double variable, rounded to the nearest whole number?

20. What happens if you try to print a number (int, float, or double) with a field width and the field width is too small? What if the field width is too big?

21. Name some operators that can be used for writing floating-point expressions.

22. Describe what happens when we attempt to assign an int value to a float variable.

23. Describe what happens when we attempt to assign a float value to an int variable.

24. Write a statement to print the following: Use \n to end a line of output.

25. Write a statement to increase the value of the int variable quantity by 10.

26. Write a statement to decrease the value of the int variable quantity by 5.

27. Write a statement to double the value of the int variable quantity.

28. Write a statement to set a to 2 times b plus 3 times c.

29. The double variable price holds the price of an item. Write a statement to increase the price by (a) $12.50 (b) 25%.

30. What will happen when the computer attempts to execute the following:

```
p   7|
q = 3 + p;
p = p + r;
printf("%d\n", p);
```

31. Suppose rate = 15. What is printed by each of the following?

```
printf("Maria earns rate dollars an hour\n");
printf("Maria earns %d dollars an hour\n", rate);
```

32. If m is 3770 and n is 123, what is printed by each of the following?

```
(a) printf("%d%d\n", n, m);
(b) printf("%d\n%d\n", n, m);
```

CHAPTER 3

Programs with Sequence Logic

In this chapter, we will explain the following:

- The idea of reading data supplied by a user

- How the `scanf` statement works

- How to read numeric data using `scanf`

- How to read string data using `gets`

- Important principles of program writing using several examples

3.1 Introduction

In the last chapter, we introduced some of C's basic data types—int, double, and float—and used simple statements to illustrate their use. We now go a step further and introduce several programming concepts by writing programs using these types.

The programs in this chapter will be based on *sequence* logic—that simply means the statements in the programs are executed one after the other, from the first to the last. This is the simplest kind of logic, also called *straight-line* logic. In the next chapter we will write programs that use *selection* logic—the ability of a program to test some *condition* and take different courses of action based on whether the condition is true or false.

3.2 Read Data Supplied by a User

Consider, again, Program P1.3.

Program P1.3

```
// This program prints the sum of 14 and 25. It shows how
// to declare variables in C and assign values to them.
#include <stdio.h>
int main() {
    int a, b, sum;
    a = 14;
    b = 25;
```

```
    sum = a + b;
    printf("%d + %d = %d\n", a, b, sum);
}
```

C allows us to declare a variable and give it an initial value in one statement so we could write the program more concisely (without the comment) as Program P3.1:

Program P3.1

```
#include <stdio.h>
int main() {
    int a = 14;
    int b = 25;
    int sum = a + b;
    printf("%d + %d = %d\n", a, b, sum);
}
```

And since, as discussed earlier, we do not really need the variable sum, this program can be written as Program P3.2.

Program P3.2

```
#include <stdio.h>
int main() {
    int a = 14;
    int b = 25;
    printf("%d + %d = %d\n", a, b, a + b);
}
```

This program is very restrictive. If we wish to add two other numbers, we will have to change the numbers 14 and 25 in the program to the ones required. We would then have to re-compile the program. And each time we want to add two different numbers, we would have to change the program. This can become very tedious.

It would be nice if we could write the program in such a way that when we *run* the program, we will have the opportunity to tell the program which numbers we wish to add. In this way, the numbers would not be tied to the program, and the program would be more *flexible*. When we "tell" the program the numbers, we say we are supplying *data* to the program. But how do we get the program to "ask" us for the numbers and how do we "tell" the program what the numbers are?

We can get the program to *prompt* us for a number by printing a message such as:

```
Enter first number:
```

using a printf statement. The program must then wait for us to type the number and, when it is typed, *read* it. This can be done with the scanf statement. (Strictly speaking, printf and scanf are functions, but the distinction is not too important for us.) Before we look at this statement, let us rewrite the algorithm using these new ideas:

```
prompt for the first number
read the number
prompt for the second number
read the number
find the sum
print the sum
```

We can *implement* this algorithm in C as Program P3.3.

Program P3.3

```c
//prompt for two numbers and find their sum
#include <stdio.h>
int main() {
    int a, b;
    printf("Enter first number: ");
    scanf("%d", &a);
    printf("Enter second number: ");
    scanf("%d", &b);
    printf("%d + %d = %d\n", a, b, a + b);
}
```

When run, the first printf statement will print:

```
Enter first number:
```

The scanf statement, explained shortly, will cause the computer to wait for the user to type a number.

Suppose she types 23; the screen will look like this:

```
Enter first number: 23
```

When she presses the "Enter" or "Return" key on the keyboard, scanf *reads* the number and stores it in the variable a.

The next printf statement then prompts:

```
Enter second number:
```

Again, scanf causes the computer to wait for the user to enter a number. Suppose she enters 18; scanf reads the number, and stores it in the variable b. At this stage, the number 23 is stored in a and 18 is stored in b. We can picture this as follows:

a [23]   b [18]

The program then executes the last printf statement and prints the following:

23 + 18 = 41

At the end, the screen will look as follows. Underlined items are typed by the user, and everything else is printed by the computer:

```
Enter first number: 23
Enter second number: 18
23 + 18 = 41
```

Since the user is free to enter *any* numbers, the program will work for whatever numbers are entered, provided the numbers are small enough to be stored in an int variable. If not, strange results will be printed.

3.3 scanf

In Program P3.3, the statement

```
scanf("%d", &a);
```

causes the computer to wait for the user to type a number. Since a is an integer variable, scanf expects the next item in the data to be an integer or a value (like 3.8, say) that can be converted into an integer but dropping the fractional part. If it is not (for example, if it is a letter or a special character) the program will give an error message such as "Invalid numeric format" and stop. We say the program will *crash*. If the data *is* valid, the number will be stored in the variable a. The statement

```
scanf("%d", &b);
```

works in a similar manner.

The statement consists of:

- The word scanf
- Left and right brackets
- Two items (called *arguments*) inside the brackets, separated by a comma

As with `printf`, the first item is a string called the *format string*. In this example, the string consists of the *format specification* %d only. It specifies the *type* of data to be read. Here, %d is used to indicate that an *integer* value is to be read.

The second argument specifies *where* to store the value read. Even though we want the value stored in a, `scanf` *requires* us to specify this by writing &a. The quick explanation is that we must tell `scanf` the *address* of the memory location where the value is to be stored; &a stands for "address of a." You will need to take it on faith that in order to *read* a value into a variable using `scanf`, the variable must be preceded by &, as in &a and &b. Note that this applies to the `scanf` statement *only*. Other than this, the variable is used in its normal form (without &) as in:

```
printf("%d + %d = %d\n", a, b, a + b);
```

We can use `scanf` to read more than one value at a time. For example, suppose we want to read three integer values for variables a, b, and c. To do so, we would need to write %d three times in the format specification, thus:

```
scanf("%d %d %d", &a, &b, &c);
```

When this statement is executed, it looks for three integers. The first one is stored in a, the second in b, and the third in c. It is up to the user to ensure that the next three items in the data are integers. If this is not so, an "Invalid numeric format" message will be printed and the program will crash.

When entering the data, the numbers must be separated by one or more spaces, like this:

```
42 -7 18
```

When using `scanf`, data can be supplied in flexible ways. The *only* requirement is that the data be supplied *in the correct order*. In this example, the three numbers could be supplied as above or like this:

```
42
-7
18
```

or this:

```
42 -7
18
```

or even with a blank line, like this:

```
42

-7 18
```

Spaces, tabs and blank lines (so-called *whitespace*) do not matter; scanf will simply keep reading data, ignoring spaces, tabs and blank lines, until it finds the three integers. However, we emphasize that if any invalid character is encountered while reading the data, the program will crash. For instance, if the user types

```
42 -7 v8
```

    or

```
42 = 18 24
```

the program will crash. In the first case, v8 is not a valid integer; and, in the second case, = is not a valid character for an integer.

3.3.1 Read Data Into a float Variable

If we wish to read a floating-point number into a float variable x, we can use

```
scanf("%f", &x);
```

The specification %f is used to read a value into a float (but not double, see next section) variable. When executed, scanf expects to find a valid floating-point constant in the data. For example, any of the following will be acceptable:

```
4.265
-707.96
2.345E+1
```

In the last case, there must be no spaces, for instance, between the 5 and the E or between the E and the + or between the + and the 1. The following will all be invalid for reading the number 23.45:

```
2.345 E+1
2.345E +1
2.345E+ 1
```

3.3.2 Read Data Into a double Variable

If we wish to read a floating-point number into a double variable, y, we can use

```
scanf("%lf", &y);
```

The specification %lf (percent ell f) is used to read a value into a double variable. Apart from the specification, data is entered the same way for float and double variables. Be careful—you *cannot* use %f for *reading* data into a double variable. If you do, your variable will contain nonsense, since the value read will be stored in 32 bits rather than 64 bits, the size of double (see Section 2.6). However, as you have seen, you *can* use %f for *printing* the value of a double variable.

When entering data for a float/double variable, an integer is acceptable. If you enter 42, say, it will be interpreted as 42.0. But, as discussed above, if you enter a floating-point constant (e.g., 2.55) for an int variable, it will be truncated (to 2, in this example).

If you need to, you can read values into more than one variable using one scanf statement. If x and y are double variables, you can use

```
scanf("%lf %lf", &x, &y);
```

to read values into x and y. When executed, scanf expects to find two valid floating-point (or integer) constants next in the data. The first is stored in x and the second in y. Any number of spaces or blank lines can come before, between, or after the numbers.

You can also read values for int, double, or float variables in the same scanf statement. You just have to ensure that you use the correct specification for each variable. Suppose item and quantity are int, and price is double. The statement

```
scanf("%d %lf %d", &item, &price, &quantity);
```

expects to find three numbers next in the data.

- The first must be an int constant that will be stored in item.

- The second must be a double (or int) constant that will be stored in price.

- The third must be an int constant that will be stored in quantity.

The following are all valid data for this scanf statement:

```
4000 7.99 8.7  // 8.7 is truncated to 8
3575 10 44     // price will be interpreted as 10.00
5600 25.0 1
```

As usual, any amount of whitespace may be used to separate the numbers.
The following are all invalid data for this scanf statement:

```
4000 7.99 x.8  // x.8 is not an integer constant
25cm 10 44     // 25cm is not an integer constant
560 25 amt = 7 // a is not a valid numeric character
```

When scanf fetches a number, it remains poised just after the number; a subsequent scanf will continue to read data from that point. To illustrate, suppose some data is typed as

```
4000 7.99 8
```

and consider the statements

```
scanf("%d", &item);
scanf("%lf", &price);
scanf("%d", &quantity);
```

The first `scanf` will store 4000 in `item`. On completion, it remains poised at the space after 4000. The next `scanf` will continue reading from that point and will store 7.99 in `price`. This `scanf` will stop at the space after 7.99. The third `scanf` will continue reading from that point and store 8 in `quantity`. This `scanf` will stop at the character after 8; this may be a space or the *end-of-line* character. Any subsequent `scanf` will continue reading from that point.

It is useful to imagine a "data pointer" moving through the data as data items are read. At any time, it marks the position in the data from which the next `scanf` will start looking for the next item of data.

3.4 Read Strings

In Section 2.6, we saw how to declare a variable to hold a string value. For example, the declaration

```
char item[50];
```

lets us store a string value (of maximum length 49) in `item`. We also saw how we can assign a string value to `item` using the standard string function, `strcpy`.

Now we show you how to read a value from the input into `item`. There are several ways to do this in C. We will use the `gets` (usually pronounced *get s* not *gets*) statement (more precisely, a function), as in:

```
gets(item);
```

This reads characters and stores them in `item` starting from the current position of the data pointer until the end-of-line is reached. The end-of-line character is *not* stored. The data pointer is positioned at the beginning of the next line.

For example, if the data line is

```
Right front headlamp
```

then the string `Right front headlamp` is stored in `item`. The *effect* is the same as if we had written

```
strcpy(item, "Right front headlamp");
```

The alert reader will notice that we did not put an & before `item`, as we have been doing for reading numbers with `scanf`. For now, just note that `item` is a "character array" and the rule in C is that we must not put & before an *array name* when reading data into it. You may understand this better after we discuss arrays in Chapter 8. The quick explanation is that an *array name* denotes the "address of the first element of the array" so there is no need for & to get the address. For now, just think of it as a rule that you need to follow.

Consider the following statements (assume the declaration `char name[50]`):

```
printf("Hi, what's your name? ");
gets(name);
printf("Delighted to meet you, %s\n", name);
```

When executed,

- The printf for comment will not use your name.

- gets will wait for you to type your name. When typed, the name will be stored in the variable name.

- printf will then print a greeting using your name.

Your computer screen will look as follows (assuming Birdie is typed as the name):

```
Hi, what's your name? Birdie
Delighted to meet you, Birdie
```

3.5 Examples

We now write programs to solve a few problems. You should try solving the problems before looking at the solutions. In the sample runs, the underlined items are typed by the user; everything else is printed by the computer.

3.5.1 Problem 1 - Average

Write a program to request three integers and print their average to one decimal place. The program should work as follows:

```
Enter 3 integers: 23 7 10
Their average is 13.3
```

A solution is shown as Program P3.4.

Program P3.4

```
//request 3 integers; print their average
#include <stdio.h>
int main() {
    int a, b, c;
    double average;
    printf("Enter 3 integers: ");
    scanf("%d %d %d", &a, &b, &c);
    average = (a + b + c) / 3.0;
    printf("\nTheir average is %3.1f\n", average);
}
```

Points to note about Program P3.4:

- The variable average is declared as double instead of int since the average may not be a whole number.

- If whole numbers are not entered in the data, the program will crash or, at best, give incorrect results.

- We use 3.0 instead of 3 in calculating the average. This forces a floating-point division to be performed. If we had used 3, an integer division would be performed, giving 13.0 as the answer for the sample data, above.

- In the last printf, the first \n is used to print the blank line in the output.

- We could have declared average and assigned to it in one statement, like this:

  double average = (a + b + c) / 3.0;

- The variable average is not really necessary in this program. We could calculate and print the average in the printf statement with

  printf("\nTheir average is %3.1f\n", (a + b + c) / 3.0);

3.5.2 Problem 2 - Square

Write a program to request a whole number and print the number and its square. The program should work as follows:

```
Enter a whole number: 6
Square of 6 is 36
```

A solution is shown as Program P3.5.

Program P3.5

```
//request a whole number; print its square
#include <stdio.h>
int main() {
    int num, numSq;
    printf("Enter a whole number: ");
    scanf("%d", &num);
    numSq = num * num;
    printf("\nSquare of %d is %d\n", num, numSq);
}
```

Points to note about Program P3.5:

- The spaces in the output is valuable, and need to appear before and after `is` to leave spaces around `is`. If these spaces are omitted, the sample output will be

  `Square of6is36`

- The variable numSq is not really necessary. It can be omitted altogether and the same output printed with

  `printf("\nSquare of %d is %d\n", num, num * num);`

- The program assumes an integer will be entered; if anything other than an integer is entered, the program will crash or give incorrect results. To cater for numbers with a point, declare num (and numSq, if used) as double.

3.5.3 Problem 3 - Banking

The following data are given for a customer in a bank: name, account number, average balance, and number of transactions made during the month. It is required to calculate the interest earned and service charge.

The interest is calculated as follows:

`interest = 6% of average balance`

and the service charge is calculated by this:

`service charge = 50 cents per transaction`

Write a program to read the data for the customer, calculate the interest and service charge, and print the customer's name, average balance, interest, and service charge.

The following is a sample run of the program:

```
Name? Alice Wonder
Account number? 4901119250056048
Average balance? 2500
Number of transactions? 13
Name: Alice Wonder
Average balance: $2500.00
Interest: $150.00
Service charge: $6.50
```

A solution is shown as Program P3.6.

Program P3.6

```c
//calculate interest and service charge for bank customer
#include <stdio.h>
int main() {
    char customer[30], acctNum[30];
    double avgBalance, interest, service;
    int numTrans;
    printf("Name? ");
    gets(customer);
    printf("Account number? ");
    gets(acctNum);
    printf("Average balance? ");
    scanf("%lf", &avgBalance);
    printf("Number of transactions? ");
    scanf("%d", &numTrans);
    interest = avgBalance * 0.06;
    service = numTrans * 0.50;
    printf("\nName: %s\n", customer);
    printf("Average balance: $%3.2f\n", avgBalance);
    printf("Interest: $%3.2f\n", interest);
    printf("Service charge: $%3.2f\n", service);
}
```

This problem is more complicated than those we have seen so far. It involves more data and more processing. But we can simplify its solution if we tackle it in small steps.

Firstly, let us outline an algorithm for solving the problem. This can be:

```
prompt for and read each item of data
calculate interest earned
calculate service charge
print required output
```

The logic here is fairly straightforward and a little thought should convince us that these are the steps required to solve the problem.

Next, we must choose variables for the data items we need to store.

- For the customer's name, we need a string variable—we call it `customer`.

- We may be tempted to use an integer variable for the account number but this is not a good idea for two reasons: an account number may contain letters (as in CD55887700); or it may be a very long integer, too big to fit in an `int` variable. For these reasons, we use a string variable that we call `acctNum`.

- The average balance may contain a decimal point and must be stored in a `double` variable; we call it `avgBalance`.

- The number of transactions is a whole number so we use an `int` variable, `numTrans`.

Next, we need variables to store the interest and service charge. Since these may contain a decimal point, we must use double variables—we call them interest and service.

Prompting for and reading the data are fairly straightforward, given what we have covered so far. We need only emphasize that when numeric data is being entered, it must be a numeric constant. We cannot, for instance, enter the average balance as $2500 or as 2,500. We must enter it as 2500 or 2500.0 or 2500.00.

The calculation of the interest and service charge presents the biggest challenge. We must specify the calculation in a form that the computer can understand and execute.

We cannot, for instance, write

```
interest = 6% of avgBalance;
```

or even

```
interest = 6% * avgBalance;
```

or

```
service = 50 cents per transaction;
```

We must express each right-hand side as a proper arithmetic expression, using appropriate constants, variables, and operators. Therefore, "6% of average balance" must be expressed as

```
avgBalance*0.06
```

or

```
0.06*avgBalance
```

and "50 cents per transaction" must be expressed as

```
0.50*numTrans
```

or

```
numTrans*0.5
```

or something similar, even

```
numTrans/2.0
```

Printing the output is fairly straightforward. Even though, for example, we cannot use $ when entering data for average balance, we can print a dollar sign in front of it when we print its value. All we need to do is print $ as part of a string. How this is done is shown in the program. Similarly, we print the interest and service charge labeled with a dollar sign.

We use the specification %3.2f for printing avgBalance. We intentionally use a small field width of 3 so that avgBalance is printed using only the exact number of print columns needed for printing its value. This ensures that its value is printed right next to the dollar sign. Similar remarks apply to interest and service.

3.5.4 Problem 4 – Tickets

At a football match, tickets are sold in three categories: reserved, stands, and grounds. For each of these categories, you are given the ticket price and the number of tickets sold. Write a program to prompt for these values and print the amount of money collected from each category of tickets. Also print the total number of tickets sold and the total amount of money collected.

We will write the program to operate as follows when run:

```
Reserved price and tickets sold? 100 500
Stands price and tickets sold? 75 4000
Grounds price and tickets sold? 40 8000
Reserved sales: $50000.00
Stands sales: $300000.00
Grounds sales: $320000.00
12500 tickets were sold
Total money collected: $670000.00
```

As shown, we prompt for and read two values at a time, the price and the number of tickets sold.

For each category, the sales is calculated by multiplying the ticket price by the number of tickets sold.

The total number of tickets sold is calculated by adding the number of tickets sold for each category.

The total money collected is calculated by adding the sales for each category.

An outline of the algorithm for solving the problem is as follows:

```
prompt for and read reserved price and tickets sold
calculate reserved sales
prompt for and read stands price and tickets sold
calculate stands sales
prompt for and read grounds price and tickets sold
calculate grounds sales
calculate total tickets
calculate total sales
print required output
```

A solution is shown as Program P3.7. The price can be entered as an integer or double constant; the number of tickets *must* be entered as an integer constant.

Program P3.7

```c
//calculate ticket sales for football match
#include <stdio.h>
int main() {
    double rPrice, sPrice, gPrice;
    double rSales, sSales, gSales, tSales;
    int rTickets, sTickets, gTickets, tTickets;
```

```
    printf("Reserved price and tickets sold? ");
    scanf("%lf %d", &rPrice, &rTickets);
    rSales = rPrice * rTickets;
    printf("Stands price and tickets sold? ");
    scanf("%lf %d", &sPrice, &sTickets);
    sSales = sPrice * sTickets;
    printf("Grounds price and tickets sold? ");
    scanf("%lf %d", &gPrice, &gTickets);
    gSales = gPrice * gTickets;
    tTickets = rTickets + sTickets + gTickets;
    tSales = rSales + sSales + gSales;
    printf("\nReserved sales: $%3.2f\n", rSales);
    printf("Stands sales: $%3.2f\n", sSales);
    printf("Grounds sales: $%3.2f\n", gSales);
    printf("\n%d tickets were sold\n", tTickets);
    printf("Total money collected: $%3.2f\n", tSales);
}
```

EXERCISES 3

1. For each of the following, give examples of data that will be read correctly and
    examples of data that will cause the program to crash. Assume the declaration

    ```
    int i, j; double x, y;);
    ```

    (a) scanf("%d %d", &i, &j);
    (b) scanf("%lf %lf", &x, &y);
    (c) scanf("%d %lf %d", &i, &x, &j);

2. For 1(c), state what will be stored in i, x, and j for each of the following sets
    of data:

    (a) 14 11 52
    (b) -7 2.3 52
    (c) 0 6.1 7.0
    (d) 1.0 8 -1

3. Write a program that requests a user to enter a weight in kilograms, and converts it
    to pounds. (1 kilogram = 2.2 pounds.)

4. Write a program that requests a length in centimeters and converts it to inches.
    (1 inch = 2.54 cm.)

5. Assuming that 12 and 5 are entered as data, identify the logic error in the following statements (a, b, c, d, and e are int):

```
scanf("%d %d", &a, &b);
c = (a - b) * 2;
d = e + a;
e = a / (b + 1);
printf("%d %d %d\n", c, d, e);
```

When the error is corrected, what is printed?

6. What is printed by the following (a, b, and c are int)?

```
a = 13;
b = a + 12;
printf("%d %d\n", a, b);
c = a + b;
a = a + 11;
printf("%d %d %d\n", a, b, c);
```

7. Write a program that requests a price and a discount percent. The program prints the original price, the discount amount, and the amount the customer must pay.

8. Same as 7, but assume that 15% tax must be added to the amount the customer must pay.

9. Write a program to calculate electricity charges for a customer. The program requests a name, previous meter reading, and current meter reading. The difference in the two readings gives the number of units of electricity used. The customer pays a fixed charge of $25 plus 20 cents for each unit used.

   Print all the data, the number of units used, and the amount the customer must pay, appropriately labeled.

10. Modify 9 so that the program requests the fixed charge and the rate per unit.

11. Write a program to request a student's name and marks in four subjects. The program must print the name, total marks, and average mark, appropriately labeled.

12. Write a program that requests a person's gross salary, deductions allowed and rate of tax (e.g., 25, meaning 25%), and calculates his net pay as follows:

   Tax is calculated by applying the rate of tax to the gross salary minus the deductions.

   Net pay is calculated by gross salary minus tax.

   Print the gross salary, tax deducted, and net pay, appropriately labeled.

   Also print the percentage of the gross salary that was paid in tax.

   Make up appropriate sets of data for testing the program.

13. Write a program that, when run, works as follows (underlined items are typed by the user):

    ```
    Hi, what's your name? Alice
    Welcome to our show, Alice
    How old are you? 27
    Hmm, you don't look a day over 22
    Tell me, Alice, where do you live? Princes Town
    Oh, I've heard Princes Town is a lovely place
    ```

14. A ball is thrown vertically upwards with an initial speed of U meters per second. Its height H after time T seconds is given by

    ```
    H = UT - 4.9T2
    ```

    Write a program that requests U and T and prints the height of the ball after T seconds.

15. Write a program to calculate the cost of carpeting a rectangular room in a house. The program must do the following:

    • Request the length and breadth of the room (assume they are in meters).

    • Request the cost per square meter of the carpet.

    • Calculate the area of the room.

    • Calculate the cost of the carpet for the room.

    • Print the area and the cost, appropriately labeled.

16. Write a program which, given a length in inches, converts it to yards, feet, and inches. (1 yard = 3 feet, 1 foot = 12 inches). For example, if the length is 100 inches, the program should print 2 yd 2 ft 4 in.

CHAPTER 4

▉ ▉ ▉

Programs with Selection Logic

In this chapter, we will explain the following:

- What are Boolean expressions

- How C represents Boolean values

- How to write programs using if

- How to write programs using if...else

- Where semicolons are required, where they are optional, and where they must *not* be put

- How a program should be tested

- Why symbolic constants are useful and how to use them in a C program

4.1 Introduction

In the last chapter, we showed how to write programs using sequence logic—programs whose statements are executed "in sequence" from the first to the last.

In this chapter, the programs will use *selection* logic—they will *test* some *condition* and take different courses of action based on whether the condition is true or false. In C, selection logic is implemented using the if and the if...else statements.

4.2 Boolean Expressions

A *Boolean expression* (named after the famous English mathematician George Boole) is one that is either true or false. The simplest kinds of Boolean expressions are those that compare one value with another. Some examples are:

```
k is equal to 999
a is greater than 100
a2 + b2 is equal to c2
b2 is greater than or equal to 4ac
s is not equal to 0
```

Each of these can be either true or false. These are examples of a special kind of Boolean expression called relational expressions. Such expressions simply check if one value is equal to, not equal to, greater than, greater than or equal to, less than, and less than or equal to another value. We write them using relational operators.

The C relational operators (with examples) are:

==	equal to	k == 999, a*a + b*b == c*c
!=	not equal to	s != 0, a != b + c
>	greater than	a > 100
>=	greater than or equal to	b*b >= 4.0*a*c
<	less than	n < 0
<=	less than or equal to	score <= 65

Boolean expressions are normally used to control the flow of program execution. For example, we may have a variable (h, say) which starts off with a value of 0. We keep increasing it by 1 and we want to know when its value reaches 100. We say we wish to know when the *condition* h == 100 is true. A condition is the common name for a Boolean expression.

The real power of programming lies in the ability of a program to *test* a *condition* and decide whether it is true or false. If it is true, the program can perform one set of actions; and if it is false, it can perform another set or simply do nothing at all.

For example, suppose the variable score holds the score obtained by a student in a test, and the student passes if her score is 50 or more and fails if it is less than 50. A program can be written to *test* the *condition*

```
score >= 50
```

If it is true, the student passes; if it is false, the student fails. In C, this can be written as:

```
if (score >= 50) printf("Pass\n");
else printf("Fail\n");
```

When the computer gets to this statement, it compares the current value of score with 50. If the value is greater than or equal to 50, we say that the condition score >= 50 is true. In this case the program prints Pass. If the value of score is less than 50, we say that the condition score >= 50 is false. In this case, the program prints Fail.

In this chapter, we will see how Boolean expressions are used in if and if...else statements and, in the next chapter, we will see how they are used in while statements.

4.2.1 AND, &&

With the relational operators, we can create *simple* conditions. But sometimes, we need to ask if one thing is true AND another thing is true. We may also need to know if one of two things is true. For these situations, we need *compound* conditions. To create compound conditions, we use the *logical operators* AND, OR, and NOT.

For example, suppose we want to know if the value of h lies between 1 and 99, inclusive. We want to know if h is greater than or equal to 1 AND if h is less than or equal to 99. In C, we express this as:

```
(h >= 1) && (h <= 99)
```

In C, the symbol for AND is &&.
Note the following:

- The variable h *must be repeated* in both conditions. It is tempting, but wrong, to write

  ```
  h >= 1 && <= 99 //this is wrong
  ```

- The brackets around h >= 1 and h <= 99 are not *required*, but it is not wrong to put them. This is so since && (and ||, see next) have *lower precedence* than the relational operators. Without the brackets,

  ```
  h >= 1 && h <= 99
  ```

  would be interpreted by C like this:

  ```
  (h >= 1) && (h <= 99)
  ```

- This is the same as with the brackets.

4.2.2 OR, ||

If n is an integer representing a month of the year, we can check if n is invalid by testing if n is less than 1 OR n is greater than 12. In C, we express this as:

```
(n < 1) || (n > 12)
```

In C, the symbol for OR is ||. As discussed above, the brackets are not required and we could write the expression as

```
n < 1 || n > 12
```

This tests if n is invalid. Of course, we can test if n is valid by testing if

```
n >= 1 && n <= 12
```

Which test we use depends on how we wish to express our logic. Sometimes it's convenient to use the valid test, sometimes the invalid one.

4.2.3 NOT, !

If p is some Boolean expression, then NOT p reverses the truth value of p. In others words, if p is true then NOT p is false; if p is false then NOT p is true. In C, the symbol for NOT is the exclamation mark, !. Using the example above, since

```
n >= 1 && n <= 12
```

tests for valid n, the condition NOT (n >=1 && n <= 12) tests for invalid n. This is written in C as

```
!(n >= 1 && n <= 12)
```

This is equivalent to n < 1 || n > 12. Those familiar with de Morgan's laws will know that

```
not (a and b) = (not a) or (not b)
```

and

```
not(a or b) = (not a) and (not b)
```

In general, if p and q are Boolean expressions, we have the following:

- p && q is true when both p and q are true and false, otherwise;
- p || q is true when either p or q is true and false only when both p and q are false;
- !p is true when p is false and false when p is true.

This is summarized in the following table (with T for true and F for false):

P	q	&&	||	!p
T	T	T	T	F
T	F	F	T	F
F	T	F	T	T
F	F	F	F	T

Most of the programs in this book will use simple conditions. A few will use compound conditions.

4.2.3.1 The data type bool in C99

The original C standard and the later ANSI C standard did not define a Boolean data type. Traditionally, C has used the concept of the *value of an expression* to denote true/false. A numeric expression can be used in any context where a true/false value is required. The expression is considered true if its value is *nonzero* and false if its value is zero.

The latest C99 standard defines the type bool. However, in this book, we will use the traditional approach mainly because many popular C compilers do not support the C99 standard as yet. Also as you will see, we can easily live without bool. The vast majority of our Boolean expressions would be relational expressions used in if and while statements. If we ever need a "Boolean" variable, we can use an int variable with 1 representing true and 0 representing false.

4.3 The `if` Construct

Let us write a program for the following problem:

A computer repair shop charges $100 per hour for labor plus the cost of any parts used in the repair. However, the minimum charge for any job is $150. Prompt for the number of hours worked and the cost of parts (which could be $0) and print the charge for the job.

We will write the program so that it works as follows:

```
Hours worked? 2.5
Cost of parts? 20
Charge for the job: $270.00
```

or

```
Hours worked? 1
Cost of parts? 25
Charge for the job: $150.00
```

The following algorithm describes the steps required to solve the problem:

```
prompt for and read the hours worked
prompt for and read the cost of parts
calculate charge = hours worked * 100 + cost of parts
if charge is less than 150 then set charge to 150
print charge
```

This is another example of an algorithm written in *pseudocode*—an informal way of specifying programming logic.

The algorithm introduces a new statement—the if statement. The expression

```
charge is less than 150
```

is an example of a *condition*. If the condition is true, the statement after then (called the *then part*) is executed; if it is false, the statement after then is *not* executed.

Program P4.1 shows how to express this algorithm as a C program.

69

Program P4.1

```
//print job charge based on hours worked and cost of parts
#include <stdio.h>
int main() {
    double hours, parts, jobCharge;
    printf("Hours worked? ");
    scanf("%lf", &hours);
    printf("Cost of parts? ");
    scanf("%lf", &parts);
    jobCharge = hours * 100 + parts;
    if (jobCharge < 150) jobCharge = 150;
    printf("\nCharge for the job: $%3.2f\n", jobCharge);
}
```

For this program, we choose to use three variables—hours, parts and jobCharge, all of type double since we may need to enter floating-point values for hours worked and cost of parts.

It is very important that you make an extra effort to understand the if statement since it is one of the most important statements in programming. It is the if statement that can make a program appear to think.

The condition

```
charge is less than 150
```

of the pseudocode algorithm is expressed in our program as

```
jobCharge < 150
```

When the program is executed, the job charge is calculated in the normal way (hours * 100 + parts). The if statement then tests if this value, jobCharge, is less than 150; if it is, then jobCharge is set to 150. If it is not less than 150, jobCharge remains as it is. The statement

```
if (jobCharge < 150) jobCharge = 150;
```

is a simple example of the if *construct*. Observe that the word then is *not* used in C. In general, the construct takes the following form in C:

```
if (<condition>) <statement>
```

The word if and the brackets around <condition> are *required* by C. You must supply <condition> and <statement> where <condition> is a Boolean expression and <statement> can be either a one-line statement or a block—one or more statements enclosed by { and }. If <condition> is true, <statement> is executed; if <condition> is false, <statement> is *not* executed. In either case, the program continues with the statement, if any, after <statement>.

In the program, `<condition>` is

```
jobCharge + 150
```
and `<statement>` is
```
jobCharge = 150;
```

To give an example where `<statement>` is a block, suppose we want to exchange the values of two variables a and b but only if a is bigger than b. This can be done with the following, assuming, as an example, that a = 15, b = 8, and c is a temporary variable:

```
if (a > b)
{
    c = a;   //store a in c; c becomes 15
    a = b;   //store b in a; a becomes 8
    b = c;   //store old value of a, 15,in b
}
```

Here, `<statement>` is the part from { to }, a block containing three assignment statements. If a is greater than b, the block is executed (and the values are exchanged); if a is *not* greater than b, the block is *not* executed (and the values remain as they are). In passing, be aware that exchanging the values of two variables requires *three* assignment statements; it *cannot* be done with *two*. If you are not convinced, try it.

In general, if there are several things that we want to do if a condition is true; we must enclose them within { and } to create a block. This will ensure that we satisfy C's rule that `<statement>` is a single statement or a block.

It is good programming practice to *indent* the statements in the block. This makes it easy to see at a glance which statements are in the block. If we had written the above as follows, the structure of the block would not be so easy to see:

```
if (a > b)
{
c = a;  //store a in c; c becomes 15
a = b;  //store b in a; a becomes 8
b = c;  //store old value of a, 15,in b
}
```

When we are writing *pseudocode*, we normally use the following format:

```
if <condition> then
    <statement1>
    <statement2>
    etc.
endif
```

The construct is terminated with `endif`, a convention used by many programmers. Note, again, that we indent the statements to be executed if `<condition>` is true. We emphasize that `endif` is not a C word but merely a convenient word used by programmers in writing pseudocode.

The example illustrates one style of writing a block in an if statement. This style matches { and } as follows:

```
if (<condition>)
{
    <statement1>;
    <statement2>;
    etc.
}
```

Here, { and } line up with if and the statements are indented. This makes it easy to recognize what's in the body. For a small program, it probably doesn't matter, but as program size increases, it will become more important for the layout of the code to reflect its structure. In this book, we will use the following style (as you would know by now, the *compiler* doesn't care which style is used):

```
if (<condition>) {
    <statement1>;
    <statement2>;
    etc.
}
```

We will put { on the first line after the right bracket and let } match up with if; the statements in the block are indented. We believe this is as clear as the first style and it's one less line in the program! Which style you use is a matter of personal preference; choose one and use it consistently.

4.3.1 Find the Sum of Two Lengths

Suppose that a length is given in meters and centimeters, for example, 3m 75cm. You are given two pairs of integers representing two lengths. Write a program to prompt for two lengths and print their sum such that the centimeter value is less than 100.

For example, the sum of 3m 25cm and 2m 15cm is 5m 40cm, but the sum of 3m 75cm and 5m 50cm is 9m 25cm.

Assume the program works as follows:

```
Enter values for m and cm: 3 75
Enter values for m and cm: 5 50

Sum is 9m 25cm
```

Observe that the data must be entered with digits only. If, for instance, we type 3m 75cm we will get an error since 3m is not a valid integer constant. Our program will assume that the first number entered is the meter value and the second number is the centimeter value.

We find the sum by adding the two meter values and adding the two centimeter values. If the centimeter value is less than 100, there is nothing more to do. But if it is not, we must subtract 100 from it and add 1 to the meter value. This logic is expressed as follows.

```
m = sum of meter values
cm = sum of centimeter values
if cm >= 100 then
    subtract 100 from cm
    add 1 to m
endif
```

As a *boundary* case, we must check that our program works if cm is exactly 100. As an exercise, verify that it does.

Program P4.2 solves the problem as described.

Program P4.2

```c
//find the sum of two lengths given in meters and cm
#include <stdio.h>
int main() {
    int m1, cm1, m2, cm2, mSum, cmSum;
    printf("Enter values for m and cm: ");
    scanf("%d %d", &m1, &cm1);
    printf("Enter values for m and cm: ");
    scanf("%d %d", &m2, &cm2);
    mSum = m1 + m2;      //add the meters
    cmSum = cm1 + cm2; //add the centimeters
    if (cmSum >= 100) {
        cmSum = cmSum - 100;
        mSum = mSum + 1;
    }
    printf("\nSum is %dm %dcm\n", mSum, cmSum);
}
```

We use the variables m1 and cm1 for the first length, m2 and cm2 for the second length, and mSum and cmSum for the sum of the two lengths.

The program assumes that the centimeter part of the given lengths is less than 100 and it works correctly if this is so. But what if the lengths were 3m 150cm and 2m 200cm?

The program will print 6m 250cm. (As an exercise, follow the logic of the program to see why.) While this is correct, it is not in the correct format since we require the centimeter value to be less than 100. We can modify our program to work in these cases as well by using integer division and % (the *remainder* operator).

The following pseudocode shows how:

```
m = sum of meter values
cm = sum of centimeter values
if cm >= 100 then
    add cm / 100 to m
    set cm to cm % 100
endif
```

Using the above example, m is set to 5 and cm is set to 350. Since cm is greater than 100, we work out 350 / 100 (this finds how many 100s there are in cm) which is 3, using integer division; this is added to m, giving 8. The next line sets cm to 350 % 100, which is 50. So the answer we get is 8m 50cm, which is correct *and* in the correct format.

Note that the statements in the "then part" *must* be written in the order shown. We must use the (original) value of cm to work out cm / 100 before changing it in the next statement to cm % 100. As an exercise, work out what value will be computed for the sum if these statements are reversed. (The answer will be 5m 50cm, which is wrong. Can you see why?)

These changes are reflected in Program P4.3.

Program P4.3

```
//find the sum of two lengths given in meters and cm
#include <stdio.h>
int main() {
    int m1, cm1, m2, cm2, mSum, cmSum;
    printf("Enter values for m and cm: ");
    scanf("%d %d", &m1, &cm1);
    printf("Enter values for m and cm: ");
    scanf("%d %d", &m2, &cm2);
    mSum = m1 + m2; //add the meters
    cmSum = cm1 + cm2; //add the centimeters
    if (cmSum >= 100) {
        mSum = mSum + cmSum / 100;
        cmSum = cmSum % 100;
    }
    printf("\nSum is %dm %dcm\n", mSum, cmSum);
}
```

The following is a sample run of this program:

```
Enter values for m and cm: 3 150
Enter values for m and cm: 2 200

Sum is 8m 50cm
```

The astute reader may recognize that we do not even need the if statement. Consider this:

```
mSum = m1 + m2; //add the meters
cmSum = cm1 + cm2; //add the centimeters
mSum = mSum + cmSum / 100;
cmSum = cmSum % 100;
```

where the last two statements come from the if statement.

We know therefore that this will work if cmSum is greater than or equal to 100 since, when that is the case, these four statements are executed.

What if cmSum is less than 100? Originally, the last two statements would not have been executed since the if condition would have been false. *Now* they are executed. Let us see what happens. Using the example of 3m 25cm and 2m 15cm, we get mSum as 5 and cmSum as 40.

In the next statement 40 / 100 is 0 so mSum does not change and in the last statement 40 % 100 is 40 so cmSum does not change. So the answer will be printed correctly as

```
Sum is 5m 40cm
```

You should begin to realize by now that there is usually more than one way to express the logic of a program. With experience and study, you will learn which ways are better and why.

4.4 The if...else Construct

Let us write a program for the following problem:

A student is given 3 tests, each marked out of 100. The student passes if his average mark is greater than or equal to 50 and fails if his average mark is less than 50. Prompt for the 3 marks and print Pass if the student passes and Fail if he fails.

We will write the program assuming it works as follows:

```
Enter 3 marks: 60 40 56

Average is 52.0 Pass
```

or

```
Enter 3 marks: 40 60 36

Average is 45.3 Fail
```

The following algorithm describes the steps required to solve the problem:

```
prompt for the 3 marks
calculate the average
if average is greater than or equal to 50 then
    print "Pass"
else
    print "Fail"
endif
```

The part from if to endif is an example of the if...else *construct*.
The condition

```
average is greater than or equal to 50
```

is another example of a relational expression. If the condition is true, the statement after then
(the *then part*) is executed; if it is false, the statement after else (the *else part*) is executed.
    The whole *construct* is terminated with endif.
When you write pseudocode, what is important is that the logic intended is unmistakably
clear. Note again how indentation can help by making it easy to identify the then part and the
else part.
    In the end, though, you must express the code in some programming language for it to be run
on a computer. Program P4.4 shows how to do this for the above algorithm.

Program P4.4

```c
//request 3 marks; print their average and Pass/Fail
#include <stdio.h>
int main() {
    int mark1, mark2, mark3;
    double average ;
    printf("Enter 3 marks: ");
    scanf("%d %d %d", &mark1, &mark2, &mark3);
    average = (mark1 + mark2 + mark3) / 3.0;
    printf("\nAverage is %3.1f", average);
    if (average >= 50) printf(" Pass\n");
    else printf(" Fail\n");
}
```

Study carefully the if...else construct in the program. It reflects the logic expressed on the
previous page. Note, again, that the word then is omitted in C.
In general, the if...else construct in C takes the form shown below.

```
if (<condition>) <statement1> else <statement2>
```

The words if and else, and the brackets, are *required* by C. You must supply <condition>,
<statement1> and <statement2>. Each of <statement1> and <statement2> can be a one-line
statement or a block. If <condition> is true, <statement1> is executed and <statement2> is
skipped; if <condition> is false, <statement1> is skipped and <statement2> is executed. When
the if construct is executed, *either* <statement1> *or* <statement2> is executed, but not both.
If <statement1> and <statement2> are one-line statements, you can use this layout:

```
if (<condition>) <statement1>
else <statement2>
```

If <statement1> and <statement2> are blocks, you can use the following layout:

```
if (<condition>) {
    ...
}
else {
    ...
}
```

In describing the various constructs in C, we normally use the phrase "where <statement> can be a one-line statement or a block."

It is useful to remember that, in C, for one-line statements, the semicolon is considered *part of* the statement. Examples are:

```
a = 5;
printf("Pass\n");
scanf("%d", &n);
```

So, in those cases where one-line statements are used, the semicolon, being part of the statement, must be present. In Program P4.4, in the if...else statement,

<statement1> is
```
printf("Pass\n");
```

and <statement2> is

```
printf("Fail\n");
```

However, for a block or compound statement, the right brace, }, ends the block. So, in those cases where a block is used, there is no need for an additional semicolon to end the block.

It is sometimes useful to remember that the entire if...else construct (from if to <statement2>) is considered by C to be *one* statement and can be used in any place where one statement is required.

4.4.1 Calculate Pay

For an example that requires blocks, suppose we have values for hours worked and rate of pay (the amount paid per hour) and wish to calculate a person's regular pay, overtime pay, and gross pay based on the following:

If hours worked is less than or equal to 40, regular pay is calculated by multiplying hours worked by rate of pay and overtime pay is 0. If hours worked is greater than 40, regular pay is calculated by multiplying 40 by the rate of pay and overtime pay is calculated by multiplying the hours *in excess of* 40 by the rate of pay by 1.5. Gross pay is calculated by adding regular pay and overtime pay.

For example, if hours is 36 and rate is 20 dollars per hour, regular pay is $720 (36 times 20) and overtime pay is $0. Gross pay is $720.

And if hours is 50 and rate is 12 dollars per hour, regular pay is $480 (40 times 12) and overtime pay is $180 (excess hours 10 times 12 times 1.5). Gross pay is $660 (480 + 180).

The above description could be expressed in pseudocode as follows:

```
if hours is less than or equal to 40 then
    set regular pay to hours x rate
    set overtime pay to 0
else
    set regular pay to 40 x rate
    set overtime pay to (hours - 40) x rate x 1.5
endif
set gross pay to regular pay + overtime pay
```

We use indentation to highlight the statements to be executed if the condition "hours is less than or equal to 40" is true and those to be executed if the condition is false. The whole *construct* is terminated with endif.

The next step is to convert the pseudocode to C. When we do, we have to make sure that we stick to C's rules for writing an if...else statement. In this example, we have to ensure that both the then and else parts are written as blocks since they both consist of more than one statement. Using the variables hours (hours worked), rate (rate of pay), regPay (regular pay), ovtPay (overtime pay), and grossPay (gross pay), we write the C code, thus:

```
if (hours <= 40) {
    regPay = hours * rate;
    ovtPay = 0;
} //no semicolon here; } ends the block
else {
    regPay = 40 * rate;
    ovtPay = (hours - 40) * rate * 1.5;
} //no semicolon here; } ends the block
grossPay = regPay + ovtPay;
```

Note the two comments. It would be wrong to put a semicolon after the first } since the if statement continues with an else part. If we were to put one, it effectively ends the if statement and C assumes there is no else part. When it finds the word else, there will be no if with which to match it and the program will give a "misplaced else" error.

There is no need for a semicolon after the last } but putting one would do no harm.

Problem: Write a program to prompt for hours worked and rate of pay. The program then calculates and prints regular pay, overtime pay, and gross pay, based on the above description. The following algorithm outlines the overall logic of the solution:

```
prompt for hours worked and rate of pay
if hours is less than or equal to 40 then
    set regular pay to hours x rate
    set overtime pay to 0
```

```
else
    set regular pay to 40 x rate
    set overtime pay to (hours - 40) x rate x 1.5
endif
set gross pay to regular pay + overtime pay
print regular pay, overtime pay and gross pay
```

This algorithm is implemented as Program P4.5. All the variables are declared as double so that fractional values can be entered for hours worked and rate of pay.

Program P4.5

```c
#include <stdio.h>
int main() {
    double hours, rate, regPay, ovtPay, grossPay;
    printf("Hours worked? ");
    scanf("%lf", &hours);
    printf("Rate of pay? ");
    scanf("%lf", &rate);
    if (hours <= 40) {
        regPay = hours * rate;
        ovtPay = 0;
    }
    else {
        regPay = 40 * rate;
        ovtPay = (hours - 40) * rate * 1.5;
    }
    grossPay = regPay + ovtPay;
    printf("\nRegular pay: $%3.2f\n", regPay);
    printf("Overtime pay: $%3.2f\n", ovtPay);
    printf("gross pay: $%3.2f\n", grossPay);
}
```

A sample run of this program is shown here:

```
Hours worked? 50
Rate of pay? 12

Regular pay: $480.00
Overtime pay: $180.00
Gross pay: $660.00
```

You should verify that the results are indeed correct.

Note that even though hours and rate are double, *data* for them can be supplied in any valid numeric format—here we use the integers 50 and 12. These values would be converted to double format before being stored in the variables. We could, if we wished, have typed 50.0 and 12.00, for example.

4.5 On Program Testing

When we write a program we should test it thoroughly to ensure that it is working correctly. As a minimum, we should test *all paths* through the program. This means that our *test data* must be chosen so that each statement in the program is executed at least once.

For Program P4.5, the sample run tests only when the hours worked is greater than 40. Based on this test alone, we cannot be sure that our program will work correctly if the hours worked is less than or equal to 40. To be sure, we must run another test in which the hours worked is less than or equal to 40. The following is such a sample run:

```
Hours worked? 36
Rate of pay? 20

Regular pay: $720.00
Overtime pay: $0.00
Gross pay: $720.00
```

These results are correct, which gives us greater assurance that our program is correct. We should also run a test when the hours is exactly 40; we must always test a program at its "boundaries." For this program, 40 is a boundary—it is the value at which overtime begins to be paid.

What if the results are incorrect? For example, suppose overtime pay is wrong. We say the program contains a *bug* (an error), and we must *debug* (remove the error from) the program. In this case, we can look at the statement(s) that calculate the overtime pay to see if we have specified the calculation correctly. If this fails to uncover the error, we must painstakingly "execute" the program by hand using the test data that produced the error. If done properly, this will usually reveal the cause of the error.

4.6 Symbolic Constants

In Program 4.1, we used two constants—100 and 150—denoting the labor charge per hour and the minimum job cost, respectively. What if these values change after the program has been written? We would have to find all occurrences of them in the program and change them to the new values.

This program is fairly short so this would not be too difficult to do. But imagine what the task would be like if the program contained hundreds or even thousands of lines of code. It would be difficult, time consuming, and error prone to make all the required changes.

We can make life a little easier by using *symbolic constants* (also called *manifest* or *named* constants)—identifiers that we set to the required constants in one place. If we need to change the value of a constant, the change would have to be made in one place only. For example, in Program P4.1, we could use the symbolic constants ChargePerHour and MinJobCost. We would set ChargePerHour to 100 and MinJobCost to 150.

In C, we use the #define directive to define symbolic constants, among other uses. We show ̶Ì̶o̶m̶ ̶Ì̶y̶r̶ ̶o̶f̶ ̶w̶i̶t̶h̶i̶n̶g̶ ̶P̶r̶o̶g̶r̶a̶m̶ ̶P̶4̶.̶1̶ ̶a̶n̶ ̶P̶r̶o̶g̶r̶a̶m̶ ̶P̶4̶.̶6̶.̶

Program P4.6

```c
//This program illustrates the use of symbolic constants
//Print job charge based on hours worked and cost of parts
#include <stdio.h>
#define ChargePerHour 100
#define MinJobCost 150
int main() {
    double hours, parts, jobCharge;
    printf("Hours worked? ");
    scanf("%lf", &hours);
    printf("Cost of parts? ");
    scanf("%lf", &parts);
    jobCharge = hours * ChargePerHour + parts;
    if (jobCharge < MinJobCost) jobCharge = MinJobCost;
    printf("\nCharge for the job: $%3.2f\n", jobCharge);
}
```

4.6.1 The #define Directive

Directives in C normally come at the top of the program. For our purposes, the #define directive takes the following form:

#define identifier followed by the "replacement text"

In the program, we used

#define ChargePerHour 100

Note that this is not a normal C statement and a semicolon is not needed to end it. Here, the identifier is ChargePerHour and the replacement text is the constant 100. In the body of the program, we use the identifier instead of the constant.

When the program is compiled, C performs what is called a "pre-processing" step. It replaces all occurrences of the identifier by its replacement text. In program P4.6, it replaces all occurrences of ChargePerHour by 100 and all occurrences of MinJobCost by 150. After this is done, the program is compiled. It is up to the programmer to ensure that, when the identifier is replaced, the resulting statement makes sense.

Effectively, the directives say that the identifier ChargePerHour is equivalent to the constant 100 and the identifier MinJobCost is equivalent to 150.

For example, the pre-processing step changes

```
if (jobCharge < MinJobCost) jobCharge = MinJobCost;
```

to

```
if (jobCharge < 150) jobCharge = 150;
```

Suppose, for instance, that the minimum job cost changes from 150 to 180. We would just need to change the value in the #define directive, thus:

```
#define MinJobCost 180
```

No other changes would be needed.

In this book, we will use the *convention* of starting a symbolic constant identifier with an uppercase letter. Note, however, that C allows you to use any valid identifier.

4.6.2 Example – Symbolic Constants

For a slightly bigger example, consider program P4.5. There, we used two constants—40 and 1.5—denoting the maximum regular hours and the overtime rate factor, respectively. We rewrite program P4.5 as program P4.7 using the symbolic constants MaxRegularHours (set to 40) and OvertimeFactor (set to 1.5).

Program P4.7

```c
#include <stdio.h>
#define MaxRegularHours 40
#define OvertimeFactor 1.5
int main() {
    double hours, rate, regPay, ovtPay, grossPay;
    printf("Hours worked? ");
    scanf("%lf", &hours);
    printf("Rate of pay? ");
    scanf("%lf", &rate);
    if (hours <= MaxRegularHours) {
        regPay = hours * rate;
        ovtPay = 0;
    }
    else {
        regPay = MaxRegularHours * rate;
        ovtPay = (hours - MaxRegularHours) * rate * OvertimeFactor;
    }
    grossPay = regPay + ovtPay;
    printf("\nRegular pay: $%3.2f\n", regPay);
    printf("Overtime pay: $%3.2f\n", ovtPay);
    printf("Gross pay: $%3.2f\n", grossPay);
}
```

Suppose, for instance, the maximum regular hours changes from 40 to 35. Program P4.7 would be easier to change than Program P4.6, since we would need to change the value in the #define directive only, like this:

```
#define MaxRegularHours 35
```

No other changes would be needed.

The numbers 40 and 1.5 used in Program P4.5 are referred to as *magic numbers*—they appear in the program for no apparent reason, as if by magic. Magic numbers are a good sign that a program may be restrictive, tied to those numbers. As far as possible, we must write our programs without magic numbers. Using symbolic constants can help to make our programs more flexible and easier to maintain.

4.7 More Examples

We now write programs to solve two more problems. Their solutions will illustrate how to use if...else statements to determine which of several alternatives to take. In the sample runs, the underlined items are typed by the user; everything else is printed by the computer.

4.7.1 Print a Letter Grade

Write a program to request a score in a test and print a letter grade based on the following:

score < 50	F
50 <= score < 75	B
score >= 75	A

The program should work as follows:

Enter a score: 70

Grade B

A solution is shown as Program P4.8.

Program P4.8

```c
//request a score; print letter grade
#include <stdio.h>
int main() {
    int score;
    printf("Enter a score: ");
    scanf("%d", &score);
    printf("\nGrade ");
    if (score < 50) printf("F\n");
    else if (score < 75) printf("B\n");
    else printf("A\n");
}
```

The second printf prints a blank line followed by the word Grade followed by one space but does not end the line. When the letter grade *is* determined, it will be printed on this same line.
We saw that the if...else statement takes the form

```c
if (<condition>) <statement1> else <statement2>
```

where <statement1> and <statement2> can be any statements. In particular, either one (or both) can be an if...else statement. This allows us to write so-called *nested if* statements. This is especially useful when we have several related conditions to test, as in this example. In the program, we can think of the part:

```c
if (score < 50) printf("F\n");
else if (score < 75) printf("B\n");
else printf("A\n");
```

as

```c
if (score < 50) printf("F\n");
else <statement>
```

where <statement> is this if...else statement:

```c
if (score < 75) printf("B\n");
else printf("A\n");
```

If score is less than 50, the program prints F and ends. If not, it follows that score must be greater than or equal to 50.

Knowing this, the first else part checks if score is less than 75. If it is, the program prints B and ends. If not, it follows that score must be greater than or equal to 75.

Knowing this, the second else part (else printf("A\n"); which matches the second if) prints A and ends.

To make sure the program is correct, you should run it with at least 3 different scores (one 70, 45, 97) to verify that each of the 3 grades is printed correctly. You should also test it at the "boundary" numbers, 50 and 75.

Note the preferred style for writing else if's. If we had followed our normal indenting style, we would have written

```
if (score < 50) printf("F\n");
else
   if (score < 75) printf("B\n");
   else printf("A\n");
```

This, of course, would still be correct. However, if we had more cases, the indentation would go too deep and would look awkward. Also, since the different ranges for score are really alternatives (rather than one being within the other), it is better to keep them at the same indentation level. The statements here were all one-line printf statements so we chose to write them on the same line as if and else. However, if they were blocks, it would be better to write it like this:

```
if (score < 50) {
   ...
}
else if (score < 75) {
   ...
}
else {
   ...
}
```

As an exercise, modify the program to print the correct grade based on the following:

score < 50	F
50 <= score < 65	C
50 <= score < 80	B
score >= 80	A

4.7.2 Classify a Triangle

Given three integer values representing the sides of a triangle, print:

- Not a triangle if the values cannot be the sides of any triangle. This is so if any value is negative or zero, or if the length of any side is greater than or equal to the sum of the other two;

- Scalene if the triangle is scalene (all sides different);

- Isosceles if the triangle is isosceles (two sides equal);
- Equilateral if the triangle is equilateral (three sides equal).

The program should work as follows:

```
Enter 3 sides of a triangle: 7 4 7

Isosceles
```

A solution is shown as Program P4.9.

Program P4.9

```c
//request 3 sides; determine type of triangle
#include <stdio.h>
int main() {
    int a, b, c;
    printf("Enter 3 sides of a triangle: ");
    scanf("%d %d %d", &a, &b, &c);
    if (a <= 0 || b <= 0 || c <= 0) printf("\nNot a triangle\n");
    else if (a >= b + c || b >= c + a || c >= a + b)
        printf("\nNot a triangle\n");
    else if (a == b && b == c) printf("\nEquilateral\n");
    else if (a == b || b == c || c == a) printf("\nIsosceles\n");
    else printf("\nScalene\n");
}
```

The first task is to establish that we, in fact, have a valid triangle. The first if checks if any of the sides is negative or zero. If so, Not a triangle is printed. If they are all positive, we go to the else part that itself consists of an if...else statement.

Here, the if checks if any one side is greater than or equal to the sum of the other two. If so, Not a triangle is printed. If not, then we have a valid triangle and must determine its type by executing the else part beginning

```
if (a == b ...
```

It is easiest to do this by first checking if it is equilateral. If two different *pairs of sides* are equal—if (a == b && b == c)—then all three are equal and we have an equilateral triangle.

If it is not equilateral, then we check if it is isosceles. If any two sides are equal—if (a == b || b == c || c == a)—we have an isosceles triangle.

If it is neither equilateral nor isosceles, then it must be scalene.

As an exercise, modify the program to determine if the triangle is right angled. It is right angled if the sum of the squares of two sides is equal to the square of the third side.

EXERCISES 4

1. An auto repair shop charges as follows. Inspecting the vehicle costs $75. If no work needs to be done, there is no further charge. Otherwise, the charge is $75 per hour for labor plus the cost of parts, with a minimum charge of $120. If any work is done, there is no charge for inspecting the vehicle.

    Write a program to read values for hours worked and cost of parts (either of which could be 0) and print the charge for the job.

2. Write a program that requests two weights in kilograms and grams and prints the sum of the weights. For example, if the weights are 3kg 500g and 4kg 700g, your program should print 8kg 200g.

3. Write a program that requests two lengths in feet and inches and prints the sum of the lengths. For example, if the lengths are 5 ft. 4 in. and 8 ft. 11 in., your program should print 14 ft. 3 in. (1 ft. = 12 in.)

4. A variety store gives a 15% discount on sales totaling $300 or more. Write a program to request the cost of three items and print the amount the customer must pay.

5. Write a program to read two pairs of integers. Each pair represents a fraction. For example, the pair 3 5 represents the fraction 3/5. Your program should print the sum of the given fractions. For example, give the pairs 3 5 and 2 3, your program should print 19/15, since 3/5 + 2/3 = 19/15.

    Modify the program so that it prints the sum with the fraction reduced to a proper fraction; for this example, your program should print 1 4/15.

6. Write a program to read a person's name, hours worked, hourly rate of pay, and tax rate (a number representing a percentage, e.g., 25 meaning 25%). The program must print the name, gross pay, tax deducted, and gross pay.

    Gross pay is calculated as described in Section 4.4.1. The tax deducted is calculated by applying the tax rate to 80% of gross pay. And the net pay is calculated by subtracting the tax deducted from the gross pay.

    For example, if the person works 50 hours at $20/hour and the tax rate is 25%, his gross pay would be (40 x 20) + (10 20 1.5) = $1100. He pays 25% tax on 80% of $1100, that is, 25% of $880 = $220. His net pay is 1100 - 220 = $880.

7. Write a program to read integer values for month and year and print the number of days in the month. For example, 4 2005 (April 2005) should print 30, 2 2004 (February 2004) should print 29 and 2 1900 (February 1900) should print 28.

    A leap year, n, is divisible by 4; however, if n is divisible by 100 then it is a leap year only if it is also divisible by 400. So 1900 is not a leap year but 2000 is.

8. In an English class, a student is given three term tests (marked out of 25) and an end-of-term test (marked out of 100). The end-of-term test counts the same as the three term tests in determining the final mark (out of 100). Write a program to read marks for the three term tests followed by the mark for the end-of-term test. The program then prints the final mark and an indication of whether the student passes or fails. To pass, the final mark must be 50 or more.

    For example, given the data `20 10 15 56`, the final mark is calculated by
    $(20+10+15)/75*50 + 56/100*50 = 58$

9. Write a program to request two times given in 24-hour clock format and find the time (in hours and minutes) that has elapsed between the first time and the second time. You may assume that the second time is later than the first time. Each time is represented by two numbers: e.g., `16 45` means the time 16:45, that is, 4:45 p.m.

    For example, if the two given times are `16 45` and `23 25` your answer should be 6 hours 40 minutes.

    Modify the program so that it works as follows: if the second time is sooner than the first time, take it to mean a time for the *next* day. For example, given the times `20:30` and `6:15`, take this to mean 8.30 p.m. to 6.15 a.m. of the next day. Your answer should be 9 hours 45 minutes.

10. A bank pays interest based on the amount of money deposited. If the amount is less than $5,000, the interest is 4% per annum. If the amount is $5,000 or more but less than $10,000, the interest is 5% per annum. If the amount is $10,000 or more but less than $20,000, the interest is 6% per annum. If the amount is $20,000 or more, the interest is 7% per annum.

    Write a program to request the amount deposited and print the interest earned for one year.

11. For any year between 1900 and 2099, inclusive, the month and day on which Easter Sunday falls can be determined by the following algorithm:

```
set a to year minus 1900
set b to the remainder when a is divided by 19
set c to the integer quotient when 7b + 1 is divided by 19
set d to the remainder when 11b + 4 - c is divided by 29
set e to the integer quotient when a is divided by 4
set f to the remainder when a + e + 31 - d is divided by 7
set g to 25 minus the sum of d and f
if g is less than or equal to 0 then
    set month to 'March'
    set day to 31 + g
else
    set month to 'April'
    set day to g
endif
```

Write a program that requests a year between 1900 and 2099, inclusive, and checks if the year is valid. If it is, print the day on which Easter Sunday falls in that year. For example, if the year is 1999, your program should print April 4.

12. Write a program to prompt for the name of an item, its previous price, and its current price. Print the percentage increase or decrease in the price. For example, if the previous price is $80 and the current price is $100, you should print increase of 25%; if the previous price is $100 and the current price is $80, you should print decrease of 20%.

13. A country charges income tax as follows based on one's gross salary. No tax is charged on the first 20% of salary. The remaining 80% is called *taxable income*. Tax is paid as follows:

- 10% on the first $15,000 of taxable income;

- 20% on the next $20,000 of taxable income;

- 25% on all taxable income in excess of $35,000.

Write a program to read a value for a person's salary and print the amount of tax to be paid. Also print the *average tax rate*, that is, the percentage of salary that is paid in tax. For example, on a salary of $20,000, a person pays $1700 in tax.

The average tax rate is 1700/20000*100 = 8.5%.

CHAPTER 5

■ ■ ■

Programs with Repetition Logic

In this chapter, we will explain the following:

- How to use the `while` construct to perform "looping" in a program

- How to find the sum and average of an arbitrary set of numbers

- How to get a program to "count"

- How to find the largest and smallest of an arbitrary set of numbers

- How to read data from a file

- How to write output to a file

- How to use the `for` construct to perform "looping" in a program

- How to produce tables using `for`

5.1 Introduction

In Chapter 3, we showed you how to write programs using sequence logic—programs whose statements are executed "in sequence" from the first to the last.

In Chapter 4, we showed you how to write programs for problems that require selection logic. These programs used the `if` and the `if...else` statements.

In this chapter, we discuss problems that require repetition logic. The idea is to write statements once and get the computer to execute them repeatedly as long as some condition is true. We will see how to express repetition logic using the `while` and `for` statements.

5.2 The while Construct

Consider the problem of writing a program to find the sum of some numbers that the user enters one at a time. The program will prompt the user to enter numbers as follows:

```
Enter a number: 13
Enter a number: 8
Enter a number: 16
```

and so on. We want to let the user enter as many numbers as he wishes. Since we can have no idea how many that will be, and the amount could vary from one run of the program to the next, we must let the user "tell" us when he wishes to stop entering numbers.

How does he "tell" us? Well, the only time the user "talks" to the program is when he types a number in response to the prompt. If he wishes to stop entering numbers, he can enter some "agreed-upon" value; when the program reads this value, it will know that the user wishes to stop.

In this example, we can use 0 as the value that tells the program that the user wishes to stop. When a value is used this way, it is referred to as a sentinel or end-of-data value. It is sometimes called a rogue value—the value is not to be taken as one of the actual data values.

What can we use as a sentinel value? Any value that cannot be confused with an actual data value would be okay. For example, if the data values are all positive numbers, we can use 0 or –1 as the sentinel value. When we prompt the user, it is a good idea to remind him what value to use as the sentinel value.

Assume we want the program to run as follows:

```
Enter a number (0 to end): 24
Enter a number (0 to end): 13
Enter a number (0 to end): 55
Enter a number (0 to end): 32
Enter a number (0 to end): 19
Enter a number (0 to end): 0

The sum is 143
```

How do we get the program to run like that? We want to be able to express the following logic in a form the computer could understand:

> *As long as the user does not enter 0, keep prompting him for another number and add it to the sum*

It seems obvious that we must, at least, prompt him for the first number. If this number is 0, we must print the sum (which, of course, would be 0 at this time). If the number is not 0, we must add it to the sum and prompt for another number. If *this* number is 0, we must print the sum. If this number is not 0, we must add it to the sum and prompt for another number. If *this* number is 0..., and so on.

The process will come to an end when the user enters 0.

This logic is expressed quite neatly using a while construct (also called a while statement or while loop):

```
//Algorithm for finding sum
set sum to 0
get a number, num
while num is not 0 do
    add num to sum
    get another number, num
endwhile
print sum
```

Note, particularly, that we get a number before we enter the while loop. This is to ensure that the while condition make sense the first time. (It would not make sense if num had no value.)

To find the sum, we need to:

- Choose a variable to hold the sum; we will use sum.

- Initialize sum to 0 (before the while loop).

- Add a number to sum (inside the while loop). One number is added each time through the loop.

On exit from the loop, sum contains the sum of all the numbers entered.

The while construct lets us execute one or more statements repeatedly as long as some *condition* is true. Here, the two statements

```
add num to sum
get another number, num
```

are executed repeatedly as long as the condition num is not 0 is true.

In *pseudocode*, the while construct is usually written as follows:

```
while <condition> do
    statements to be executed repeatedly
endwhile
```

The statements to be executed repeatedly are called the *body* of the while construct (or, simply, the body of the loop). The construct is executed as follows:

1. <condition> is tested.

2. If true, the body is executed and we go back to step 1; if false, we continue with the statement, if any, after endwhile.

We now show how the algorithm is executed using the sample data entered above. For easy reference, the data was entered in the following order:

```
24  13  55  32  19  0
```

Initially, num is undefined and sum is 0. We show this as follows:

num [   ]   sum [0]

24 is entered and stored in num;
num is not 0 so we enter the while loop;
num (24) is added to sum (0), giving:

num [24]   sum [24]

13 is entered and stored in num;
num is not 0 so we enter the while loop;
num (13) is added to sum (24), giving:

num [13]   sum [37]

55 is entered and stored in num;
num is not 0 so we enter the while loop;
num (55) is added to sum (37), giving:

num [55]   sum [92]

32 is entered and stored in num;
num is not 0 so we enter the while loop;
num (32) is added to sum (92), giving:

num [32]   sum [124]

19 is entered and stored in num;
num is not 0 so we enter the while loop;
num (19) is added to sum (124), giving:

num [19]   sum [143]

0 is entered and stored in num;
num *is* 0 so we exit the while loop and go to print sum with

num [0]   sum [143]

sum is now 143 so the algorithm prints 143.

When a while construct is being executed, we say the program is looping or the while loop is being executed.

It remains to show how to express this algorithm in C. Program P5.1 shows how.

Program P5.1

```c
//print the sum of several numbers entered by a user
#include <stdio.h>
int main() {
    int num, sum = 0;
    printf("Enter a number (0 to end): ");
    scanf("%d", &num);
    while (num != 0) {
        sum = sum + num;
        printf("Enter a number (0 to end): ");
        scanf("%d", &num);
    }
    printf("\nThe sum is %d\n", sum);
}
```

Of particular interest is the while statement. The pseudocode

```
while num is not 0 do
    add num to sum
    get another number, num
endwhile
```

is expressed in C as

```c
while (num != 0) {
    sum = sum + num;
    printf("Enter a number (0 to end): ");
    scanf("%d", &num);
}
```

When the program is run, what would happen if the very first number entered was 0? Since num is 0, the while condition is immediately false so we drop out of the while loop and continue with the printf statement. The program will print the correct answer:

```
The sum is 0
```

In general, if the while condition is false the first time it is tested, the body is not executed at all.

Formally, the while construct in C is defined as follows:

while (<condition>) <statement>

The word while and the brackets are required. You must supply <condition> and <statement>. <statement> must be a single statement or a block—one or more statements enclosed by { and }. First, <condition> is tested; if true, <statement> is executed and <condition> is tested again. This is repeated until <condition> becomes false; when this happens, execution continues with the statement, if any, after `<statement>`. If `<condition>` is `false` the first time, `<statement>` is not executed and execution continues with the following statement, if any.

In Program P5.1, `<condition>` is `num != 0` and `<statement>` is the block

```
{
    sum = sum + num;
    printf("Enter a number (0 to end): ");
    scanf("%d", &num);
}
```

Whenever we want to execute several statements if `<condition>` is true, we must enclose the statements by { and }. Effectively, this makes them into one statement, a compound statement, satisfying C's syntax rule that requires one statement as the body.

5.2.1 Highest Common Factor

Let us write a program to find the *highest common factor*, HCF (also called the *greatest common divisor*, GCD), of two numbers. The program will run as follows:

```
Enter two numbers: 42 24

Their HCF is 6
```

We will use Euclid's algorithm for finding the HCF of two integers, m and n. The algorithm is as follows:

```
1. if n is 0, the HCF is m and stop
2. set r to the remainder when m is divided by n
3. set m to n
4. set n to r
5. go to step 1
```

Using m as 42 and n as 24, step through the algorithm and verify that it gives the correct answer, 6.

Steps 2, 3, and 4 are executed as long as n is not 0. Hence, this algorithm can be expressed using a `while` loop as follows:

```
while n is not 0 do
    set r to m % n
    set m to n
    set n to r
endwhile
HCF is m
```

We can now write Program P5.2, which finds the HCF of two numbers entered.

Program P5.2

```
//find the HCF of two numbers entered by a user
#include <stdio.h>
int main() {
    int m, n, r;
    printf("Enter two numbers: ");
    scanf("%d %d", &m, &n);
    while (n != 0) {
        r = m % n;
        m = n;
        n = r;
    }
    printf("\nTheir HCF is %d\n", m);
}
```

Note that the while condition is n != 0 and the while body is the block

```
{
    r = m % n;
    m = n;
    n = r;
}
```

The algorithm and, hence, the program, works whether m is bigger than n or not. Using the example above, if m is 24 and n is 42, when the loop is executed the first time, it will set m to 42 and n to 24. In general, if m is smaller than n, the first thing the algorithm does is swap their values.

5.3 Keep a Count

Program P5.1 finds the sum of a set of numbers entered. Suppose we want to *count* how many numbers were entered, not counting the end-of-data 0. We could use an integer variable n to hold the count. To get the program to keep a count, we need to do the following:

- Choose a variable to hold the count; we choose n.

- Initialize n to 0.

- Add 1 to n in the appropriate place. Here, we need to add 1 to n each time the user enters a nonzero number.

- Print the count.

Program P5.3 is the modified program for counting the numbers.

Program P5.3

```
//print the sum and count of several numbers entered by a user
#include <stdio.h>
int main() {
    int num, sum = 0, n = 0;
    printf("Enter a number (0 to end): ");
    scanf("%d", &num);
    while (num != 0) {
        n = n + 1;
        sum = sum + num;
        printf("Enter a number (0 to end): ");
        scanf("%d", &num);
    }
    printf("\n%d numbers were entered\n", n);
    printf("The sum is %d\n", sum);
}
```

The following is a sample run of the program:

```
Enter a number (0 to end): 24
Enter a number (0 to end): 13
Enter a number (0 to end): 55
Enter a number (0 to end): 32
Enter a number (0 to end): 19
Enter a number (0 to end): 0

5 numbers were entered
The sum is 143
```

Comments on Program P5.3

- We declare and initialize n and sum to 0 *before* the while loop.

- The statement

  n = n + 1;

  adds 1 to n. We say n is *incremented* by 1. Suppose n has the value 3.

- When the right-hand side is evaluated, the value obtained is 3 + 1 = 4. This value is stored in the variable on the left-hand side, that is, n. The net result is that 4 is stored in n.

- This statement is placed *inside* the loop so that n is incremented each time the loop body is executed. Since the loop body is executed when num is not 0, the value of n is always the amount of numbers entered so far.

- When we exit the while loop, the value in n will be the amount of numbers entered, not counting 0. This value is then printed.

- Observe that if the first number entered were 0, the while condition would be immediately false and control will go directly to the first printf statement after the loop with n and sum both having the value 0. The program will print, correctly:

```
0 numbers were entered
The sum is 0
```

- If one number is entered, the program will print "1 numbers were entered"—not very good English. Use an if statement to fix this.

5.3.1 Find Average

Program P5.3 can be easily modified to find the average of the numbers entered. As we saw above, on exit from the while loop, we know the sum (sum) and how many numbers were entered (n). We can add a printf statement to print the average to 2 decimal places, say, like this:

```
printf("The average is %3.2f\n", (double) sum/n);
```

For the data in the sample run, the output will be

```
5 numbers were entered
The sum is 143
The average is 28.60
```

As explained in Section 2.5.4, note the use of the cast (double) to force a floating-point calculation. Without it, since sum and n are int, an integer division would be performed, giving 28.

Alternatively, we could declare sum as double, and print the sum and average with this:

```
printf("The sum is %3.0f\n", sum);
printf("The average is %3.2f\n", sum/n);
```

However, there is still a problem. If the user enters 0 as the first number, execution will reach the last printf statement with sum and n both having the value 0. The program will attempt to divide 0 by 0, giving the error "Attempt to divide by 0." This is an example of a *runtime* (or *execution*) error.

To cater to this situation, we could use the following after the while loop:

```
if (n == 0) printf("\nNo numbers entered\n");
else {
    printf("\n%d numbers were entered\n", n);
    printf("The sum is %d\n", sum);
    printf("The average is %3.2f\n", (double) sum/n);
}
```

The moral of the story is that, whenever possible, you should try to anticipate the ways in which your program might fail and cater to them. This is an example of what is called *defensive programming*.

5.4 Increment and Decrement Operators

There are a number of operators that originated with C and give C its unique flavor. The best known of these is the increment operator, ++. In the last program, we used

```
n = n + 1;
```

to add 1 to n. The statement

```
n++;
```

does the same thing. The operator ++ adds 1 to its argument, which must be a variable. It can be written as a prefix (++n) or as a suffix (n++).

Even though ++n and n++ both add 1 to n, in certain situations, the side effect of ++n is different from n++. This is so because ++n increments n *before* using its value, whereas n++ increments n *after* using its value. As an example, suppose n has the value 7. The statement

```
a = ++n;
```

first increments n and *then assigns* the value (8) to a. But the statement

```
a = n++;
```

first assigns the value 7 to a and *then increments* n to 8. In both cases, though, the end result is that n is assigned the value 8.

As an exercise, what is printed by the following?

```
n = 5;
printf("Suffix: %d\n", n++);
printf("Prefix: %d\n", ++n);
```

The decrement operator -- is similar to ++ except that it subtracts 1 from its variable argument. For example, --n and n-- are both equivalent to

```
n = n - 1;
```

As explained above, --n subtracts 1 and then uses the value of n; n-- uses the value of n and then subtracts 1 from it. It would be useful to do the above exercise with ++ replaced by --.

5.5 Assignment Operators

So far, we have used the assignment operator = to assign the value of an expression to a variable, as in the following:

c = a + b

The entire construct consisting of the variable = and the expression is referred to as an *assignment expression*. When the expression is followed by a semicolon, it becomes an *assignment statement*. The *value* of an assignment expression is simply the value assigned to the variable. For example, if a is 15 and b is 20, then the assignment expression

c = a + b

assigns the value 35 to c. The value of the (entire) assignment expression is also 35.

Multiple assignments are possible, as in

a = b = c = 13

The operator = evaluates from right to left, so the above is equivalent to

a = (b = (c = 13))

The rightmost assignment is done first, followed by the one to the left, and so on.

C provides other assignment operators, of which += is the most widely used. In Program P5.3, above, we used the statement

sum = sum + num;

to add the value of num to sum. This can be written more neatly using += as:

sum += num; //add num to sum

To add 3 to n, we could write

n += 3

which is the same as

n = n + 3

Other assignment operators include -=, *=, /=, and %=. If op represents any of +, -, *, /, or %, then

variable op= expression

is equivalent to

variable = variable op expression

We point out that we could write all our programs without using increment, decrement, or the special assignment operators. However, sometimes, they permit us to express certain operations more concisely, more conveniently, and, possibly, more clearly.

5.6 Find Largest

Suppose we want to write a program that works as follows: the user will type some numbers and the program will find the largest number typed. The following is a sample run of the program (underlined items are typed by the user):

```
Enter a number (0 to end): 36
Enter a number (0 to end): 17
Enter a number (0 to end): 43
Enter a number (0 to end): 52
Enter a number (0 to end): 50
Enter a number (0 to end): 0

The largest is 52
```

The user will be prompted to enter numbers, one at a time. We will assume that the numbers entered are all positive integers. We will let the user enter as many numbers as she likes. However, in this case, she will need to tell the program when she wishes to stop entering numbers. To do so, she will type 0.

Finding the largest number involves the following steps:

- Choose a variable to hold the largest number; we choose bigNum.

- Initialize bigNum to a very small value. The value chosen should be such that no matter what number is entered, its value would be greater than this initial value. Since we are assuming that the numbers entered would be positive, we can initialize bigNum to 0.

- As each number (num, say) is entered, it is compared with bigNum; if num is greater than bigNum, then we have a bigger number and bigNum is set to this new number.

- When all the numbers have been entered and checked, bigNum will contain the largest one.

These ideas are expressed in the following algorithm:

```
set bigNum to 0
get a number, num
while num is not 0 do
    if num is bigger than bigNum, set bigNum to num
    get a number, num
endwhile
print bigNum
```

Like before, we get the first number *before* we enter the while loop. This is to ensure that the while condition makes sense (*is defined*) the first time. It would not make sense if num had no value. If it is not 0, we enter the loop. Inside the loop, we process the number (compare it with bigNum, etc.) after which we get another number. *This* number is then used in the next test of the while condition. When the while condition is false (num is 0), the program continues with the print statement *after* the loop.

This algorithm is implemented as shown in Program P5.4.

Program P5.4

```c
//find the largest of a set of numbers entered
#include <stdio.h>
int main() {
    int num, bigNum = 0;
    printf("Enter a number (0 to end): ");
    scanf("%d", &num);
    while (num != 0) {
        if (num > bigNum) bigNum = num; //is this number bigger?
        printf("Enter a number (0 to end): ");
        scanf("%d", &num);
    }
    printf("\nThe largest is %d\n", bigNum);
}
```

Let us "step through" this program using the sample data entered at the beginning of this section. For easy reference, the data was entered in the following order:

36   17   43   52   50   0

Initially, num is undefined and bigNum is 0. We show this as:

num   [   ]   bignum   [0   ]

36 is entered and stored in num;
num is not 0 so we enter the while loop;
num (36) is compared with bigNum (0);
36 is bigger so bigNum is set to 36, giving:

num   [36   ]   bignum   [36   ]

17 is entered and stored in num;
num is not 0 so we enter the while loop;
num (17) is compared with bigNum (36);
17 is not bigger so bigNum remains at 36, giving:

| num | 17 | | bignum | 36 |

43 is entered and stored in num;
num is not 0 so we enter the while loop;
num (43) is compared with bigNum (36);
43 is bigger so bigNum is set to 43, giving:

| num | 43 | | bignum | 43 |

52 is entered and stored in num;
num is not 0 so we enter the while loop;
num (52) is compared with bigNum (43);
52 is bigger so bigNum is set to 52, giving:

| num | 52 | | bignum | 52 |

50 is entered and stored in num;
num is not 0 so we enter the while loop;
num (50) is compared with bigNum (52);
50 is not bigger so bigNum remains at 52, giving:

| num | 50 | | bignum | 52 |

0 is entered and stored in num;
num *is* 0 so we exit the while loop and go to printf with

| num | 0 | | bignum | 52 |

bigNum is now 52 and the printf statement prints

The largest is 52

5.7 Find Smallest

In addition to finding the largest of a set of items, we are sometimes interested in finding the smallest. We will find the smallest of a set of integers. To do so involves the following steps:

- Choose a variable to hold the smallest number; we choose smallNum.

- Initialize smallNum to a very big value. The value chosen should be such that no matter what number is entered, its value would be smaller than this initial value. If we have an idea of the numbers we will get, we can choose an appropriate value.

- For instance, if we know that the numbers will contain at most 4 digits, we can use an initial value such as 10000. If we do not know this, we can set smallNum to the largest integer value defined by the compiler (32767 for 16-bit integers). Similarly, when we are finding the largest, we can initialize bigNum (say) to a very small number like -32767.

- Another possibility is to read the first number and set smallNum (or bigNum) to it, provided it is not 0. For variety, we will illustrate this method.

- As each number (num, say) is entered, it is compared with smallNum; if num is smaller than smallNum, then we have a smaller number and smallNum is set to this new number.

- When all the numbers have been entered and checked, smallNum will contain the smallest one.

These ideas are expressed in the following algorithm:

```
get a number, num
if num is 0 then stop //do nothing and halt the program
set smallNum to num
while num is not 0 do
    if num is smaller than smallNum, set smallNum to num
    get a number, num
endwhile
print smallNum
```

The first number is read. If it is 0, there is nothing to do and the program halts. If it is not 0, we set smallNum to it. We could, at this stage, get another number before we execute the while statement. However, in the interest of brevity, we don't. The penalty for this is that, even though we know that num is not 0 and it is not smaller than smallNum (it is the same), we still do these tests before getting the next number.

This algorithm is implemented as shown in Program P5.5.

Program P5.5

```
//find the smallest of a set of numbers entered
#include <stdio.h>
int main() {
    int num;
    printf("Enter a number (0 to end): ");
    scanf("%d", &num);
    if (num == 0) return; //halt the program
    int smallNum = num;
    while (num != 0) {
        if (num < smallNum) smallNum = num;
        printf("Enter a number (0 to end): ");
        scanf("%d", &num);
    }
    printf("\nThe smallest is %d\n", smallNum);
}
```

In C, the keyword return can be used in main to halt the program by "returning" to the operating system. We will discuss return in more detail in Chapter 7.

When run, if numbers are entered in the following order:

```
36   17   43   52   50   0
```

the program will print

```
The smallest is 17
```

and if the numbers entered are

```
36   -17   43   -52   50   0
```

the program will print

```
The smallest is -52
```

5.8 Read Data from a File

So far, we have written our programs assuming that data to be supplied is typed at the keyboard. We have fetched the data using scanf for reading numbers and gets for reading strings. Typically, the program prompts the user for the data and waits for the user to type the data. When the data is typed, the program reads it, stores it in a variable (or variables), and continues with its execution. This mode of supplying data is called *interactive* since the user is interacting with the program.

We say we have been reading data from the "standard input." C uses the predefined identifier stdin to refer to the standard input. When your program starts up, C assumes that stdin is the keyboard. Similarly, the predefined identifier stdout refers to the standard output, the screen. So far, our programs have written output to the screen.

We can also supply data to a program by storing the data in a file. When the program needs data, it fetches it directly from the file, without user intervention. Of course, we have to ensure that the appropriate data has been stored in the file in the correct order and format. This mode of supplying data is normally referred to as *batch* mode. (The term *batch* is historical and comes from the old days when data had to be "batched" before being submitted for processing.)

For example, suppose we need to supply an item number (int) and a price (double) for several items. If the program is written assuming that the data file contains several pairs of numbers (an int constant followed by a double constant), then we must ensure that the data in the file conforms to this.

Suppose we create a file called input.txt and *type* data in it. This file is a *file of characters* or a *text* file. Depending on the programming environment provided by your C compiler, it may be possible to assign stdin to input.txt—we say *redirect* the standard input to input.txt. Once this is done, your program will read data from the file rather than the keyboard. Similarly, it may be possible to redirect the standard output to a file, output.txt, say. If done, your printf's will write output to the file, rather than the screen.

We will take a slightly different approach, which is a bit more general since it will work with any C program and does not depend on the particular compiler or operating system you happen to be using.

Suppose we want to be able to read data from the file input.txt. The first thing we need to do is declare an identifier called a "file pointer." This can be done with the statement.

```
FILE * in; // read as "file pointer in"
```

The word FILE must be spelt as shown, with all uppercase letters. The spaces before and after * may be omitted. So you could write FILE* in, FILE *in or even FILE*in. We have used the identifier in; any other will do, such as inf, infile, inputFile, payData.

The second thing we must do is associate the file pointer in with the file input.txt and tell C we will be reading data from the file. This is done using the *function* fopen, as follows:

```
in = fopen("input.txt", "r");
```

This tells C to "open the file input.txt for reading": "r" indicates reading. (We will use "w" if we want the file to be opened for "writing," that is, to receive output.) If we wish, we could accomplish both things with one statement, thus:

```
FILE * in = fopen("input.txt", "r");
```

Once this is done, the "data pointer" will be positioned at the beginning of the file. We can now write statements that will read data from the file. We will see how shortly.

It is up to us to ensure that the file exists and contains the appropriate data. If not, we will get an error message such as "File not found." If we need to, we can specify the *path* to the file.

Suppose the file is located at C:\testdata\input.txt.

We can tell C we will be reading data from the file with this:

```
FILE * in = fopen("C:\\testdata\\input.txt", "r");
```

Recall that the escape sequence \\ is used to represent \ within a string. If the file is on a flash drive with assigned letter E, we can use:

```
FILE * in = fopen("E:\\input.txt", "r");
```

5.8.1 fscanf

We use the statement (more precisely, the function) fscanf to read data from the file. It is used in exactly the same way as scanf except that the first argument is the file pointer in. For example, if num is int, the statement

```
fscanf(in, "%d", &num);
```

will read an integer from the file input.txt (the one associated with in) and store it in num. Note that the first argument is the file pointer and not the name of the file.

When we have finished reading data from the file, we should *close* it. This is done with fclose, as follows:

```
fclose(in);
```

There is one argument, the file pointer (not the name of the file). This statement breaks the association of the file pointer in with the file input.txt. If we need to, we could now link the identifier in with another file (paydata.txt, say) using:

```
in = fopen("paydata.txt", "r");
```

Note that we do not repeat the FILE * part of the declaration, since it has already been declared as FILE *. Subsequent fscanf(in, ...) statements will read data from the file paydata.txt.

5.8.2 Find Average of Numbers in a File

To illustrate the use of fscanf, let us rewrite Program P5.3 to read several numbers from a file and find their average. Previously, we discussed how to find the average. We just need to make the changes to read the numbers from a file. Suppose the file is called input.txt and contains several positive integers with 0 indicating the end, for example,

```
24 13 55 32 19 0
```

Program P5.6 shows how to define the file as the place from which the data will be read and how to find the average.

Program P5.6

```c
//read numbers from a file and find their average; 0 ends the data
#include <stdio.h>
int main() {
    FILE * in = fopen("input.txt", "r");
    int num, sum = 0, n = 0;
    fscanf(in, "%d", &num);
    while (num != 0) {
        n = n + 1;
        sum = sum + num;
        fscanf(in, "%d", &num);
    }
    if (n == 0) printf("\nNo numbers supplied\n");
    else {
        if (n == 1) printf("\n1 number supplied\n");
        else printf("\n%d numbers supplied\n", n);
        printf("The sum is %d\n", sum);
        printf("The average is %3.2f\n", (double) sum/n);
    }
    fclose(in);
}
```

Comments on Program P5.6

- FILE * and fopen are used so that the fscanf statement would fetch data from the file input.txt.

- Since the data is being read directly from the file, the question of prompting for data does not arise. The printf statements that prompted for data are no longer necessary.

- The program makes sure that n is not 0 before attempting to find the average.

- When run, the program reads the data from the file and prints the results without any user intervention.

- If the data file contains

  24 13 55 32 19 0

  the output will be

  5 numbers were supplied
  The sum is 143
  The average is 28.60

- The numbers in the file could be supplied in "free format"—any amount could be put on a line. For example, the sample data could have been typed on one line as above or as follows:

```
24 13
55 32
19 0
```

or like this:

```
24 13
55
32 19
0
```

or like this:

```
24
13
55
32
19
0
```

- As an exercise, add statements to the program so that it also prints the largest and smallest numbers in the file.

■ **File cannot be found** when you try to run this program, it may not run properly because it cannot find the file input.txt. This may be because the compiler is looking for the file in the wrong place. Some compilers expect to find the file in the same folder/directory as the program file. Others expect to find it in the same folder/directory as the compiler. Try placing input.txt in each of these folders, in turn, and run the program. If this does not work, then you will need to specify the complete path to the file in the fopen statement. For example, if the file is in the folder data that is in the folder CS10E, which is on the C: drive, you will need to use the following statement:

```
FILE * in = fopen("C:\\CS10E\\data\\input.txt", "r");
```

5.9 Send Output to a File

So far, our programs have read data from the standard input (the keyboard) and sent output to the standard output (the screen). We have just seen how to read data from a file. We now show you how you can send output to a file.

This is important because when we send output to the screen, it is lost when we exit the program or when we switch off the computer. If we need to save our output, we must write it to a file. Then the output is available as long as we wish to keep the file.

The process is similar to reading from a file. We must declare a "file pointer" (we use out) and associate it with the actual file (output.txt, say) using fopen. This can be done with

```
FILE * out = fopen("output.txt", "w");
```

This tells C to "open the file output.txt for writing"; "w" indicates writing. When this statement is executed, the file output.txt is created if it does not already exist. If it exists, its contents are destroyed. In other words, whatever you write to the file will replace its original contents. Be careful that you do not open for writing a file whose contents you wish to keep.

5.9.1 fprintf

We use the statement (more precisely, the function) fprintf to send output to the file. It is used in exactly the same way as printf except that the first argument is the file pointer out. For example, if sum is int with value 143, the statement

```
fprintf(out, "The sum is %d\n", sum);
```

will write

```
The sum is 143
```

to the file output.txt.

Note that the first argument is the *file pointer* and *not* the name of the file.

When we have finished writing output to the file, we must close it. This is especially important for output files since, the way some compilers operate, this is the only way to ensure that all output is sent to the file. (For instance, they send output to a temporary buffer in memory; only when the buffer is full is it sent to the file. If you do not close the file, some output may be left in the buffer and never sent to the file.) We close the file with fclose, as follows:

```
fclose(out);
```

There is one argument, the file pointer (not the name of the file). This statement breaks the association of the file pointer out with the file output.txt. If we need to, we could now link the identifier out with another file (payroll.txt, say) using:

```
out = fopen("payroll.txt", "w");
```

Note that we do not repeat the FILE * part of the declaration, since out has already been declared as FILE *. Subsequent fprintf(out, ...) statements will send output to the file payroll.txt.

For an example, we rewrite Program P5.6 as Program P5.7 by adding the fopen and fprintf statements. The only difference is that P5.6 sends its output to the screen while P5.7 sends its output to the file output.txt.

Program P5.7

```
//read numbers from a file and find their average; 0 ends the data
#include <stdio.h>
int main() {
    FILE * in = fopen("input.txt", "r");
    FILE * out = fopen("output.txt", "w");
    int num, sum = 0, n = 0;
    fscanf(in, "%d", &num);
    while (num != 0) {
        n = n + 1;
        sum = sum + num;
        fscanf(in, "%d", &num);
    }
    if (n == 0) fprintf(out, "No numbers entered\n");
    else {
        fprintf(out, "%d numbers were entered\n", n);
        fprintf(out, "The sum is %d\n", sum);
        fprintf(out, "The average is %3.2f\n", (double) sum/n);
    }
    fclose(in);
    fclose(out);
}
```

As explained in Section 5.8, you can, if you wish, specify the complete path to your file in the fopen statement. For instance, if you want to send the output to the folder Results on a flash drive (with assigned letter F), you can use

```
FILE * out = fopen("F:\\Results\\output.txt", "w");
```

When you run Program P5.7, it will appear as if nothing has happened. However, if you check your file system, using the file path you specified, you will find the file output.txt. Open it to view your results.

5.10 Payroll

So far, our programs have read data from the standard input (the keyboard) and sent output to the standard output (the screen). We have just seen how to read data from a file. We now show you how you can send output to a file.

The data for each employee consists of a first name, a last name, the number of hours worked, and the rate of pay. The data will be stored in a file paydata.txt and output will be sent to the file payroll.txt.

In order to show you another way to read a string, we will assume that the data is stored in the file as follows:

```
Maggie May 50 12.00
Akira Kanda 40 15.00
Richard Singh 48 20.00
Jamie Barath 30 18.00
END
```

We use the "first name" END as the end-of-data marker.

Regular pay, overtime pay, and net pay will be calculated as described in Section 4.4.1. The employee name, hours worked, rate of pay, regular pay, overtime pay, and net pay are printed under a suitable heading. In addition, we will write the program to do the following:

- Count how many employees are processed.

- Calculate the total wage bill (total net pay for all employees).

- Determine which employee earned the highest pay and how much. We will ignore the possibility of a tie.

For the sample data, the output should look like this:

Name	Hours	Rate	Regular	Overtime	Net
Maggie May	50.0	12.00	480.00	180.00	660.00
Akira Kanda	40.0	15.00	600.00	0.00	600.00
Richard Singh	48.0	20.00	800.00	240.00	1040.00
Jamie Barath	30.0	18.00	540.00	0.00	540.00

```
Number of employees: 4
Total wage bill: $2840.00
Richard Singh earned the most pay of $1040.00
```

An outline of the algorithm for reading the data is as follows:

```
read firstName
while firstName is not "END" do
    read lastName, hours, rate
    do the calculations
    print results for this employee
    read firstName
endwhile
```

We will use the specification %s in fscanf for reading the names. Suppose we have declared firstName as

```
char firstName[20];
```

We can read a string into firstName with the statement

```
fscanf(in, "%s", firstName);
```

The specification %s must be matched with a character array, like firstName. As mentioned in Section 3.4, when an *array name* is an argument to scanf (or fscanf), we must not write & before it.

%s is used for reading a string of characters *not containing* any whitespace characters. Beginning with the *next* non-whitespace character, characters are stored in firstName until the *next* whitespace character is encountered. It is up to us to make sure that the array is big enough to hold the string.

Because a whitespace character ends the reading of a string, %s *cannot be used to read a string containing blanks.* For this reason, we will use separate variables for first name (firstName) and last name (lastName).

For example, suppose the next piece of data contains (◊ denotes a space):

◊◊◊Robin◊◊◊◊Hood◊◊

The statement

```
fscanf(in, "%s", firstName);
```

will skip over spaces until it reaches the first non-whitespace character R. Starting with R, it stores characters in firstName until it reaches the next space, the one after n. Reading stops and Robin is stored in firstName. The data pointer is positioned at the space after n. If we now execute

```
fscanf(in, "%s", lastName);
```

fscanf will skip over spaces until it reaches H. Starting with H, it stores characters in lastName until it reaches the space after d. Reading stops and Hood is stored in lastName. If d were the last character on the line, the end-of-line character (which is whitespace) would have stopped the reading.

Because of the way %s works, we will need to read the first and last names separately. However, in order to get the output to line up neatly as shown on the previous page, it would be more convenient to have the entire name stored in one variable (name, say). Suppose Robin is stored in firstName and Hood is stored in lastName. We will copy firstName to name with

```
strcpy(name, firstName);
```

We will then add a space with

```
strcat(name, " ");
```

strcat is a predefined string function that allows us to join (concatenate) two strings. It stands for "**str**ing con**cat**enation". If s1 and s2 are strings, strcat(s1, s2) will add s2 to the end of s1. It assumes that s1 is big enough to hold the joined strings.

We will then add lastName with

`strcat(name, lastName);`

Using our example, at the end of all this, name will contain Robin Hood.

In our program, we will use the specification %-15s to print name. This will print name left justified in a field width of 15. In other words, all names will be printed using 15 print columns. This is necessary for the output to line up neatly. To cater for longer names, you can increase the field width.

To use the string functions, we must write the directive

```
#include <string.h>
```

at the head of our program if we want to use the string functions supplied by C.

Our program will need to check if the value in firstName is the string "END". Ideally, we would like to say something like

```
while (firstName != "END") {  //cannot write this in C
```

but we cannot do so since C does not allow us to compare *strings* using the relational operators. What we *can* do is use the predefined string function strcmp (**string compare**).

If s1 and s2 are strings, the expression strcmp(s1, s2) returns the following values:

- 0 if s1 is identical to s2

- < 0 if s1 is less than s2 (in alphabetical order)

- > 0 if s1 is greater than s2 (in alphabetical order)

For example,

```
strcmp("hello", "hi") is < 0
strcmp("hi","hello") is > 0
strcmp("allo","allo") is 0
```

Using strcmp, we can write the while condition as

```
while (strcmp(firstName, "END") != 0)
```

If strcmp(firstName, "END") is not 0, it means that firstName does not contain the word END so we have not reached the end of the data; the while loop is entered to process that employee.

When faced with a program that requires so many things to be done, it is best to start by working on part of the problem, getting it right, and then tackling the other parts. For this problem, we can start by getting the program to read and process the data without counting, finding the total or finding the highest-paid employee.

Program P5.8 is based on program P4.7 (Section 4.6.2).

Program P5.8

```
#include <stdio.h>
#include <string.h>
#define MaxRegularHours 40
#define OvertimeFactor 1.5
int main() {
    FILE * in = fopen("paydata.txt", "r");
    FILE * out = fopen("payroll.txt", "w");
    char firstName[20], lastName[20], name[40];
    double hours, rate, regPay, ovtPay, netPay;

    fprintf(out,"Name   Hours Rate  Regular  Overtime  Net\n\n");
    fscanf(in, "%s", firstName);
    while (strcmp(firstName, "END") != 0) {
        fscanf(in, "%s %lf %lf", lastName, &hours, &rate);
        if (hours <= MaxRegularHours) {
            regPay = hours * rate;
            ovtPay = 0;
        }
        else {
            regPay = MaxRegularHours * rate;
            ovtPay = (hours - MaxRegularHours) * rate * OvertimeFactor;
        }
        netPay = regPay + ovtPay;

        //make one name out of firstName and lastName
        strcpy(name,firstName); strcat(name," "); strcat(name,lastName);
        fprintf(out, "%-15s %5.1f %6.2f", name, hours, rate);
        fprintf(out, "%9.2f %9.2f %7.2f\n", regPay, ovtPay, netPay);
        fscanf(in, "%s", firstName);
    }
    fclose(in);
    fclose(out);
}
```

Comments on Program P5.8

- We use the "file pointers" in and out for reading data from paydata.txt and sending output to payroll.txt.

- Since data is being read from a file, prompts are not required.

- We use fscanf for reading data and fprintf for writing output.

- We use fclose to close the files.

- We print a heading with the following statement:

  fprintf(out,"Name   Hours Rate Regular Overtime Net\n\n");

- To get the output to line up nicely, you will need to fiddle with the spaces between the words and the field widths in the statements that print the results. For example, there are 13 spaces between e and H, 3 spaces between s and R, 2 between e and R, 2 between r and O, and 5 between e and N.

- You should experiment with the field widths in the fprintf statements (which write one line of output) to see what effect it has on your output.

- We use a while loop to process several employees. When the "first name" END is read, the program knows it has reached the end of the data. It closes the files and stops.

Now that we've got the basic processing right, we can add the statements to perform the other tasks. Program P5.9 is the complete program that counts the employees, calculates the total wage bill, and determines the employee who earned the highest salary.

Counting the employees and finding the total wage bill are fairly straightforward. We use the variables numEmp and wageBill, which are initialized to 0 *before* the loop. They are incremented *inside* the loop and their final values are printed *after* the loop. If you have difficulty following the code, you need to reread Sections 5.1 and 5.2. We use numEmp++ to add 1 to numEmp and wageBill += netPay to add netPay to wageBill.

The variable mostPay holds the most pay earned by any employee. It is initialized to 0. Each time we calculate netPay for the current employee, we compare it with mostPay. If it is bigger, we set mostPay to the new amount and save the name of the employee (name) in bestPaid.

Program P5.9

```c
#include <stdio.h>
#include <string.h>
#define MaxRegularHours 40
#define OvertimeFactor 1.5
int main() {
    FILE * in = fopen("paydata.txt", "r");
    FILE * out = fopen("payroll.txt", "w");
    char firstName[20], lastName[20], name[40], bestPaid[40];
    double hours, rate, regPay, ovtPay, netPay;
    double wageBill = 0, mostPay = 0;
    int numEmp = 0;

    fprintf(out,"Name   Hours Rate  Regular  Overtime  Net\n\n");
    fscanf(in, "%s", firstName);
    while (strcmp(firstName, "END") != 0) {
        numEmp++;
        fscanf(in, "%s %lf %lf", lastName, &hours, &rate);

        if (hours <= MaxRegularHours) {
            regPay = hours * rate;
            ovtPay = 0;
        }
```

```
        else {
            regPay = MaxRegularHours * rate;
            ovtPay = (hours - MaxRegularHours) * rate * OvertimeFactor;
        }
        netPay = regPay + ovtPay;

        //make one name out of firstName and lastName
        strcpy(name,firstName); strcat(name," "); strcat(name,lastName);

        fprintf(out, "%-15s %5.1f %6.2f", name, hours, rate);
        fprintf(out, "%9.2f %9.2f %7.2f\n", regPay, ovtPay, netPay);

        if (netPay > mostPay) {
            mostPay = netPay;
            strcpy(bestPaid, name);
        }
        wageBill += netPay;
        fscanf(in, "%s", firstName);
    } //end while

    fprintf(out, "\nNumber of employees: %d\n", numEmp);
    fprintf(out, "Total wage bill: $%3.2f\n", wageBill);
    fprintf(out,"%s earned the most pay of $%3.2f\n",bestPaid, mostPay);
    fclose(in);   fclose(out);
}
```

5.11 The for Construct

In Chapters 3, 4, and 5 we showed you three kinds of logic that can be used for writing programs—sequence, selection, and repetition. Believe it or not, with these three, you have all the logic control structures you need to express the logic of any program. It has been proven that these three structures are all you need to formulate the logic to solve any problem that can be solved on a computer.

It follows that all you need are if and while statements to write the logic of any program. However, many programming languages provide additional statements because they allow you to express some kinds of logic *more conveniently* than using if and while. The for statement is a good example.

Whereas while lets you repeat statements as long as some condition is true, for lets you repeat statements *a specified number of times* (25 times, say). Consider the following *pseudocode* example of the for construct (more commonly called the for loop):

```
for h = 1 to 5 do
    print "I must not sleep in class"
endfor
```

This says to execute the `print` statement 5 times, with h assuming the values 1, 2, 3, 4, and 5, one value for each of the 5 times. The effect is to print the following:

```
I must not sleep in class
I must not sleep in class
I must not sleep in class
I must not sleep in class
I must not sleep in class
```

The construct consists of:

- the word `for`
- the *loop variable* (h, in the example)
- `=`
- the *initial* value (1, in the example)
- the word `to`
- the *final value* (5, in the example)
- the word `do`
- one or more statements to be executed each time through the loop; these statements make up the *body* of the loop
- the word `endfor`, indicating the end of the construct

We emphasize that `endfor` is not a C word and does not appear in any C program. It is just a convenient word used by programmers when writing pseudocode to indicate the end of a `for` loop.

In order to highlight the structure of the loop and make it more readable, we line up `for` and `endfor`, and indent the statements in the body.

The part of the construct between `for` and `do` is called the *control part* of the loop. This is what determines how many times the body is executed. In the example, the control part is h = 1 to 5. This works as follows:

- h is set to 1 and the body (`print`) is executed
- h is set to 2 and the body (`print`) is executed
- h is set to 3 and the body (`print`) is executed
- h is set to 4 and the body (`print`) is executed
- h is set to 5 and the body (`print`) is executed

The net effect is that, in this case, the body is executed 5 times.

In general, if the control part is h = `first` to `last`, it is executed as follows:

- if `first` > `last`, the body is not executed at all; execution continues with the statement, if any, after `endfor`; otherwise

- h is set to `first` and the body is executed

- 1 is added to h; if the value of h is less than or equal to `last`, the body is executed again

- 1 is added to h; if the value of h is less than or equal to `last`, the body is executed again

- and so on

When the value of h reaches `last`, the body is executed for the last time and control goes to the statement, if any, after `endfor`.

The net effect is that the body is executed for each value of h between `first` and `last`, inclusive.

5.11.1 The for Statement in C

The pseudocode construct

```
for h = 1 to 5 do
    print "I must not sleep in class"
endfor
```

is implemented in C as follows:

```
for (h = 1; h <= 5; h++)
    printf("I must not sleep in class\n");
```

assuming that h is declared as `int`. However, it is more common to declare h in the `for` statement itself, like this:

```
for (int h = 1; h <= 5; h++)
    printf("I must not sleep in class\n");
```

In this case, though, note that the scope of h extends only to the body of the `for` (see next).

■ **Caution** The ability to declare the loop variable in the `for` statement was not allowed in early versions of C. If you are using an older compiler, you will get an error. In that case, just declare the loop variable *before* the `for` statement.

In C, the body of the `for` must be a single statement or a block. In the example, it is the single `printf` statement. If it were a block, we would write it in the following form:

```
for (int h = 1; h <= 5; h++) {
    <statement1>
    <statement2>
    etc.
}
```

When we declare the loop variable (h in the example) in the for statement, h is "known" (can be used) within the block only. If we attempt to use h *after* the block, we will get an "undeclared variable" error message.

Program P5.10 illustrates how the for statement is used to print the following five times:

```
I must not sleep in class
```

As you could probably figure out, if you want to print 100 lines, say, all you have to do is change 5 to 100 in the for statement.

Program P5.10

```
#include
int main() {
    int h;
    for (h = 1; h <= 5; h++)
        printf("I must not sleep in class\n");
}
```

The general form of the for statement in C is

```
for (<expr1>;  <expr2>;  <expr3>)
    <statement>
```

The word for, the brackets, and the semicolons are required. You must supply <expr1>, <expr2>, <expr3>, and <statement>.

In detail, the for statement consists of

- The word for
- A left bracket, (
- <expr1>, called the initialization step; this is the first step performed when the for is executed.
- A semicolon, ;
- <expr2>, the condition which controls whether or not <statement> is executed.
- A semicolon, ;
- <expr3>, called the reinitialization step
- A right bracket,)
- <statement>, called the body of the loop. This can be a simple statement or a block.

When a for statement is encountered, it is executed as follows:

1. <expr1> is evaluated.

2. <expr2> is evaluated. If it is false, execution continues with the statement, if any, after <statement>. If it is true, <statement> is executed, followed by <expr3>, and this step (2) is repeated.

This can be expressed more concisely as follows:

```
<expr1>;
while (<expr2>) {
    <statement>;
    <expr3>;
}
```

Consider the following:

```
for (h = 1; h <= 5; h++)
printf("I must not sleep in class\n");
```

- h = 1 is <expr1>

- h <= 5 is <expr2>

- h++ is <expr3>

- <statement> is printf(...);

This code is executed as follows:

1. h is set to 1

2. The test h <= 5 is performed. It is true, so the body of the loop is executed (one line is printed). The reinitialization step h++ is then performed, so h is now 2.

3. The test h <= 5 is again performed. It is true, so the body of the loop is executed (a second line is printed); h++ is performed, so h is now 3.

4. The test h <= 5 is again performed. It is true, so the body of the loop is executed (a third line is printed); h++ is performed, so h is now 4.

5. The test h <= 5 is again performed. It is true, so the body of the loop is executed (a fourth line is printed); h++ is performed, so h is now 5.

6. The test h <= 5 is again performed. It is true, so the body of the loop is executed (a fifth line is printed); h++ is performed, so h is now 6.

7. The test h <= 5 is again performed. It is now false, so execution of the for loop ends and the program continues with the statement, if any, after printf(...).

On exit from the for loop, the value of h (6, in this case) is available and may be used by the programmer, if required. Note, however, that if h was declared in the for statement, it would be unavailable outside the loop.

If we need a loop to count backwards (from 5 down to 1, say), we can write

```
for (int h = 5; h >= 1; h--)
```

The loop body is executed with h taking on the values 5, 4, 3, 2, and 1.

We can also count upwards (or downwards) in steps other than 1. For example, the statement

```
for (int h = 10; h <= 20; h += 3)
```

will execute the body with h taking on the values 10, 13, 16 and 19. And the statement

```
for (int h = 100; h >= 50; h -= 10)
```

will execute the body with h taking on the values 100, 90, 80, 70, 60, and 50.

In general, we can use whatever expressions we need to get the effect that we want.

In Program P5.10, h takes on the values 1, 2, 3, 4, and 5 inside the loop. We have not used h in the body but it is available, if needed. We show a simple use in Program P5.11 in which we number the lines by printing the value of h.

Program P5.11

```
#include <stdio.h>
int main() {
    for (int h = 1; h <= 5; h++)
        printf("%d. I must not sleep in class\n", h);
}
```

When run, this program will print the following:

```
1. I must not sleep in class
2. I must not sleep in class
3. I must not sleep in class
4. I must not sleep in class
5. I must not sleep in class
```

The initial and final values in the for statement do not have to be constants; they can be variables or expressions. For example, consider this:

```
for (h = 1; h <= n; h++) ...
```

How many times would the body of this loop be executed? We cannot say unless we know the value of n when this statement is encountered. If n has the value 7, then the body would be executed 7 times.

This means that *before* the computer gets to the for statement, n must have been assigned some value and it is *this* value which determines how many times the loop is executed. If a value has not been assigned to n, the for statement would not make sense and the program will crash (or, at best, give some nonsensical output).

To illustrate, we can modify Program P5.11 to ask the user how many lines she wants to print. The number entered is then used to control how many times the loop is executed and, hence, how many lines are printed.

The changes are shown in Program P5.12.

Program P5.12

```c
#include <stdio.h>
int main() {
    int n;
    printf("How many lines to print? ");
    scanf("%d", &n);
    printf("\n"); //print a blank line
    for (int h = 1; h <= n; h++)
        printf("%d. I must not sleep in class\n", h);
}
```

A sample run is shown below. We will show shortly how to neaten the output.

```
How many lines to print? 12

1. I must not sleep in class
2. I must not sleep in class
3. I must not sleep in class
4. I must not sleep in class
5. I must not sleep in class
6. I must not sleep in class
7. I must not sleep in class
8. I must not sleep in class
9. I must not sleep in class
10. I must not sleep in class
11. I must not sleep in class
12. I must not sleep in class
```

Note that we do not (and cannot) know beforehand what number the user will type. However, that is not a problem. We simply store the number in a variable (n is used) and use n as the "final value" in the for statement. Thus, the number the user types will determine how many times the body is executed.

Now the user can change the number of lines printed simply by entering the desired value in response to the prompt. No change is needed in the program. Program P5.12 is much more *flexible* than P5.11.

5.11.2 A Bit of Aesthetics

In the above run, while the output is correct, the numbers do not line up very nicely with the result that the I's do not line up properly. We can get things to line up by using a field width when printing h. For this example, 2 will do. However, if the number could run into the hundreds, we must use at least 3 and for thousands at least 4, and so on.

In Program P5.12, if we change the printf statement to this:

```
printf("%2d. I must not sleep in class\n", h);
```

the following, more neatly looking output, would be printed:

```
How many lines to print? 12

 1. I must not sleep in class
 2. I must not sleep in class
 3. I must not sleep in class
 4. I must not sleep in class
 5. I must not sleep in class
 6. I must not sleep in class
 7. I must not sleep in class
 8. I must not sleep in class
 9. I must not sleep in class
10. I must not sleep in class
11. I must not sleep in4 class
12. I must not sleep in class
```

5.12 Multiplication Tables

The for statement is quite handy for producing multiplication tables. To illustrate, let us write a program to produce a "2 times" table from 1 to 12. The following should be printed by the program:

```
 1 x 2 =  2
 2 x 2 =  4
 3 x 2 =  6
 4 x 2 =  8
 5 x 2 = 10
 6 x 2 = 12
 7 x 2 = 14
 8 x 2 = 16
 9 x 2 = 18
10 x 2 = 20
11 x 2 = 22
12 x 2 = 24
```

A look at the output reveals that each line consists of three parts:

1. A number on the left that increases by 1 for each new line.

2. A fixed part " x 2 = " (note the spaces) that is the same for each line.

3. A number on the right; this is derived by multiplying the number on the left by 2.

We can produce the numbers on the left by using this statement:

```
for (int m = 1; m <= 12; m++)
```

We then print m each time through the loop. And we can produce the number on the right by multiplying m by 2.

Program P5.13 shows how to write it. When run, it will produce the table above.

Program P5.13

```
#include <stdio.h>
int main() {
    for (int m = 1; m <= 12; m++)
        printf("%2d x 2 = %2d\n", m, m * 2);
}
```

Note the use of the field width 2 (in %2d) for printing m and m * 2. This is to ensure that the numbers line up as shown in the output. Without the field width, the table would not look neat—try it and see.

What if we want to print a "7 times" table? What changes would be needed? We would just need to change the printf statement to

```
printf("%2d x 7 = %2d\n", m, m * 7);
```

Similarly, if we want a "9 times" table, we would have to change the 7s to 9s. And we would have to keep changing the program for each table that we want.

A better approach is to let the user tell the computer which table he wants. The program will then use this information to produce the table requested. Now when the program is run, it will prompt:

```
Enter type of table:
```

If the user wants a "7 times" table, he will enter 7. The program will then go ahead and produce a "7 times" table. Program P5.14 shows how.

Program P5.14

```
#IIII IIIAA <stdio.h>
int main() {
    int factor;
    printf("Type of table? ");
    scanf("%d", &factor);
    for (int m = 1; m <= 12; m++)
        printf("%2d x %d = %2d\n", m, factor, m * factor);
}
```

Since we do not know beforehand what type of table would be requested, we cannot use 7, say, in the format string, since the user may want a "9 times" table. We must print the variable factor which holds the type of table.

The following is a sample run:

```
Type of table? 7

 1 x 7 =  7
 2 x 7 = 14
 3 x 7 = 21
 4 x 7 = 28
 5 x 7 = 35
 6 x 7 = 42
 7 x 7 = 49
 8 x 7 = 56
 9 x 7 = 63
10 x 7 = 70
11 x 7 = 77
12 x 7 = 84
```

We now have a program that can produce any multiplication table from 1 to 12. But there is nothing sacred about the range 1 to 12 (special, maybe, since that's what we all learned in school). How can we *generalize* the program to produce *any* table in any range? We must let the user tell the program what type of table and what range he wants. And in the program, we will need to replace the numbers 1 and 12 by variables, (start and finish, say).

All these changes are reflected in Program P5.15.

Program P5.15

```
#include <stdio.h>
int main() {
    int factor, start, finish;
    printf("Type of table? ");
    scanf("%d", &factor);
    printf("From? ");
    scanf("%d", &start);
    printf("To? ");
    scanf("%d", &finish);
    printf("\n");
    for (int m = start; m <= finish; m++)
        printf("%2d x %d = %2d\n", m, factor, m * factor);
}
```

The following sample run shows how to produce a "6 times" table from 10 to 16.

```
Type of table? 6
From? 10
To? 16

10 x 6 = 60
11 x 6 = 66
12 x 6 = 72
13 x 6 = 78
14 x 6 = 84
15 x 6 = 90
16 x 6 = 96
```

To cater for bigger numbers, we would need to increase the field width of 2 in the printf statement if we want the numbers to line up neatly.

Comment on Program P5.15

The program assumes that start is less than or equal to finish. What if this is not so? For example, suppose the user enters 20 for start and 15 for finish. The for statement becomes

```
for (int m = 20; m <= 15; m++)
```

m is set to 20; since this value is immediately bigger than the final value 15, the body is not executed at all, and the program ends with nothing printed.

To cater for this possibility, we can let the program *validate* the values of start and finish to ensure that the "From" value is less than or equal to the "To" value. One way of doing this is to write the following.

```
if (start > finish)
    printf("Invalid data: From value is bigger than To value\n");
else {
    printf("\n");
    for (int m = start; m <= finish; m++)
        printf("%2d x %d = %2d\n", m, factor, m * factor);
}
```

Validating data entered is yet another example of *defensive programming*. Also, it is better to print a message informing the user of the error rather than have the program do nothing. This makes the program more *user friendly*.

Another option here is *not* to treat a bigger start value as an error but simply print the table in reverse order, going from largest to smallest. Yet another possibility is to swap the values of start and finish and print the table in the normal way. These variations are left as exercises.

5.13 Temperature Conversion Table

Some countries use the Celsius scale for measuring temperature while others use the Fahrenheit scale. Suppose we want to print a table of temperature conversions from Celsius to Fahrenheit. The table runs from 0 degrees C to 100 degrees C in steps of 10, thus:

Celsius	Fahrenheit
0	32
10	50
20	68
30	86
40	104
50	122
60	140
70	158
80	176
90	194
100	212

For a Celsius temperature, C, the Fahrenheit equivalent is $32 + 9C/5$.

If we use c to hold the Celsius temperature, we can write a for statement to let c take on the values 0, 10, 20, ..., up to 100, with

```
for (c = 0; c <= 100; c += 10)
```

Each time the loop is executed, c is incremented by 10. Using this, we write Program P5.16 to produce the table.

Program P5.16

```c
#include <stdio.h>
int main() {
    double c, f;
    printf("Celsius  Fahrenheit\n\n");
    for (c = 0; c <= 100; c += 10) {
        f = 32 + 9 * c / 5;
        printf("%5.0f %9.0f\n", c, f);
    }
}
```

An interesting part of the program are the printf statements. In order to get the temperatures centered under the heading, we need to do some counting. Consider the heading

```
Celsius  Fahrenheit
```

with the C in column 1 and 2 spaces between s and F.

Assume we want the Celsius temperatures lined up under i and the Fahrenheit temperatures lined up under n (see output above).

By counting, we find that i is in column 5 and n is in column 15.

From this, we can figure out that the value of c must be printed in a field width of 5 (the first 5 columns) and the value of f must be printed in the next 10 columns. We use a field width of 9 for f since there is already one space between f and % in printf(...).

We print c and f without a decimal point using 0 as the number of decimal places in the format specification. If any temperature is not a whole number, the 0 specification will print it *rounded* to the nearest whole number, as in the table below.

```
Celsius  Fahrenheit

   20         68
   22         72
   24         75
   26         79
   28         82
   30         86
   32         90
   34         93
   36         97
   38        100
   40        104
```

As an exercise, rewrite Program P5.16 so that it requests threes values for start, finish, and incr and produces a conversion table with Celsius temperatures going from start to finish by incr. Follow the ideas of the previous section for producing any multiplication table. For example, if start is 20, finish is 40 and incr is 2, the program should produce the following table (with Fahrenheit temperatures rounded to the nearest whole number):

As another exercise, write a program that produces a table from Fahrenheit to Celsius. For a Fahrenheit temperature, F, the Celsius equivalent is 5(F - 32)/9.

5.14 Expressive Power of for

In C, the for statement can be used for a lot more than just counting the number of times a loop is executed. This is possible because <expr1>, <expr2>, and <expr3> can be any expressions; they are not even required to be related in any way. So, for instance, <expr1> can be h = 1, <expr2> can test if a is equal to b, and <expr3> can be k++ or any other expression the programmer desires. The following is perfectly valid:

```
for (h = 1;  a == b;  k++)
```

It is also possible to omit any of <expr1>, <expr2>, or <expr3>. However, the semicolons must be included. Thus, to omit <expr3>, one can write

```
for (<expr1>; <expr2>; ) <statement>
```

In this case,

1.   <expr1> is evaluated; then

2.   <expr2> is evaluated. If it is false, execution continues after <statement>.
     If it is true, <statement> is executed and this step (2) is repeated.

This is equivalent to

```
<expr1>;
while (<expr2>) <statement>
```

If, in addition, we omit <expr1>, we will have

```
for ( ; expr2 ; ) <statement>   // note the semicolons
```

Now, <expr2> is evaluated. If it is false, execution continues after <statement>. If it is true, <statement> is executed, followed by another evaluation of <expr2>, and so on. The net effect is that <statement> is executed as long as <expr2> is true—the same effect achieved by

```
while (<expr2>) <statement>
```

Most times, <expr1> will initialize some variable, <expr2> will test it, and <expr3> will change it. But more is possible. For instance, the following is valid:

```
for (lo = 1, hi = n; lo <= hi; lo++, hi--) <statement>
```

Here, <expr1> consists of two assignment statements separated by a comma; <expr3> consists of two expressions separated by a comma. This is very useful when two variables are related and we want to highlight the relationship. In this case, the relationship is captured in one place, the for statement. We can easily see how the variables are initialized and how they are changed.

This feature comes in very handy when dealing with arrays. We will see examples in Chapter 8. For now, we leave you with the example of printing all pairs of integers that add up to a given integer, n.

The code is:

```
int lo, hi;
//assume n has been assigned a value
for (lo = 1, hi = n - 1; lo <= hi; lo++, hi--)
    printf("%2d %2d\n", lo, hi);
```

If n is 10, this code will print the following:

```
1   9
2   8
3   7
4   6
5   5
```

The variables lo and hi are initialized to the first pair. After a pair is printed, lo is incremented by 1 and hi is decremented by 1 to get the next pair. When lo passes hi, all pairs have been printed.

5.15 The do...while Statement

We have seen that the while statement allows a loop to be executed zero or more times. However, there are situations in which it is convenient to have a loop executed at least once. For example, suppose we want to prompt for a number representing a day of the week, with 1 for Sunday, 2 for Monday, and so on. We also want to ensure that the number entered is valid, that it lies in the range 1 to 7. In this case, at least one number must be entered. If it is valid, we move on; if not, we must prompt again for another number and must do so as long as the number entered is invalid. We could express this logic using a while statement as follows:

```
printf("Enter a day of the week  (1-7): ");
scanf("%d", &day); //assume int day
while (day < 1 || day > 7) { //as long as day is invalid
    printf("Enter a day of the week  (1-7): ");
    scanf("%d", &day);
}
```

While this will work, we can express it a bit neater using a do...while statement. The general form of the do...while statement in C is

```
do
    <statement>
while (<expression>);
```

The words do and while, the brackets, and the semicolon are required. You must supply <statement> and <expression>.

When a do...while is encountered,

1. <statement> is executed

2. <expression> is then evaluated; if it is true (non-zero), repeat from step 1. If it is false (zero), execution continues with the statement, if any, after the semicolon.

As long as <expression> is true, <statement> is executed. It is important to note that because of the way the construct is written, <statement> is always executed at least once.

Using do...while, we can express the logic above as follows:

```
do {
    printf("Enter a day of the week  (1-7): ");
    scanf("%d", &day);
} while (day < 1 || day > 7); //as long as day is invalid
```

Note how much neater this looks. Here, <statement> is the block delimited by { and }, and <expression> is day < 1 || day > 7.

We illustrate the use of do...while with two more examples.

5.15.1 Highest Common Factor

Previously, we wrote Program P5.2 to find the HCF of two integers using Euclid's algorithm. We now rewrite the program using do...while to ensure that the two numbers entered are indeed positive integers. We also re-code the algorithm using do...while instead of while. This is shown as Program P5.17.

Program P5.17

```
#include <stdio.h>
int main() {
    int m, n, r;

    do {
        printf("Enter two positive integers: ");
        scanf("%d %d", &m, &n);
    } while (m <= 0 || n <= 0);
    // At this point, both m and n are positive
    printf("\nThe HCF of %d and %d is ", m, n);

    do {
        r = m % n;
        m = n;
        n = r;
    } while (n > 0);

    printf("%d\n", m);
}
```

Program P5.17 requests two positive values. The first do...while keeps asking until two positive values are entered. When this occurs, the program continues with the calculation of the HCF. On exit from the second do...while, the value of n is 0 and the value of m is the HCF. The following is a sample run of program P5.17:

```
Enter two positive integers: 84 -7
Enter two positive integers: 46 0
Enter two positive integers: 200 16

The HCF of 200 and 16 is 8
```

5.15.2 Interest at the Bank

Consider the following problem:

A man deposits $1000 in a bank at an interest rate of 10% per year. At the end of each year, the interest earned is added to the amount on deposit and this becomes the new deposit for the next year. Write a program to determine the year in which the amount accumulated first exceeds $2000. For each year, print the deposit at the beginning of the year and the interest earned for that year until the target is reached.

A solution to this problem is given in Program P5.18.

Program P5.10

```c
#include <stdio.h>
int main() {
    int year;
    double initialDeposit, interestRate, target, deposit, interest;

    printf("Initial deposit? ");
    scanf("%lf", &initialDeposit);
    printf("Rate of interest? ");
    scanf("%lf", &interestRate);
    printf("Target deposit? ");
    scanf("%lf", &target);

    printf("\nYear Deposit Interest\n\n");
    deposit = initialDeposit;
    year = 0;
    do {
        year++;
        interest = deposit * interestRate / 100;
        printf("%3d %8.2f %8.2f\n", year, deposit, interest);
        deposit += interest;
    } while (deposit <= target);
    printf("\nDeposit exceeds $%7.2f at the end of year %d\n", target, year);
}
```

The program uses the following variables:

initialDeposit	1000, in the example
interestRate	10, in the example
target	2000, in the example
deposit	the deposit at any given time

As long as the end-of-year deposit has not exceeded the target, we calculate interest for another year. Program P5.18 does not cater for the case when the initial deposit is greater than the target. If this is required, a while statement may be used (exercise!). The following is a sample run of P5.18:

```
Initial deposit? 1000
Rate of interest? 10
Target deposit? 2000

Year Deposit Interest

1   1000.00    100.00
2   1100.00    110.00
3   1210.00    121.00
4   1331.00    133.10
5   1464.10    146.41
6   1610.51    161.05
7   1771.56    177.16
8   1948.72    194.87

Deposit exceeds $2000.00 at the end of year 8
```

EXERCISES 5

1. What is an end-of-data marker? Give the other names for it.

2. Write a program to read data for several items from a file. For each item, the price and a discount percent is given. Choose an appropriate end-of-data marker. For each item, print the original price, the discount amount, and the amount the customer must pay. At the end, print the number of items and the total amount the customer must pay.

3. An auto repair shop charges as follows. Inspecting the vehicle costs $75. If no work needs to be done, there is no further charge. Otherwise, the charge is $75 per hour for labor plus the cost of parts, with a minimum charge of $120. If any work is done, there is no charge for inspecting the vehicle.

4. Write a program to read several sets of hours worked and cost of parts and, for each, print the charge for the job. Choose an appropriate end-of-data marker. (You cannot choose 0 since either hours or parts could be 0.) At the end, print the total charge for all jobs.

5. Write a program to calculate electricity charges for several customers. The data for each customer consists of a name, the previous meter reading, and the current meter reading. The difference in the two readings gives the number of units of electricity used. The customer pays a fixed charge of $25 plus 20 cents for each unit used. The data is stored in a file.

6. Assume that the fixed charge and the rate per unit are the same for all customers and are given on the first line. This is followed by the data for the customers. Each set of data consists of two lines: a name on the first line and the meter readings on the second line. The "name" xxxx ends the data. Print the information for the customers under a suitable heading. Also,

- Count how many customers were processed

- Print the total due to the electricity company

- Find the customer whose bill was the highest

7. A file contains data for several persons. The data for each person consists of their gross salary, deductions allowed and rate of tax (e.g., 25, meaning 25%). Tax is calculated by applying the rate of tax to (gross salary minus deductions). Net pay is calculated by gross salary minus tax.

   Under an appropriate heading, print the gross salary, tax deducted, net pay, and the percentage of the gross salary that was paid in tax.

   For each person, the data consists of two lines: a name on the first line and gross salary, deductions allowed and rate of tax on the second line. The "name" xxxx ends the data. Also,

- Count how many persons were processed

- Print totals for gross salary, tax deducted and net pay

- Find the person who earned the highest net pay

8. Write a program that reads several lengths in inches and, for each, converts it to yards, feet and inches. (1 yard = 3 feet, 1 foot = 12 inches). For example, if a length is 100, the program should print 2 yd 2 ft 4 in. Choose an appropriate end-of-data marker.

9. Each line of data in a file consists of two lengths. Each length is given as two numbers representing feet and inches. A line consisting of 0 0 only ends the data. For each pair of lengths, print their sum. For example, if the lengths are **5 ft. 4 in.** and **8 ft. 11 in.**, your program should print **14 ft. 3 in.** The line of data for this example would be given as

   5 4 8 11

10. You are given a file containing an unknown amount of numbers. Each number is one of the numbers 1 to 9. A number can appear zero or more times and can appear anywhere in the file. The number 0 indicates the end of the data. Some sample data are:

    5 3 7 7 7 4 3 3 2 2 2 6 7 4 7 7
    2 2 9 6 6 6 6 8 5 5 3 7 9 9 9 0

    Write a program to read the data *once* and print the number that appears the most in consecutive positions and the number of times it appears. Ignore the possibility of a tie. For the above data, output should be 6 5.

11. A contest was held for the promotion of SuperMarbles. Each contestant was required to guess the number of marbles in a jar. Write a program to determine the Grand Prize winner (ignoring the possibility of a tie) based on the following:

    The first line of data contains a single integer (answer, say) representing the actual number of marbles in the jar. Each subsequent line contains a contestant's ID number (an integer), and an integer representing that contestant's guess. The data is terminated by a line containing 0 only.

    The Grand Prize winner is that contestant who guesses closest to answer *without exceeding it*. There is no winner if all guesses are too big.

    Assume all data are valid. Print the number of contestants and the ID number of the winner, if any.

12. The manager of a hotel wants to calculate the cost of carpeting the rooms in the hotel. All the rooms are rectangular in shape. He has a file, rooms.in, which contains data for the rooms. Each line of data consists of the room number, the length, and breadth of the room (in meters), and the cost per square meter of the carpet for that room. For example, the data line:

    ```
    325  3.0  4.5  40.00
    ```

    means that room 325 is 3.0 meters by 4.5 meters, and the cost of the carpet for that room is $40.00 per square meter. The last line of the file contains 0 only, indicating the end of the data.

    Write a program to do the following, sending output to the file rooms.out:

    • Print a suitable heading and under it, for each room, print the room number, the area of the room, and the cost of the carpet for the room;

    • Print the number of rooms processed;

    • Print the total cost of carpeting all the rooms;

    • Print the number of the room that will cost the most to carpet (ignore ties).

13. The price of an item is p dollars. Due to inflation, the price of the item is expected to increase by r% each year. For example, the price might be $79.50 and inflation might be 7.5%. Write a program which reads values for p and r, and, starting with year 1, prints a table consisting of year and year-end price. The table ends when the year-end price is at least twice the original price.

14. A fixed percentage of water is taken from a well each day. Request values for W and P where

    • W is the amount (in liters) of water in the well at the start of the first day

    • P is the percentage of the water in the well taken out each day

Write a program to print the number of the day, the amount taken for that day, and the amount remaining at the end of the day. The output should be terminated when 30 days have been printed or the amount remaining is less than 100 liters, whichever comes first. For example, if W is 1000 and P is 10, the output should start as follows:

Day	Amount Taken	Amount Remaining
1	100	900
2	90	810
3	81	729

15. Write a program to print the following 99 times:

When you have nothing to say, it is a time to be silent

16. Write a program to print 8 copies of your favorite song.

17. Write a program to print a table of squares from 1 to 10. Each line of the table consists of a number and the square of that number.

18. Write a program to request a value for n and print a table of squares from 1 to n.

19. Write a program to request values for first and last, and print a table of squares from first to last.

20. Write a program to print 100 mailing labels for

The Computer Store
57 First Avenue
San Fernando

21. Write a program to print a conversion table from miles to kilometers. The table ranges from 5 to 100 miles in steps of 5. (1 mile = 1.61 km).

22. Write a program which requests a user to enter an amount of money. The program prints the interest payable per year for rates of interest from 5% to 12% in steps of 0.5%.

23. Write a program to request a value for n; the user is then asked to enter n numbers, one at a time. The program calculates and prints the sum of the numbers. The following is a sample run:

How many numbers? 3
Enter a number? 12
Enter a number? 25
Enter a number? 18

The sum of the 3 numbers is 55

24. Write a program to request an integer n from 1 to 9 and print a line of output consisting of ascending digits from 1 to n followed by descending digits from n-1 to 1. For example, if n = 5, print the line

    123454321

25. Solve problem 10, above, assuming that the first line of data contains the number of rooms (n, say) to carpet. This is followed by n lines of data, one line for each room.

26. Solve problem 12, above, but this time print the table for exactly 30 days. If necessary, continue printing the table even if the amount of water falls below 100 liters.

CHAPTER 6

■ ■ ■

Characters

In this chapter, we will explain the following:

- Some important features of character sets

- How to work with character constants and values

- How to declare character variables in C

- How you can use characters in arithmetic expressions

- How to read, manipulate, and print characters

- How to test for end-of-line using \n

- How to test for end-of-file using EOF

- How to compare characters

- How to read characters from a file

- How to convert a number from character to integer

6.1 Character Sets

Most of us are familiar with a computer or typewriter keyboard (called the *standard English keyboard*). On it, we can type the letters of the alphabet (both uppercase and lowercase), the digits and other 'special' characters like +, =, <, >, &, and %—these are the so-called *printable* characters.

On a computer, each character is assigned a unique integer value, called its *code*. This code may be different from one computer to another depending on the *character set* being used. For example, the code for A might be 33 on one computer but 65 on another.

Inside the computer, this integer code is stored as a sequence of bits; for example, the 6-bit code for 33 is 100001 and the 7-bit code for 65 is 1000001.

Nowadays, most computers use the ASCII (American Standard Code for Information Interchange) character set for representing characters. This is a 7-bit character standard that includes the letters, digits, and special characters found on a standard keyboard. It also includes *control* characters such as backspace, tab, line feed, form feed, and carriage return.

141

The ASCII codes run from 0 to 127 (the range of numbers that can be stored using 7 bits). The ASCII character set is shown in Appendix B. Interesting features to note are the following:

- The digits **0** to **9** occupy codes **48** to **57**.

- The uppercase letters **A** to **Z** occupy codes **65** to **90**.

- The lowercase letters **a** to **z** occupy codes **97** to **122**.

Note, however, that even though the ASCII set is *defined* using a 7-bit code, it is stored on most computers in 8-bit bytes—a 0 is added at the front of the 7-bit code. For example, the 7-bit ASCII code for A is 1000001; on a computer, it is stored as 01000001, occupying one byte.

In this book, as far as is possible, we will write our programs making no assumptions about the underlying character set. Where it is unavoidable, we will assume that the ASCII character set is used. For instance, we may need to assume that the uppercase letters are assigned consecutive codes, similarly for lowercase letters. This may not necessarily be true for another character set. Even so, we will not rely on the specific values of the codes, only that they are consecutive.

6.2 Character Constants and Values

A character constant is a single character enclosed in single quotes such as 'A', '+' and '5'. Some characters cannot be represented like this because we cannot type them. Others play a special role in C (e.g. ', \). For these, we use an *escape sequence* enclosed in single quotes. Some examples are shown in the following table:

char	description	Code
'\n'	new line	10
'\f'	form feed	12
'\t'	tab	9
'\''	single quote	39
'\\'	backslash	92

The character constant '\0' is special in C; it is the character whose code is 0, normally referred to as the *null character*. One of its special uses is to indicate the end of a string in memory (see Chapter 8).

The *character value* of a character constant is the character represented, without the single quotes. Thus, the character value of 'T' is T and the character value of '\\' is \.

A character constant has an *integer value* associated with it—the numeric code of the character represented. Thus, the integer value of 'T' is 84 since the ASCII code for T is 84. The integer value of '\\' is 92 since the ASCII code for \ is 92. And the integer value of '\n' is 10 since the ASCII code for the newline character is 10.

We could print the *character* value using the specification %c in `printf`, and we could print the integer value using %d. For example, the statement

```
printf("Character: %c, Integer: %d\n", 'T', 'T');
```

will print

```
Character: T, Integer: 84
```

6.3 The Type char

In C, we use the keyword `char` to declare a variable in which we wish to store a character. For example, the statement

```
char ch;
```

declares ch as a *character variable*. We could, for instance, assign a character constant to ch, as follows:

```
ch = 'R';     //assign the letter R to ch
ch = '\n';    //assign the newline character, code 10, to ch
```

We could print the character value of a character variable using %c in `printf`. And we could print the integer value of a character variable using %d. For instance,

```
ch = 'T';
printf("Mr. %c\n", ch);
printf("Mr. %d\n", ch);
```

will print

```
Mr. T
Mr. 84
```

6.4 Characters in Arithmetic Expressions

C allows us to use variables and constants of type char directly in arithmetic expressions. When we do, it uses the *integer value* of the character. For example, the statement

```
int n = 'A' + 3;
```

assigns 68 to n since the code for 'A' is 65.
Similarly, we can assign an integer value to a char variable. For example,

```
char ch = 68;
```

In this case, "the character whose code is 68" is assigned to ch; this character is 'D'.
For a more useful example, consider the following:

```
int d = '5' - '0';
```

The *integer* 5 is assigned to d since the code for '5' is 53 and the code for '0' is 48.

Note that the code for a digit in character form is **not** the same as the value of the digit; for instance, the code for the character '5' is 53 but the value of the digit 5 is 5. Sometimes we know that a character variable contains a digit and we want to get the (integer) value of the digit.

The above statements show how we can get the value of the digit – we simply subtract the code for '0' from the code for the digit. It does not matter what the actual codes for the digits are; it matters only that the codes for 0 to 9 are consecutive. (Exercise: check this for yourself assuming a different set of code values for the digits.)

In general, if ch contains a digit character ('0' to '9'), we can obtain the integer value of the digit with the statement

```
d = ch - '0';
```

6.4.1 Uppercase To/From Lowercase

Suppose ch contains an uppercase letter and we want to convert it to its equivalent lowercase letter. For example, assume ch contains 'H' and we want to change it to 'h'. First we observe that the ASCII codes for 'A' to 'Z' range from 65 to 90 and the codes for 'a' to 'z' range from 97 to 122. We further observe that the difference between the codes for the two cases of a letter is always 32; for example,

```
'r' - 'R' = 114 - 82 = 32
```

Hence we can convert a letter from uppercase to lowercase by adding 32 to the uppercase code. This can be done with

```
ch = ch + 32;
```

If ch contains 'H' (code 72), the above statement adds 32 to 72 giving 104; the "character whose code is 104" is assigned to ch, that is, 'h'. We have changed the value of ch from 'H' to 'h'. Conversely, to convert a letter from lowercase to uppercase, we subtract 32 from the lowercase code.

By the way, we do not really need to know the codes for the letters. All we need is the difference between the uppercase and lowercase codes. We can let C tell us what the difference is by using 'a' - 'A', like this:

```
ch = ch + 'a' - 'A';
```

This works no matter what the actual codes for the letters are. It assumes, of course, that ch contains an uppercase letter and the difference between the uppercase and lowercase codes is the same for all letters.

6.5 Read and Print Characters

Many programs revolve around the idea of reading and writing one character at a time, and developing the skill of writing such programs is a very important aspect of programming. We can use scanf to read a *single* character from the standard input (the keyboard) into a char variable (ch, say) with:

```
scanf("%c", &ch);
```

The *next* character in the data is stored in ch. It is very important to note a big difference between reading a number and reading a character. When reading a number, scanf will skip over any amount of whitespace until it finds the number. When reading a character, the *very next character* (whatever it is, even if it's a space) is stored in the variable.

While we can use scanf, reading a character is important enough that C provides a special function getchar for reading characters from the standard input. (Strictly speaking, getchar is what's called a *macro*, but the distinction is not important for our purposes.) For the most part, we can think that getchar returns the next character in the data. However, it *actually* returns the numeric code of the next character. For this reason, it is usually assigned to an int variable, as in:

```
int c = getchar(); // the brackets are required
```

But it can also be assigned to a char variable, as in:

```
char ch = getchar(); // the brackets are required
```

To be precise, getchar returns the next byte in the data – to all intents and purposes, this is the next character. If we call getchar when there is no more data, it returns **-1**.

To be more precise, it returns the value designated by the symbolic constant EOF (all uppercase) defined in stdio.h. This value is usually, though not always, -1. The actual value is system dependent, but EOF will always denote the value returned on the system on which the program is run. We can, of course, always find out what value is returned by printing EOF, thus:

```
printf("Value of EOF is %d \n", EOF);
```

For an example, consider the statement:

```
char ch = getchar();
```

Suppose the data typed by the user is this:

```
Hello
```

When ch = getchar() is executed, the first character H is read and stored in ch. We can then use ch in whatever way we like. Suppose we just want to print the first character read. We could use:

```
printf("%c \n", ch);
```

145

This would print

H

on a line by itself. We could, of course, label our output as in the following statement:

```
printf("The first character is %c \n", ch);
```

This would print

```
The first character is H
```

Finally, we don't even need ch. If all we want to do is print the first character in the data, we could do so with:

```
printf("The first character is %c \n", getchar());
```

If we want to print the numeric code of the first character, we could do so by using the specification %d instead of %c. These ideas are incorporated in Program P6.1.

Program P6.1

```
//read the first character in the data, print it,
//its code and the value of EOF
#include <stdio.h>
int main() {
    printf("Type some data and press 'Enter' \n");
    char ch = getchar();
    printf("\nThe first character is %c \n", ch);
    printf("Its code is %d \n", ch);
    printf("Value of EOF is %d \n", EOF);
}
```

The following is a sample run:

```
Type some data and press 'Enter'
Hello

The first character is H
Its code is 72
Value of EOF is -1
```

A word of caution: we might be tempted to write the following:

```
printf("The first character is %c \n", getchar());
printf("Its code is %d \n", getchar());  // wrong
```

But if we did, and assuming that Hello is typed as input, these statements will print:

```
The first character is H
Its code is 101
```

Why? In the first printf, getchar returns H, which is printed. In the second printf, getchar returns the *next* character, which is e; it is e's code (101) that is printed.

In Program P6.1, we *could* use an int variable (n, say) instead of ch and the program would work in an identical manner. If an int variable is printed using %c, the last (rightmost) 8 bits of the variable are interpreted as a character and this character is printed. For example, the code for H is 72 which is 01001000 in binary, using 8 bits. Assuming n is a 16-bit int, when H is read, the value assigned to n will be

```
00000000 01001000
```

If n is now printed with %c, the last 8 bits will be interpreted as a character which, of course, is H.

Similarly, if an int value n is assigned to a char variable (ch, say), the last 8 bits of n will be assigned to ch.

As mentioned, getchar returns the integer value of the character read. What does it return when the user presses "Enter" or "Return" on the keyboard? It returns the newline character \n, whose code is 10. This can be seen using Program P6.1. When the program is waiting for you to type data, if you press the "Enter" or "Return" key only, the first lines of output would be as follows (note the blank line):

```
The first character is

Its code is 10
```

Why the blank line? Since ch contains \n, the statement

```
printf("\nThe first character is %c \n", ch);
```

is effectively the same as the following (with %c replaced by the value of ch)

```
printf("\nThe first character is \n \n");
```

The \n after is ends the first line and the last \n ends the second line, effectively printing a blank line. Note, however, that the code for \n is printed correctly.

In Program P6.1, we read just the first character. If we want to read and print the first three characters, we could do this with Program P6.2.

Program P6.2

```
//read and print the first 3 characters in the data
#include <stdio.h>
int main() {
    printf("Type some data and press 'Enter' \n");
    for (int h = 1; h <= 3; h++) {
        char ch = getchar();

        printf("Character %d is %c \n", h, ch);
    }
}
```

The following is a sample run of the program:

```
Type some data and press 'Enter'
Hi, how are you?
Character 1 is H
Character 2 is i
Character 3 is ,
```

If we want to read and print the first 20 characters, all we have to do is change 3 to 20 in the for statement.

Suppose the first part of the data line contains an arbitrary number of blanks, including none. How do we find and print the first non-blank character? Since we do not know how many blanks to read, we cannot say something like "read 7 blanks, then the next character."

More likely, we need to say something like "as long as the character read is a blank, keep reading." We have the notion of doing something (reading a character) as long as some 'condition' is true; the condition here is whether the character is a blank. This can be expressed more concisely as follows:

```
read a character
while the character read is a blank
    read the next character
```

Program P6.3 shows how to read the data and print the first non-blank character. (This code will be written more concisely later in this section.)

Program P6.3

```
//read and print the first non-blank character in the data
#include <stdio.h>
int main() {
   printf("Type some data and press 'Enter' \n");
   char ch = getchar();     // get the first character
   while (ch == ' ')        // as long as ch is a blank
      ch = getchar();       // get another character

   printf("The first non-blank is %c \n", ch);
}
```

The following is a sample run of the program (◊ denotes a blank):

```
Type some data and press 'Enter'
◊◊◊Hello
The first non-blank is H
```

The program will locate the first non-blank character regardless of how many blanks precede it.

As a reminder of how the while statement works, consider the following portion of code from Program P6.3 with different comments:

```
char ch = getchar();  //executed once; gives ch a value
                      //to be tested in the while condition

while (ch == ' ')
   ch = getchar();    //executed as long as ch is ' '
```

and suppose the data entered is (◊ denotes a space):

◊◊◊Hello

The code will execute as follows:

1. The first character is read and stored in ch; it is a blank.

2. The while condition is tested; it is true.

3. The while body ch = getchar(); is executed and the second character is read and stored in ch; it is a blank.

4. The while condition is tested; it is true.

5. The while body ch = getchar(); is executed and the third character is read and stored in ch; it is a blank.

6. The while condition is tested; it is true.

7. The while body ch = getchar(); is executed and the fourth character is read and stored in ch; it is H.

8. The while condition is tested; it is false.

9. Control goes to the printf, which prints.

```
The first non-blank is H
```

What if H was the very first character in the data? The code will execute as follows:

1. The first character is read and stored in ch; it is H.

2. The while condition is tested; it is false.

3. Control goes to the printf, which prints.

```
The first non-blank is H
```

It still works! If the while condition is false the first time it is tested, the body is not executed at all.

As another example, suppose we want to print all characters up to, but not including, the first blank. To do this, we could use Program P6.4.

Program P6.4

```
//print all characters before the first blank in the data
#include <stdio.h>
int main() {
    printf("Type some data and press 'Enter' \n");
    char ch = getchar();   // get the first character
    while (ch != ' ') {    // as long as ch is NOT a blank
        printf("%c \n", ch);// print it

        ch = getchar();      // and get another character
    }
}
```

The following is a sample run of P6.4:

```
Type some data and press 'Enter'
Way to go
W
a
y
```

The body of the while consists of two statements. These are enclosed by { and } to satisfy C's rule that the while body must be a single statement or a block. Here, the body is executed as long as the character read is not a blank — we write the condition using != (not equal to).

If the character is not a blank, it is printed and the next character read. If *that* is not a blank, it is printed and the next character read. If *that* is not a blank, it is printed and the next character read. And so on, until a blank character *is* read, making the while condition false, causing an exit from the loop.

We would be amiss if we didn't enlighten you about some of the expressive power in C. For instance, in Program P6.3, we could have read the character *and* tested it in the while condition. We could have rewritten the following three lines:

```
ch = getchar();      // get the first character
while (ch == ' ')    // as long as ch is a blank
   ch = getchar();   // get another character
```

as one line

```
while ((ch = getchar()) == ' '); // get a character and test it
```

ch = getchar() is an *assignment expression* whose value is the character assigned to ch, that is, the character read. This value is then tested to see if it is a blank. The brackets around ch = getchar() are required since == has higher precedence than =. Without them, the condition would be interpreted as ch = (getchar() == ' '). This would assign the value of a condition (which, in C, is 0 for false or 1 for true) to the variable ch; this is not what we want.

Now that we have moved the statement in the body into the condition, the body is empty; this is permitted in C. The condition would now be executed repeatedly until it becomes false.

To give another example, in Program 6.4, consider the following code:

```
char ch = getchar();     // get the first character
while (ch != ' ') {      // as long as ch is NOT a blank
   printf("%c \n", ch)   // print it
   ch = getchar();       // and get another character
}
```

This could be re-coded as follows (assuming ch is declared before the loop):

```
while ((ch = getchar()) != ' ')  // get a character
   printf("%c \n", ch);          // print it if non-blank; repeat
```

Now that the body consists of just one statement, the braces are no longer required. Five lines have been reduced to two!

6.6 Count Characters

Program P6.3 prints the first non-blank character. Suppose we want to *count* how many blanks there were before the first non-blank. We could use an integer variable numBlanks to hold the count. Program P6.5 is the modified program for counting the leading blanks.

Program P6.5

```
//find and print the first non-blank character in the data;
// count the number of blanks before the first non-blank
#include <stdio.h>
int main() {
   char ch;
   int numBlanks = 0;
   printf("Type some data and press 'Enter' \n");
   while ((ch = getchar()) == ' ') // repeat as long as ch is blank
      numBlanks++;              // add 1 to numBlanks
   printf("The number of leading blanks is %d \n", numBlanks);
   printf("The first non-blank is %c \n", ch);
}
```

The following is a sample run of the program (◊ denotes a space):

```
Type some data and press 'Enter'
◊◊◊◊Hello
The number of leading blanks is 4
The first non-blank is H
```

Comments on Program P6.5:

- numBlanks is initialized to 0 *before* the while loop.

- numBlanks is incremented by 1 *inside* the loop so that numBlanks is incremented each time the loop body is executed. Since the loop body is executed when ch contains a blank, the value of numBlanks is always the number of blanks read so far.

- When we exit the while loop, the value in numBlanks will be the number of blanks read. This value is then printed.

- Observe that if the first character in the data were non-blank, the while condition would be immediately false and control will go directly to the first printf statement with numBlanks having the value 0. The program will print, correctly:

  ```
  The number of leading blanks is 0
  ```

6.6.1 Count Characters in a Line

Suppose we want to count the number of characters in a line of input. Now we must read characters until the end of the line. How does our program test for end-of-line? Recall that when the "Enter" or "Return" key is pressed by the user, the newline character, \n, is returned by getchar. The following while condition reads a character and tests for \n.

```
while ((ch = getchar()) != '\n')
```

Program P6.6 reads a line of input and counts the number of characters in it, not counting the "end-of-line" character.

Program P6.6

```
//count the number of characters in the input line
#include <stdio.h>
int main() {
   char ch;
   int numChars = 0;
   printf("Type some data and press 'Enter' \n");
   while ((ch = getchar()) != '\n') // repeat as long as ch is not \n
      numChars++;                    // add 1 to numChars

   printf("The number of characters is %d \n", numChars);
}
```

The main difference between this and Program P6.5 is that this one reads characters until the end of the line rather than until the first non-blank. A sample run is:

```
Type some data and press 'Enter'
One moment in time

The number of characters is 18
```

6.7 Count Blanks in a Line of Data

Suppose we want to count *all the blanks* in a line of data. We must still read characters until the end of the line is encountered. But now, for each character read, we must check whether it is a blank. If it is, the count is incremented. We would need two counters—one to count the number of characters in the line and the other to count the number of blanks. The logic could be expressed as:

```
set number of characters and number of blanks to 0
while we are not at the end-of-line
    read a character
    add 1 to number of characters
    if character is a blank then add 1 to number of blanks
endwhile
```

This logic is implemented as shown in Program P6.7.

Program P6.7

```
//count the number of characters and blanks in the input line
#include <stdio.h>
int main() {
    char ch;
    int numChars = 0;
    int numBlanks = 0;
    printf("Type some data and press 'Enter' \n");
    while ((ch = getchar()) != '\n') { // repeat as long as ch is not \n
        numChars++;                    // add 1 to numChars
        if (ch == ' ') numBlanks++;    // add 1 if ch is blank
    }
    printf("\nThe number of characters is %d \n", numChars);
    printf("The number of blanks is %d \n", numBlanks);
}
```

Here is a sample run:

```
Type some data and press 'Enter'
One moment in time

The number of characters is 18
The number of blanks is 3
```

The if statement tests the condition ch == ' '; if it is true (that is, ch contains a blank), numBlanks is incremented by 1. If it is false, numBlanks is not incremented; control would normally go to the next statement within the loop but there is none (the if is the last statement). Therefore, control goes back to the top of the while loop, where another character is read and tested for \n.

6.8 Compare Characters

Characters can be compared using the relational operators ==, !=, <, <=, > and >=. We've compared the char variable ch with a blank using ch == ' ' and ch != ' '.

Let us now write a program to read a line of data and print the 'largest' character, that is, the character with the highest code. For instance, if the line consisted of English words, the letter that comes latest in the alphabet would be printed. (Recall, though, that lowercase letters have higher codes than uppercase letters so that, for instance, 'g' is greater than 'T'.)

'Finding the largest character' involves the following steps:

- Choose a variable to hold the largest value; we choose bigChar.

- Initialize bigChar to a very small value. The value chosen should be such that no matter what character is read, its value would be greater than this initial value. For characters, we normally use '\0'—the null character, the 'character' with a code of 0.

- As each character (ch, say) is read, it is compared with bigChar; if ch is greater than bigChar, then we have a 'larger' character and bigChar is set to this new character.

- When all the characters have been read and checked, bigChar will contain the largest one.

These ideas are expressed in Program P6.8.

Program P6.8

```
//read a line of data and find the 'largest' character
#include <stdio.h>
int main() {
   char ch, bigChar = '\0';
   printf("Type some data and press 'Enter' \n");
   while ((ch = getchar()) != '\n')
      if (ch > bigChar) bigChar = ch; //is this character bigger?

   printf("\nThe largest character is %c \n", bigChar);
}
```

The following is a sample run; u is printed since its code is the highest of all the characters typed.

```
Type some data and press 'Enter'
Where The Mind Is Without Fear

The largest character is u
```

155

6.9 Read Characters from a File

In our examples so far, we have read characters typed at the keyboard. If we want to read characters from a file (input.txt, say), we must declare a file pointer (in, say) and associate it with the file using

```
FILE * in = fopen("input.txt", "r");
```

Once this is done, we could read the next character from the file into a char variable (ch, say) with this statement:

```
fscanf(in, "%c", &ch);
```

However, C provides the more convenient function getc (**get** a **c**haracter) for reading a character from a file. It is used as follows:

```
ch = getc(in);
```

getc takes one argument, the file pointer (not the name of the file). It reads and returns the next character in the file. If there are no more characters to read, getc returns EOF. Thus, getc works exactly like getchar except that getchar reads from the keyboard while getc reads from a file.

To illustrate, let us write a program that reads one line of data from a file, input.txt, and prints it on the screen. This is shown as Program P6.9.

Program P6.9

```
#include <stdio.h>
int main() {
    char ch;
    FILE *in = fopen("input.txt", "r");
    while ((ch = getc(in)) != '\n')
        putchar(ch);
    putchar('\n');
    fclose(in);
}
```

This program uses the standard function putchar to write a single character to the standard output. (Like getchar, putchar is a *macro* but the distinction is not important for our purposes.) It takes a character value as its only argument and writes the character in the next position in the output. However, if the character is a *control* character, the *effect* of the character is produced. For example,

```
putchar('\n');
```

will end the current output line – the same effect as if "Enter" or "Return" is pressed.

The program reads one character at a time from the file and prints it on the screen using putchar. It does this until \n is read, indicating that the entire line has been read. On exit from the while loop, it uses putchar('\n') to terminate the line on the screen.

Be careful, though. This program assumes that the line of data is terminated by an end-of-line character, \n (generated when you press "Enter" or "Return"). However, if the line is not terminated by \n, the program will 'hang'—it will be caught in a loop from which it cannot get out (we say it will be caught in an *infinite loop*). Why?

Because the while condition ((ch = getc(in)) != '\n') will never become false (this happens when ch is '\n') since there is no \n to be read. But, as discussed before, when we reach the end-of-file, the value returned by getchar, and now also by getc, is the symbolic constant EOF defined in stdio.h. Knowing this, we could easily fix our problem by testing for \n and EOF in the while condition, thus:

```
while ((ch = getc(in)) != '\n' && ch != EOF)
```

Even if \n is not present, getc(in) will return EOF when the end of the file is reached, and the condition ch != EOF would be false, causing an exit from the loop.

6.10 Write Characters to a File

Suppose we want to write characters to a file (output.txt, say). As always, we must declare a file pointer (out, say) and associate it with the file using

```
FILE * out = fopen("output.txt", "w");
```

If ch is a char variable, we can write the value of ch to the file with

```
fprintf(out, "%c", ch);
```

C also provides the function putc (**put** a **c**haracter) to do the same job. To write the value of ch to the file associated with out, we must write:

```
putc(ch, out);
```

Note that the file pointer is the second argument to putc.

6.10.1 Echo Input, Number Lines

Let us expand the example on the previous page to read data from a file and write back the same data (*echo* the data) to the screen with the lines numbered starting from 1.

The program would read the data from the file and write it to the screen, thus:

```
1. First line of data
2. Second line of data
   etc.
```

This problem is a bit more difficult than those we have met so far. When faced with such a problem, it is best to tackle it a bit at a time, solving easier versions of the problem and working your way up to solving the complete problem.

For this problem, we can first write a program that simply echoes the input *without* numbering the lines. When we get this right, we can tackle the job of numbering the lines.

An outline of the algorithm for this first version is the following:

```
read a character, ch
while ch is not the end-of-file character
    print ch
    read a character, ch
endwhile
```

This will maintain the line structure of the data file since, for instance, when \n is read from the file, it is immediately printed to the screen, forcing the current line to end.

Program P6.10 implements the above algorithm for reading the data from a file and printing an exact copy on the screen.

Program P6.10

```c
#include <stdio.h>
int main() {
    char ch;
    FILE *in = fopen("input.txt", "r");
    while ((ch = getc(in)) != EOF)
        putchar(ch);
    fclose(in);
}
```

Now that we can echo the input, we need only figure out how to print the line numbers. A simplistic approach is based on the following outline:

```
set lineNo to 1
print lineNo
read a character, ch
while ch is not the end-of-file character
    print ch
    if ch is \n
        add 1 to lineNo
        print lineNo
    endif
    read a character, ch
endwhile
```

We have simply added the statements that deal with the line numbers to the algorithm above. We can easily add the code that deals with the line numbers to Program P6.10 to get Program P6.11. Note that when we print the line number, we do not terminate the line with \n since the data must be written on the same line as the line number.

Program P6.11

```
//This program prints the data from a file numbering the lines
#include <stdio.h>
int main() {
    char ch;
    FILE *in = fopen("input.txt", "r");
    int lineNo = 1;
    printf("%2d. ", lineNo);
    while ((ch = getc(in)) != EOF) {
        putchar(ch);
        if (ch == '\n') {
            lineNo++;
            printf("%2d. ", lineNo);
        }
    }
    fclose(in);
}
```

Assume the input file contains the following:

```
There was a little girl
  Who had a little curl
Right in the middle of her forehead
```

Program P6.11 will print this:

```
1. There was a little girl
2.   Who had a little curl
3. Right in the middle of her forehead
4.
```

Almost, but not quite, correct! The little glitch is that we print an extra line number at the end. To see why, look at the if statement. When \n of the third data line is read, 1 would be added to lineNo, making it 4, which is printed by the next statement. This printing of an extra line number also holds if the input file is empty, since line number 1 would be printed in this case, but there is no such line.

To get around this problem, we must delay printing the line number until we are sure that there is at least one character on the line. We will use an `int` variable `writeLineNo`, initially set to 1. If we have a character to print and `writeLineNo` is 1, the line number is printed and `writeLineNo` is set to 0. When `writeLineNo` is 0, all that happens is that the character just read is printed.

When \n is printed to end a line of output, `writeLineNo` is set to 1. If it turns out that there is a character to print on the next line, the line number will be printed first since `writeLineNo` is 1. If there are no more characters to print, nothing further is printed; in particular, the line number is not printed.

Program P6.12 contains all the details. When run, it will number the lines without printing an extra line number.

Program P6.12

```
//This program prints the data from a file numbering the lines
#include <stdio.h>
int main() {
   char ch;
   FILE *in = fopen("input.txt", "r");
   int lineNo = 0, writeLineNo = 1;
   while ((ch = getc(in)) != EOF) {
      if (writeLineNo) {
         printf("%2d. ", ++lineNo);
         writeLineNo = 0;
      }
      putchar(ch);
      if (ch == '\n') writeLineNo = 1;
   }
   fclose(in);
}
```

We wrote the `if` condition as follows:

`if (writeLineNo)...`

If `writeLineNo` is 1 the condition evaluates to 1 and is, therefore, `true`; if it is 0, the condition is `false`. We could also have written the condition as

`if (writeLineNo == 1)...`

In the statement

`printf("%d. ", ++lineNo);`

the expression ++lineNo means that lineNo is incremented *first* before being printed. By comparison, if we had used lineNo++, then lineNo would be printed first and *then* incremented.

Exercise: Modify Program P6.12 to send the output to a file, linecopy.txt.

~~Exercise: Write a program to copy the contents of a file input.txt to a file copy.txt.~~
Hint: you just need to make minor changes to Program P6.10.

6.11 Convert Digit Characters to Integer

Let us consider how we can convert a sequence of digits into an integer. When we type the number 385, we are actually typing three individual characters – '3' then '8' then '5'. Inside the computer, the integer 385 is completely different from the three characters '3' '8' '5'. So when we type 385 and try to read it into an int variable, the computer has to convert this sequence of three characters into the integer 385.

To illustrate, the 8-bit ASCII codes for the characters '3', '8', and '5' are 00110011, 00111000, and 00110101, respectively. When typed to the screen or a file, the digits 385 are represented by this:

00110011 00111000 00110101

Assuming an integer is stored using 16 bits, the integer 385 is represented by its binary equivalent

0000000110000001

Observe that the character representation is quite different from the integer representation. When we ask scanf (or fscanf) to read an integer that we type, it must convert the character representation to the integer representation. We now show how this is done.

The basic step requires us to convert a digit character into its equivalent integer value. For example, we must convert the character '5' (represented by 00110101) into the integer 5 (represented by 0000000000000101).

Assuming that the codes for the digits 0 to 9 are consecutive (as they are in ASCII and other character sets), this can be done as follows:

integer value of digit = code for digit character – code for character '0'

For example, in ASCII, the code for '5' is 53 and the code for '0' is 48. Subtracting 48 from 53 gives us the integer value (5) of the character '5'. Once we can convert individual digits, we can construct the value of the number as we read it from left to right, using the following algorithm:

```
set num to 0
get a character, ch
while ch is a digit character
    convert ch to the digit value, d = ch - '0'
    set num to num*10 + d
    get a character, ch
endwhile
num now contains the integer value
```

The sequence of *characters* 385 is converted as follows:

```
num = 0
get '3'; convert to 3
num = num*10 + 3 = 0*10 + 3; num is now 3
get '8'; convert to 8
num = num*10 + 8 = 3*10 + 8; num is now 38
get '5'; convert to 5
num = num*10 + 5 = 38*10 + 5; num is now 385
```

There are no more digits and the final value of num is 385.

Let us use this idea to write a program that reads data character by character until it finds an integer. It constructs and prints the integer.

The program will have to read characters until it finds a digit, the first of the integer. Having found the first digit, it must construct the integer by reading characters as long as it keeps getting a digit. For example, suppose the data was this:

```
Number of items: 385, all in good condition
```

The program will read characters until it finds the first digit, 3. It will construct the integer using the 3 and then reading 8 and 5. When it reads the comma, it knows the integer has ended.

This outline can be expressed in pseudocode as follows:

```
read a character, ch
while ch is not a digit do
    read a character, ch
endwhile
//at this point, ch contains a digit
while ch is a digit do
    use ch to build the integer
    read a character, ch
endwhile
print the integer
```

How do we test if the character in ch is a digit? We must test if

```
ch >= '0' && ch <= '9'
```

If this is true, we know that the character is between '0' and '9', inclusive. Conversely, to test if ch is not a digit, we can test if

```
ch < '0' || ch > '9'
```

Putting all these ideas together gives us Program P6.13.

Program P6.13

```
#include <stdio.h>
int main() {
   printf("Type data including a number and press \"Enter\"\n");
   char ch = getchar();
   // as long as the character is not a digit, keep reading
   while (ch < '0' || ch > '9') ch = getchar() ;
   // at this point, ch contains the first digit of the number
   int num = 0;
   while (ch >= '0' && ch <= '9') { // as long as we get a digit
      num = num * 10 + ch - '0';    // update num
      ch = getchar();
   }
   printf("Number is %d\n", num);
}
```

A sample run is shown below:

```
Type data including a number and press "Enter"
hide the number &(%%)4719&*(&^ here
Number is 4719
```

This program will find the number, no matter where it is hidden in the line.

EXERCISES 6

1. Give the range of ASCII codes for (a) the digits (b) the uppercase letters (c) the lowercase letters.

2. How is the single quote represented as a character constant?

3. What is the character value of a character constant?

4. What is the numeric value of a character constant?

5. How is the expression 5 + 'T' evaluated? What is its value?

6. What value is assigned to n by n = 7 + 't'?

7. What character is stored in ch by ch = 4 + 'n'?

8. If ch = '8', what value is assigned to d by d = ch - '0'?

9. If ch contains any uppercase letter, explain how to change ch to the equivalent lowercase letter.

10. If ch contains any lowercase letter, explain how to change ch to the equivalent uppercase letter.

11. Write a program to request a line of data and print the first digit on the line.

12. Write a program to request a line of data and print the first letter on the line.

13. Write a program to request a line of data and print the number of digits and letters on the line.

14. Write a program to read a passage from a file and print how many times each vowel appears.

15. Modify Program P6.13 so that it will find negative integers as well.

16. Write a program that reads a file containing a C program and outputs the program to another file with all the // comments removed.

17. Write a program to read the data, character by character, and store the next number (with or without a decimal point) in a double variable (dv, say). For example, given the following data your program should store 43.75 in dv.

     ```
     Mary works for $43.75 per hour
     ```

18. In the programming language Pascal, comments can be enclosed by { and } or by (* and *). Write a program which reads a data file input.pas containing Pascal code and writes the code to a file output.pas, replacing each { with (* and each } with *). For example, the statements

     ```
     read(ch);     {get the first character}
     while ch = ' ' do     {as long as ch is a blank}
     read(ch);     {get another character}
     writeln('The first non-blank is ', ch);
     ```

     should be converted to

     ```
     read(ch);       (*get the first character*)
     while ch = ' ' do     (*as long as ch is a blank*)
     read(ch);     (*get another character*)
     writeln('The first non-blank is ', ch);
     ```

19. You are given the same data as in 17, but now remove the comments altogether.

20. Someone has typed a letter in a file letter.txt, but does not always start the word after a period with a capital letter. Write a program to copy the file to another file format.txt so that all words after a period now begin with a capital letter. Also ensure there is exactly one space after each period. For example, the text

     ```
     Things are fine.    we can see you now.          let us know
     when is a good time.  bye for now.
     ```

     must be rewritten as

     ```
     Things are fine. We can see you now. Let us know when is a
     good time. Bye for now.
     ```

CHAPTER 7

■ ■ ■

Functions

In this chapter, we will explain the following:

- Why functions are important in programming

- How to write functions

- What happens when a function is called

- Where functions are placed in a program

- Some important concepts relating to functions using several examples

7.1 About Functions

So far, all our programs have consisted of a single function called main. However, we have made use of predefined C functions such as printf, scanf, strcpy, and fopen. When we run a program, it starts executing with the first statement in main and ends when it reaches the last statement.

As we have seen, it is possible to write reasonably useful programs with only main. However, there are many limitations to this approach. The problem to be solved may be too complex to be solved with one function. We may need to break it up into subproblems and try to solve each of these individually. It would be impractical to solve all the subproblems in one function. It might be better to write a separate function to solve each subproblem.

Also, we may want to reuse the solution to common problems. It would be difficult to reuse a solution if it is part of the solution to a bigger problem. For example, if we need the highest common factor (HCF) of two numbers in several places, it would be best to write a routine that works out the HCF of two given numbers; we call this routine whenever we need to find the HCF of two numbers.

A well-written function performs some well-defined task; for example, skip a specified number of lines in the output or arrange some numbers in ascending order. However, quite often, a function also returns a value; for example, calculate the salary of a person and return the answer or play one turn of a game and return the score for that turn. The value returned is normally used at the point from which the function was called.

Previously, we used the string function strcmp, which returns a value that tells us the result of comparing two strings. And we have used getchar and getc to return the next character in the input.

We are now ready to learn how to write our own functions (called *user-defined* functions), and we will see several examples in the rest of this book.

165

7.2 skipLines

We have seen that we can use \n in a printf statement to print a blank line. For example, the statement

```
printf("%d\n\n%d\n", a, b);
```

will print a on one line, skip one line and print b on the next line. We can usually skip any number of lines by writing the appropriate number of \n's in the printf statement.

Sometimes we may want to skip 3 lines, sometimes 2 lines, sometimes 5 lines, and so on. It would be nice if there was a statement we could use to skip any number of lines we want. For instance, to skip 3 lines, we should be able to write

```
skipLines(3);
```

and to skip 5 lines, we write

```
skipLines(5);
```

What we want is a *function* called skipLines, which takes an *integer argument* (n, say) and skips n lines. In C, we write this function as follows:

```
void skipLines(int n) {
for (int h = 1; h <= n; h++)
    printf("\n");
}
```

Observe that the structure of the function is similar to the structure of main. It consists of a *header* (the first line, except {) followed by the *body* enclosed in braces. The word void indicates that the function does not return a value and (int n) defines n as an integer *parameter*. When the function is called, we must supply it with an integer value to match the parameter n.

This is the *definition* of the function skipLines. We *use* the function by *calling* it when we write, in main, a statement such as:

```
skipLines(3);
```

(A function can normally be called from any other function but, to focus our discussion, we will assume it is called from main.)

We say that we *call* (or *invoke*) the function with the *argument*. (In this book, we use the term 'parameter' when referring to the definition of the function and the term 'argument' when the function is *called*. Others use the terms interchangeably.) The "call" is executed as follows:

- The value of the argument is determined. In this case, it is just the constant 3 but, in general, it could be an expression.

- The value is copied to a temporary memory location. This location is passed to the function where it is labeled with the name of the parameter, n. In effect, the parameter variable n is set to the value of the argument. We can picture this as follows:

  n | 3 |

- The body of the function is executed. In this case, since n is 3, the for loop becomes

  for (int h = 1; h <= 3; h++)

  and it prints \n three times.

- When the function is finished, the location containing the argument is discarded and control returns to main to the statement following skipLines(3).

Note that we can get skipLines to print a different number of blank lines by supplying a different argument when we call it.

When the *value* of an argument is passed to a function, we say the argument is passed "by value." In C, arguments are passed "by value."

7.3 A Program with a Function

We write Program P7.1 to show how skipLines fits into a complete program.

Program P7.1

```
#include <stdio.h>
int main() {
    void skipLines(int);
    printf("Sing a song of sixpence\n");
    skipLines(2);
    printf("A pocket full of rye\n");
} //end main

void skipLines(int n) {
    for (int h = 1; h <= n; h++)
        printf("\n");
} //end skipLines
```

When we wish to use a variable in main, we must declare the variable in main. Similarly, if we want to use skipLines in main, we must tell C about it using what is called a *function prototype*. A function prototype is a *declaration* pretty much like the function header. In the program, we use the prototype:

```
void skipLines(int);
```

The prototype describes the function by stating the *return type* of the function (void, in this case), the name of the function (skipLines) and the type(s) of any argument(s) (int, in this example). If you wish, you can write a variable after the type, as in:

```
void skipLines(int a);
```

This variable will be used by the compiler only if it needs to generate an error message. In this book, we will write our prototypes using the type only.

Note that the function *prototype* is followed by a semicolon whereas the function *header* is followed by a *left brace*.

As another example, the prototype

```
int max(int, int);
```

says that max is a function that takes two integer arguments and returns an integer value.

A common mistake made by beginners is to forget to write the function prototype. However, that is not a big problem. If you forget, the compiler will remind you of it. It is like forgetting to declare a variable – the compiler will tell you about it. You just fix it and move on.

In terms of layout, the functions, including main, which make up a C program can appear in any order. However, it is customary to place main first where the overall logic of the program can be easily seen.

We emphasize that this program is for illustrative purposes only since the output could be produced more easily with this:

```
printf("Sing a song of sixpence\n\n\n");
printf("A pocket full of rye\n");
```

7.3.1 The Function Header

In our example, we used the function header

```
void skipLines(int n)
```

In general, the function header consists of:

- a *type* (such as void, int, double, char), which specifies the type of value returned by the function. If no value is returned, we use the word void. The function skipLines does not return a value so we use void.

- the name we make up for the function, skipLines in the example.

- zero or more parameters, called the *parameter list*, enclosed in brackets; one parameter n of type int is used in the example. If there are no parameters, the brackets must still be present, as in printHeading().

The function header is followed by the left brace of the body.

Parameters are specified in the same way variables are declared. In fact, they really are declarations. The following are all valid examples of headers of void functions:

```
void sample1(int m, int n)                  // 2 parameters
void sample2(double a, int n, char c)       // 3 parameters
void sample3(double a, double b, int j, int k) // 4 parameters
```

Each parameter must be declared individually and two consecutive declarations are separated by a comma. For example, it is invalid to write

```
void sample1(int m, n)  //not valid; must write (int m, int n)
```

Shortly, we will see examples of functions that return a value.

7.3.2 How a Function Gets Its Data

A function is like a mini program. In the programs we have written, we have stated what data must be supplied to the program, what processing must take place, and what the output (results) should be. We must do the same when we write a function.

When we write a function header, we use the parameter list to specify what data must be supplied to the function when it is called. The list specifies *how many* data items, the *type* of the each item, and the *order* in which they must be supplied.

For example, we wrote skipLines with an integer parameter n; this says that an integer value must be supplied to skipLines when it is called. When skipLines is called, the argument supplied becomes the specific value of n and the function is executed assuming that n has this value. In the call skipLines(3), the argument 3 is the data that skipLines needs to perform its job.

It is worth emphasizing that main gets its data by using scanf, among other functions, to read and store the data in variables. On the other hand, a function gets its data when it is called. The variables in the parameter list are set to the values of the corresponding arguments used in the call. For example, when we write the header

```
void sample(int n, char c, double b)
```

we are saying that, when we call sample, we must do so with three arguments: the first must be an int value, the second a char value and the third a double value.

Assuming that num is int, ch is char and x is double, the following are all valid calls to sample:

```
sample(25, 'T', 7.5);
sample(num, 'A', x);
sample(num, ch, 7); //an int argument can match a double parameter
sample(num + 1, ch, x / 2.0);
```

If, when a function is called, the type of an argument is not the same as the corresponding parameter, C tries to convert the argument to the required type. For example, in the call

```
sample(num, 72, 'E');
```

the value 72 is converted to char and the parameter c is set to 'H' (since the code for H is 72); the numeric value of 'E' (which is 69) is converted to the double value 69.0 and the parameter b is set to 69.0.

If it is not possible to convert the argument to the required type, you will get a "type mismatch" error, as in the call

```
sample(num, ch, "hi"); // error - cannot convert string to double
```

You will also get an error if you do not supply the required number of arguments, as in

```
sample(num, x); // error - must have 3 arguments
```

7.4 max

Finding the larger of two values is something we need to do sometimes. If a and b are two numbers, we can set the variable max to the larger of the two with this:

```
if (a > b) max = a;
else max = b;
```

If the numbers are equal, max will be set to b (the else part will be executed). We can, of course, write this statement every time we want to get the larger of two values. But this will become clumsy and awkward. It will be more convenient and readable if we can simply write something like

```
big = max(a, b);
```

or even

```
printf("The bigger is %d\n", max(a, b));
```

We can, if we write the *function* max as follows:

```
int max(int a, int b) {
    if (a > b) return a;
    return b;
}
```

The first line (except {) is the function header. It consists of

- The word int, indicating that the function returns an integer value.

- The name we make up for the function, max in the example.

- One or more parameters, called the *parameter list*, enclosed in brackets; two parameters a and b of type int are used in the example.

The *body* of the function is the part from { to }. Here, we use the if statement to determine the larger of a and b. If a is bigger, the function "returns" a; if not, it returns b.

In C, a function "returns a value" by using the return statement. It consists of the word return followed by the value to be returned. The value is returned to the place at which the function was called.

To show how max fits into an overall program and how it can be used, we write Program P7.2 that reads pairs of integers and, for each pair, prints the larger of the two. The program ends when the user types 0 0.

Program P7.2

```
#include <stdio.h>
int main() {
    int n1, n2;
    int max(int, int);
    printf("Enter two whole numbers: ");
    scanf("%d %d", &n1, &n2);
    while (n1 != 0 || n2 != 0) {
        printf("The bigger is %d\n", max(n1, n2));
        printf("Enter two whole numbers: ");
        scanf("%d %d", &n1, &n2);
    }
} //end main

int max(int a, int b) {
    if (a > b) return a;
    return b;
} //end max
```

The following is a sample run of P7.2:

```
Enter two whole numbers: 24 33
The bigger is 33
Enter two whole numbers: 10 -13
The bigger is 10
Enter two whole numbers: -5 -8
The bigger is -5
Enter two whole numbers: 0 7
The bigger is 7
Enter two whole numbers: 0 0
```

In order to call max from main, we must "declare" max in main using the function prototype

```
int max(int, int);
```

This says that max takes two integer arguments and returns an integer value.

The variables n1 and n2, declared in main, are considered as belonging to main.

When the program is run, suppose n1 is 24 and n2 is 33. When the function is called with max(n1, n2) from within printf, the following occurs:

- The values of the arguments n1 and n2 are determined. These are 24 and 33, respectively.

- Each value is copied to a temporary memory location. These locations are passed to the function max where 24 is labeled with a, the first parameter; and 33 is labeled with b, the second parameter. We can picture this as follows:

  a ⬜24⬜   b ⬜33⬜

- The if statement is executed; since a (24) is not greater than b (33), control goes to the statement return b; and 33 is returned as the value of the function. This value is returned to the place from which max was called (the printf statement).

- Just before the function returns, the locations containing the arguments are thrown away. The value returned by max (33, in our example) replaces the call to max. Thus, max(n1, n2) is replaced by 33 and printf prints

  ```
  The bigger is 33
  ```

When a function returns a value, it makes sense for this value to be used in a situation where a value is required. Above, we printed the value. We could also assign the value to a variable, as in

```
big = max(n1, n2);
```

or use it as part of an expression, as in

```
ans = 2 * max(n1, n2);
```

What does *not* make sense is to use it in a statement by itself, thus:

```
max(n1, n2); //a useless statement
```

Here, the value is not being used in any way, so the statement makes no sense at all. It is the same as if we had written a number on a line by itself, like this

```
33; //a useless statement
```

Think carefully when you call a function that returns a value. Be very clear in your mind what you intend to use the value for.

As written, max returns the larger of two integers. What if we want to find the larger of two double numbers? Could we use max? Unfortunately, no. If we called max with double values as arguments, we may get strange results when a double number is assigned to an int parameter.

On the other hand, if we wrote max with double parameters and double return type, it would work for both double and int arguments, since we can assign an int value to a double parameter without losing any information.

Note, however, that if we call max with two character arguments, it would work by returning the larger of the two codes. For example, max('A', 'C') will return 67, the code for C.

EXERCISE

Write functions to return the *smaller* of two integers and two floating-point numbers.

7.5 Print the Day

Let us write a program that requests a number from 1 to 7 and prints the name of the day of the week. For example, if the user enters 5, the program prints Thursday. Program P7.3 does the job using a series of if...else statements.

Program P7.3

```c
#include <stdio.h>
int main() {
    int d;
    printf("Enter a day from 1 to 7: ");
    scanf("%d", &d);
    if (d == 1) printf("Sunday\n");
    else if (d == 2) printf("Monday\n");
    else if (d == 3) printf("Tuesday\n");
    else if (d == 4) printf("Wednesday\n");
    else if (d == 5) printf("Thursday\n");
    else if (d == 6) printf("Friday\n");
    else if (d == 7) printf("Saturday\n");
    else printf("Invalid day\n");
}
```

Now suppose that printing the name of a day of the week was a small part of a much larger program. We wouldn't want to clutter up main with this code nor would we want to rewrite this code every time we needed to print the name of a day. It would be much nicer if we could write printDay(n) and get the appropriate name printed. We would be able to do this if we write a function printDay to do the job.

The first thing to ask is what information does printDay need to do its job. The answer is that it needs the number of the day. This immediately suggests that printDay must be written with the number of the day as a parameter. Apart from this, the body of the function will contain essentially the same code as Program P7.3. Also, printDay does not return a value so its "return type" is void.

```
void printDay(int d) {
    if (d == 1) printf("Sunday\n");
    else if (d == 2) printf("Monday\n");
    else if (d == 3) printf("Tuesday\n");
    else if (d == 4) printf("Wednesday\n");
    else if (d == 5) printf("Thursday\n");
    else if (d == 6) printf("Friday\n");
    else if (d == 7) printf("Saturday\n");
    else printf("Invalid day\n");
}
```

■ **Tip** When we write the function, we can use any variable name we want for the parameter. We never have to worry about how the function will be called. Many beginners mistakenly believe that if the function is called with printDay(n), the parameter in the header must be n. But that cannot be true since it could be called with printDay(4) or printDay(n) or printDay(j) or even printDay(n + 1). The choice is up to the calling function.

All we need to know is that whatever the value of the argument, that value will be assigned to d (or whatever variable we happen to use as the parameter), and the function will be executed assuming the parameter (d, in our case) has that value.

We now rewrite Program P7.3 as P7.4 to illustrate how the function fits into an overall program and how it can be used.

Program P7.4

```
#include <stdio.h>
int main() {
    int n;
    void printDay(int);
    printf("Enter a day from 1 to 7: ");
    scanf("%d", &n);
    printDay(n);
} //end main

void printDay(int d) {
    if (d == 1) printf("Sunday\n");
    else if (d == 2) printf("Monday\n");
    else if (d == 3) printf("Tuesday\n");
    else if (d == 4) printf("Wednesday\n");
    else if (d == 5) printf("Thursday\n");
    else if (d == 6) printf("Friday\n");
```

```
    else if (d == 7) printf("Saturday\n");
    else printf("Invalid day\n");
} //end printDay
```

Now that we have delegated the printing to a function, notice how main is much less cluttered. However, we do have to write the function prototype for printDay in main so that printDay can be called from main. Here is the prototype:

```
void printDay(int);
```

As with all C programs, execution begins with the first statement in main. This prompts the user for a number, and the program goes on to print the name of the day by calling the function printDay.

A sample run is:

```
Enter a day from 1 to 7: 4
Wednesday
```

In main, suppose n has the value 4. The call printDay(n) is executed as follows:

- The *value* of the argument n is determined. It is 4.

- The value 4 is copied to a temporary memory location. This location is passed to the function printDay where it is labeled with the name of the parameter, d. In effect, d is set to the value of the argument.

- The body of the function is executed. In this case, since d is 4, the statement printf("Wednesday\n") will be executed.

- After printing Wednesday, the function is finished. The location containing the argument is discarded and control returns to main to the statement following the call printDay(n). In this case, there are no more statements so the program ends.

7.6 Highest Common Factor

In Chapter 5, we wrote Program P5.2, which read two numbers and found their highest common factor (HCF). You should refresh your memory by taking a look at the program.

It would be nice if whenever we want to find the HCF of two numbers (m and n, say), we could make a function call hcf(m, n) to get the answer. For instance, the call hcf(42, 24) would return the answer 6. To be able to do this, we write the function as follows:

```
//returns the hcf of m and n
int hcf(int m, int n) {
    while (n != 0) {
        int r = m % n;
        m = n;
        n = r;
    }
    return m;
} //end hcf
```

The logic for finding the HCF is the same as that used in program P5.2. The difference here is that values for m and n will be passed to the function when it is called. In P5.2, we prompted the user to enter values for m and n and fetched them using scanf.

Suppose the function is called with hcf(42, 24). The following occurs:

- Each of the arguments is copied to a temporary memory location. These locations are passed to the function hcf where 42 is labeled with m, the first parameter, and 24 is labeled with n, the second parameter. We can picture this as:

    m | 42 | n | 24 |

- The while loop is executed, working out the HCF. On exit from the loop, the HCF is stored in m, which will contain 6 at this time. This is the value returned by the function to the place from where it was called.

- Just before the function returns, the locations containing the arguments are thrown away; control then returns to the place from where the call was made.

Program P7.5 tests the function by reading pairs of numbers and printing the HCF of each pair. The call to hcf is made in the printf statement. The program stops if either number is less than or equal to 0.

Program P7.5

```c
#include <stdio.h>
int main() {
    int a, b;
    int hcf(int, int);
    printf("Enter two positive numbers: ");
    scanf("%d %d", &a, &b);
    while (a > 0 && b > 0) {
        printf("The HCF is %d\n", hcf(a, b));
        printf("Enter two positive numbers: ");
        scanf("%d %d", &a, &b);
    }
} //end main

//returns the hcf of m and n
int hcf(int m, int n) {
    while (n != 0) {
        int r = m % n;
        m = n;
        n = r;
    }
    return m;
} //end hcf
```

The following is a sample run of P7.5:

```
Enter two positive numbers: 42 24
The HCF is 6
Enter two positive numbers: 32 512
The HCF is 32
Enter two positive numbers: 100 31
The HCF is 1
Enter two positive numbers: 84 36
The HCF is 12
Enter two positive numbers: 0 0
```

We emphasize again that even though the function is written with parameters m and n, it can be called with any two integer values – constants, variables, or expressions. In particular, it does not have to be called with variables named m and n. In our program, we called it with a and b.

We remind you that in order to use hcf in main, we must "declare" it using the function prototype

```
int hcf(int, int);
```

If you wish, you could write the two int declarations in main as one:

```
int a, b, hcf(int, int);
```

7.6.1 Using HCF to Find LCM

A common task in arithmetic is to find the lowest common multiple (LCM) of two numbers. For example, the LCM of 8 and 6 is 24 since 24 is the smallest number that can divide both 8 and 6 exactly.

If we know the HCF of the two numbers, we can find the LCM by multiplying the numbers and dividing by their HCF. Given that the HCF of 8 and 6 is 2, we can find their LCM by working out

$$\frac{8 \times 6}{2}$$

which is 24. In general,

```
LCM(m, n) = (m x n) / HCF(m, n)
```

Knowing this, we can easily write a function lcm which, given two arguments m and n, returns the LCM of m and n.

```
//returns the lcm of m and n
int lcm(int m, int n) {
    int hcf(int, int);
    return (m * n) / hcf(m, n);
} //end lcm
```

Since lcm uses hcf, we must declare hcf by writing its prototype. We leave it as an exercise for you to write a program to test lcm. Remember to include the function hcf in your program. You may place hcf before or after lcm.

7.7 factorial

So far, we have written several functions that illustrate various concepts you need to know in writing and using functions. We now write another one and discuss it in detail, reinforcing some of the concepts we have met thus far and introducing new ones.

Before we write the function, let us first write a program which reads an integer n and prints $n!$ (n factorial) where

```
0! = 1
n! = n(n - 1)(n - 2)...1  for n > 0
```

For example, $5! = 5.4.3.2.1 = 120$.

The program will be based on the following algorithm:

```
set nfac to 1
read a number, n
for h = 2 to n do
    nfac = nfac * h
endfor
print nfac
```

Dry run the algorithm with a value of 3 for n and convince yourself that it will print 6, the value of 3!. Check also that it produces the correct answer when n is 0 or 1. (Hint: the for loop is not executed when n is 0 or 1.)

The algorithm does not validate the value of n. For instance, n should not be negative since factorial is not defined for negative numbers. As a matter of interest, what would the algorithm print if n is negative? (Hint: the for loop is not executed.) To keep matters simple, our Program P7.6 does not validate n.

Program P7.6

```
#include <stdio.h>
int main() {
    int nfac = 1, n;
    printf("Enter a positive whole number: ");
    scanf("%d", &n);
    for (int h = 2; h <= n; h++)
        nfac = nfac * h;
    printf("%d! = %d\n", n, nfac);
}
```

A sample run of this program is shown here:

```
Enter a positive whole number: 4
4! = 24
```

We now consider the problem of writing a function (which we will call factorial) that, given an integer n, calculates and returns the value of n!. Since n! is an integer, the "return type" of the function is int.

We first write the function header. It is

```
int factorial(int n)
```

It is interesting to note that the function header is all the information we need in order to use the function correctly. Ignoring for the moment what the rest of factorial might look like, we can use it like this:

```
printf("5! = %d\n", factorial(5));
```

or like this:

```
scanf("%d", &num);
printf("%d! = %d\n", num,factorial(num));
```

In the latter case, if num is 4, printf prints:

```
4! = 24
```

The call factorial(num) returns the value 24 directly to the printf statement.

Following the logic of Program P7.6, we write the function factorial as follows:

```
int factorial(int n) {
    int nfac = 1;
    for (int h = 2; h <= n; h++)
        nfac = nfac * h;
    return nfac;
} //end factorial
```

It is worthwhile comparing Program P7.6 and the function:

- The program prompts for and reads a value for n; the function gets a value for n when the function is called, as in factorial(4). It is wrong to attempt to read a value for n in this function.

- In addition to n, both the program and the function need the variables nfac and h to express their logic.

179

- The *logic* for calculating the factorial is the same for both program and function.

- The program prints the answer (in nfac); the function returns the answer (in nfac) to the calling function. The answer is returned to the point at which factorial was called.

Other comments on factorial

- Variables declared within a function are said to be *local to the function*. Thus, nfac is a local variable, used to hold the factorial. As a matter of interest, h is local to the for statement. When factorial is called, storage is allocated to nfac and h. These variables are used to work out the factorial. Just before the function returns, nfac and h are discarded.

- You should verify that the function works properly if n is 0 or 1 (that is, it returns 1).

We now take a detailed look at what happens when factorial is called (from main, say). Consider the statements (m and fac are int):

```
m = 3;
fac = factorial(m);
```

The second statement is executed as follows:

- The *value* of the argument m is determined; it is 3.

- This value is *copied* to a temporary memory location and *this* location is passed to the function. The function labels it with the name of the parameter, n. The net effect is as if execution of the function began with the statement

```
n = 3;
```

- In programming terminology, we say that the argument m is passed "by value." The *value* of the argument is copied to a temporary location, and it is this temporary location that is passed to the function. The function has *no access* whatsoever to the *original* argument. In this example, factorial has no access to m and, hence, cannot affect it in any way.

- After n is assigned the value 3, execution of factorial proceeds as described above. Just before the function returns, the storage location occupied by n is discarded. In effect, the parameter n is treated like a local variable except that it is initialized to the value of the argument supplied.

- The value returned by the function is the last value stored in nfac. In this example, the last value assigned to nfac is 6. Therefore, the value 6 is returned to the place from which the call factorial(3) was made.

- The value 6 returned by factorial is assigned to fac.

- Execution continues with the next statement, if any.

7.7.1 Using Factorial

We illustrate how factorial can be used by writing a complete program P7.7, which prints n! for n = 0, 1, 2, 3, 4, 5, 6 and 7.

Program P7.7

```
#include <stdio.h>
int main() {
    int factorial(int);
    printf(" n    n!\n\n");

    for (int n = 0; n <= 7; n++)
        printf("%2d %5d\n", n, factorial(n));
} //end main

int factorial(int n) {
    int nfac = 1;
    for (int h = 2; h <= n; h++)
        nfac = nfac * h;
    return nfac;
} //end factorial
```

When run, this program prints the following:

```
n    n!

0    1
1    1
2    2
3    6
4    24
5    120
6    720
7    5040
```

As you can see, the value of factorial increases very quickly. Even 8! = 40320, which is too big to fit in a 16-bit integer (largest value that can be stored is 32767). As an exercise, write the loop from 0 to 8 and see what happens.

Let us take a closer look at main. The first statement is the function prototype for factorial. This is needed since factorial will be called from main.

When main is executed,

- printf prints a heading

- The for loop is executed with n assuming the values 0, 1, 2, 3, 4, 5, 6, 7. For each value of n, factorial is called with n as its argument. The factorial is calculated and returned to the place in printf from where it was called.

We have deliberately used a variable called n in main to illustrate that this n does not (and cannot) conflict with the parameter n of factorial. Suppose n in main is stored in memory location 865 and has the value 3. The call factorial(n) stores the value of n, i.e. 3, in a temporary location (472, say) and this temporary location is passed to factorial where it is known as n. This is illustrated as follows:

865 [3   ]   472 [3   ]

     n in main   n in factorial

We now have *two* locations called n. When in factorial, n refers to location 472; when in main, n refers to location 865; factorial has no access whatsoever to location 865.

It does not happen here, but if factorial were to change the value of n, it is the value in location 472 that would be changed; the value in location 865 would not be affected. When factorial finishes, location 472 is discarded – *that* n no longer exists.

From another point of view, factorial is oblivious to the actual argument that was used to call it since it sees only the argument's value, not how it was derived.

We used n in main as a loop variable to illustrate the point above. However, we could have used any variable. In particular, we could have used h and there would be no conflict with the local variable h of the function factorial. When in factorial, h refers to the local variable; when in main, h refers to the h declared in main.

7.7.2 Combinations

Suppose there are 7 people on a committee. How many subcommittees of 3 people can be formed? The answer is denoted by $^7C_3$ and calculated as follows:

$$\frac{7!}{4!\,3!}$$

This gives us a value of 35. We say there are 35 combinations of 7 objects taken 3 at a time.

In general, ^nC_r denotes the number of combinations of *n* objects taken *r* at a time and is calculated by the formula:

$$\frac{n!}{(n-r)!\,r!}$$

Using factorial, we can write a function, combinations, which, given n and r, returns the number of combinations of n objects taken r at a time. Here it is:

```
int combinations(int n, int r) {
    int factorial(int);
    return factorial(n) / (factorial(n-r) * factorial(r));
} //end combinations
```

The body consists of the function prototype for factorial and one return statement with 3 calls to factorial.

We note, in passing, that this is perhaps the easiest, but not the most efficient, way to evaluate ^nC_r. For instance, if we were calculating $^7C_3$ by hand, we would use:

$$\frac{7.6.5}{3.2.1}$$

rather than

$$\frac{7.6.5.4.3.2.1}{4.3.2.1.3.2.1}$$

that the function uses. As an exercise, write an efficient function for evaluating combinations.

To show the functions factorial and combinations in a complete program and to show how they may be used, we write a program to read values for n and r and print the number of combinations we can get from n objects taken r at a time.

Program P7.8 shows how it's done.

Program P7.8

```
#include <stdio.h>
int main() {
    int n, r, nCr, factorial(int), combinations(int, int);
    printf("Enter values for n and r: ");
    scanf("%d %d", &n, &r);
    while (n != 0) {
        nCr = combinations(n, r);
        if (nCr == 1)
            printf("There is 1 combination of %d objects taken "
                "%d at a time\n\n", n, r);
        else
            printf("There are %d combinations of %d objects taken "
                "%d at a time\n\n", nCr, n, r);
        printf("Enter values for n and r: ");
        scanf("%d %d", &n, &r);
    }
} //end main
```

183

```
int factorial(int n) {
    int nfac = 1;
    for (int h = 2; h <= n; h++)
        nfac = nfac * h;
    return nfac;
} //end factorial

int combinations(int n, int r) {
    int factorial(int);
    return factorial(n) / (factorial(n-r) * factorial(r));
} //end combinations
```

The program reads values for n and r and prints the number of combinations. This is done until a value of 0 is entered for n. The following is a sample run:

```
Enter values for n and r: 7 3
There are 35 combinations of 7 objects taken 3 at a time

Enter values for n and r: 5 2
There are 10 combinations of 5 objects taken 2 at a time

Enter values for n and r: 6 6
There is 1 combination of 6 objects taken 6 at a time

Enter values for n and r: 3 5
There are 0 combinations of 3 objects taken 5 at a time

Enter values for n and r: 0 0
```

Observe the use of if...else to get the program to "speak" correct English. In the statement, also note how a long string is broken into two pieces and each piece is put on one line. Recall that, in C, the opening and closing quotes of a string constant must be on the same line. When the program is compiled, the pieces will be joined together and stored in memory as one string.

7.8 Job Charge

In Program 4.6 we read the number of hours worked and the cost of parts and calculated the cost for a job. Let us write a function that, given the hours worked and cost of parts, returns the cost for the job. Here it is:

```
#define ChargePerHour 100
#define MinJobCost 150
double calcJobCost(double hours, double parts) {
    double jobCharge;
    jobCharge = hours * ChargePerHour + parts;
```

```
    if (jobCharge < MinJobCost) return MinJobCost;
    return jobCharge;
} //end calcJobCost
```

When we say that a function is *given* some data, this immediately implies that such data should be defined as parameters of the function. The *logic* of the function is the same as that of the program. Here, the parameter list indicates what data would be given to the function when it is called. Also, we must specify the return type of the function; it is double since the job cost is a double value.

When the function is called, as in

```
jobCost = calcJobCost(1.5, 87.50);
```

the parameter hours is set to 1.5 and parts is set to 87.50; the body of the function is then executed using these values for hours and parts.

As an exercise, write a complete program to read several values for hours worked and cost of parts and, for each pair, print the cost of the job.

7.9 Calculate Pay

In Program P4.7 we read values for hours and rate and calculated net pay. All the code was written in main. We now write a function that, given values for hours and rate, returns the value of net pay calculated as described in Section 4.3.1. The function is shown below.

```
#define MaxRegularHours 40
#define OvertimeFactor 1.5
double calcNetPay(double hours, double rate) {
    if (hours <= MaxRegularHours) return hours * rate;
    return MaxRegularHours * rate +
        (hours - MaxRegularHours) * rate * OvertimeFactor;
} //end CalcNetPay
```

If hours is less than or equal to MaxRegularHours, the first return is executed; if it is false, the second return is executed. Note that there is no need for else. If the first return is taken, we exit the function and the second return cannot be executed.

If we want to find out the net pay of someone who worked for 50 hours at $12.00 per hour, all we have to do is call calcNetPay(50, 12.00).

As an exercise, write a complete program to read several values for a name, hours worked, and rate of pay; and, for each person, print the net pay received. *Hint*: study Program P5.8.

7.10 Sum of Exact Divisors

Let us write a function to return the sum of the exact divisors of a given integer. We assume the divisors include 1 but not the given number. For example, the exact divisors of 50 are 1, 2, 5, 10 and 25. Their sum is 43. The function is shown below.

```
//returns the sum of the exact divisors of n
int sumDivisors(int n) {
    int sumDiv = 1;
    for (int h = 2; h <= n / 2; h++)
        if (n % h == 0) sumDiv += h;
    return sumDiv;
} //end sumDivisors
```

- sumDiv is used to hold the sum of the exact divisors; it is set to 1 since 1 is always an exact divisor.

- Other possible divisors are 2, 3, 4, and so on up to n/2. The for loop checks each of these in turn.

- If h is an exact divisor of n then the remainder when n is divided by h is 0, that is, n % h is 0. If this is so, h is added to sumDiv.

- The last statement returns the value of sumDiv to the place from which sumDivisors is called.

In the next example, we will see how sumDivisors may be used.

7.10.1 Classify Numbers

Positive integers can be classified based on the sum of their exact divisors. If n is an integer and s is the sum of its exact divisors (including 1 but not including n) then:

- if $s < n$, n is *deficient*; e.g., 15 (divisors 1, 3, 5; sum 9)

- if $s = n$, n is *perfect*; e.g., 28 (divisors 1, 2, 4, 7, 14; sum 28)

- if $s > n$, n is *abundant*; e.g., 12 (divisors 1, 2, 3, 4, 6; sum 16)

Let us write Program P7.9 to read several numbers and, for each, print whether it is deficient, perfect, or abundant.

Program P7.9

```
#include <stdio.h>
int main() {
    int num, sumDivisors(int);
    printf("Enter a number: ");
    scanf("%d", &num);
    while (num != 0) {
        int sum = sumDivisors(num);
        if (sum < num) printf("Deficient\n\n");
        else if (sum == num) printf("Perfect\n\n");
        else printf("Abundant\n\n");
        printf("Enter a number: ");
        scanf("%d", &num);
    }
} //end main

//returns the sum of the exact divisors of n
int sumDivisors(int n) {
    int sumDiv = 1;
    for (int h = 2; h <= n / 2; h++)
        if (n % h == 0) sumDiv += h;
    return sumDiv;
} //end sumDivisors
```

Note that we call sumDivisors once (for each number) and store the result in sum. We use sum when we need the "sum of divisors" rather than recalculating it each time.

The following is a sample run of Program P7.9:

```
Enter a number: 15
Deficient

Enter a number: 12
Abundant

Enter a number: 28
Perfect

Enter a number: 0
```

As an exercise, write a program to find all the perfect numbers less than 10,000.

7.11 Some Character Functions

In this section, we write several functions relating to characters.

Perhaps the simplest is a function that takes a character as argument; it returns 1 if the character is a digit and 0, if it is not. (Recall that, in C, a zero value is interpreted as false and a nonzero value is interpreted as true.) This description suggests that we must write a function that takes a char argument and returns an int value. We will call it isDigit. Here it is:

```
int isDigit(char ch) {
    return ch >= '0' && ch <= '9';
} //end isDigit
```

The Boolean expression (ch >= '0' && ch <= '9') is true if ch lies between '0' and '9', inclusive; that is, if ch contains a digit. Hence, if ch contains a digit, the function returns 1 (for true); if ch does not contain a digit, it returns 0 (for false).

We could have written the body of the function as

```
if (ch >= '0' && ch <= '9') return 1;
return 0;
```

but the single return statement used above is the preferred way.

Similarly, we can write the function isUpperCase, which returns 1 if its argument is an uppercase letter and 0 if it's not, thus:

```
int isUpperCase(char ch) {
    return ch >= 'A' && ch <= 'Z';
} //end isUpperCase
```

Next we have the function isLowerCase, which returns 1 if its argument is a lowercase letter and 0 if it's not.

```
int isLowerCase(char ch) {
    return ch >= 'a' && ch <= 'z';
} //end isLowerCase
```

If we wish to know if the character is a letter (either uppercase or lowercase), we can write isLetter, which uses isUpperCase and isLowerCase.

```
int isLetter(char ch) {
    int isUpperCase(char), isLowerCase(char);
    return isUpperCase(ch) || isLowerCase(ch);
} //end isLetter
```

Note that we need to include the function prototypes for isUpperCase and isLowerCase.

7.11.1 Position of a Letter in the Alphabet

Let us write a function that, given a character, returns 0 if it is not a letter of the English alphabet; otherwise it returns the *position* – an integer value – of the letter in the alphabet. The function should work if the character is either an uppercase or a lowercase letter. For example, given 'T' or 't', the function should return 20.

The function takes a char argument and returns an int value. Using the functions isUpperCase and isLowerCase, we write the function (which we call position) as follows:

```
int position(char ch) {
    int isUpperCase(char), isLowerCase(char);
    if (isUpperCase(ch)) return ch - 'A' + 1;
    if (isLowerCase(ch)) return ch - 'a' + 1;
    return 0;
} //end position
```

We use isUpperCase and isLowerCase to establish what kind of character we have. If it is neither, control goes to the last statement and we return 0.

If we have an uppercase letter, we find the distance between the letter and A by subtracting the code for A from the code for the letter. For example, the distance between A and A is 0 and the distance between A and F is 5. Adding 1 gives the position of the letter in the alphabet. Here, adding 1 gives us 1 for A and 6 for F.

If we have a lowercase letter, we find the distance between the letter and a by subtracting the code for a from the code for the letter. For example, the distance between a and b is 1 and the distance between a and z is 25. Adding 1 gives the position of the letter in the alphabet. Here, adding 1 gives us 2 for b and 26 for z.

To illustrate how the function may be used, we write Program P7.10, which reads a line of input; for each character on the line, it prints 0 if it is not a letter and its position in the alphabet if it is a letter.

Program P7.10

```
#include <stdio.h>
int main() {
    char c;
    int position(char);
    printf("Type some letters and non-letters and press 'Enter'\n");
    while ((c = getchar()) != '\n')
        printf("%c%2d\n", c, position(c));
} //end main

int isUpperCase(char ch) {
    return ch >= 'A' && ch <= 'Z';
} //end isUpperCase
```

```
int isLowerCase(char ch) {
    return ch >= 'a' && ch <= 'z';
} //end isLowerCase

int position(char ch) {
    int isUpperCase(char), isLowerCase(char);
    if (isUpperCase(ch)) return ch - 'A' + 1;
    if (isLowerCase(ch)) return ch - 'a' + 1;
    return 0;
} //end isPosition
```

Here is a sample run of P7.10:

```
Type some letters and non-letters and press "Enter"
FaT($hY&n
F     6
a     1
T     20
(     0
$     0
h     8
Y     25
&     0
n     14
```

We have written the functions isDigit, isUpperCase, isLowerCase, and isLetter to illustrate basic concepts about character functions. However, C provides a number of predefined functions (actually, macros, but the distinction is not important for us) for working with characters. Among these are isdigit (test for a digit), isupper (test for an uppercase letter), islower (test for a lowercase letter), and isalpha (test for a letter). To use these functions, you need to place the directive

```
#include <ctype.h>
```

at the head of your program. As an exercise, rewrite P7.10 using isupper and islower. Without isUpperCase, isLowerCase and their prototypes, your program would be much shorter.

7.12 Fetch the Next Integer

Previously, we wrote Program P6.13 which read the data character by character, constructed and stored the next integer found in a variable, and finally printed the integer.

Let us now write a *function*, getInt, which reads the data character by character and *returns* the next integer found. The function does not take any arguments but the brackets must still be written after the name. The code is essentially the same as in P6.13, except that we use the predefined function isdigit. Here is getInt:

```
int getInt() {
    char ch = getchar();
    // as long as the character is not a digit, keep reading
    while (!isdigit(ch)) ch = getchar() ;
    // at this point, ch contains the first digit of the number
    int num = 0;
    while (isdigit(ch)) { // as long as we get a digit
        num = num * 10 + ch - '0'; // update num
        ch = getchar();
    }
    return num;
} //end getInt
```

Note that

```
while (ch < '0' || ch > '9')
```

of program P6.13 is replaced by

```
while (!isdigit(ch))
```

and

```
while (ch >= '0' && ch <= '9')
```

is replaced by

```
while (isdigit(ch))
```

We believe this makes the program a little more readable.

The function needs the variables ch and num to do its job; ch holds the next character in the data and num holds the number constructed so far. We declare them within the function, making them local variables. This way, they will not conflict with any variables with the same names declared anywhere else in the program. This makes the function *self-contained* – it does not depend on variables declared elsewhere.

The function can be used as in

```
id = getInt();
```

This fetches the next positive integer from the input, regardless of how many and what kind of characters come before it, and stores it in id. Recall that scanf("%d", &id) works only if the next integer is preceded by zero or more *whitespace* characters. Our getInt is more general.

We test it by rewriting Program P4.2, which requests two lengths given in meters and centimeters and finds the sum. We observed then that the data must be entered with digits only. If, for instance, we had typed 3m 75cm we would have gotten an error since 3m is not a valid integer constant. With getInt, we *will* be able to enter the data in the form 3m 75cm. The new program is shown as Program P7.11.

Program P7.11

```c
//find the sum of two lengths given in meters and centimeters
#include <stdio.h>
#include <ctype.h>
int main() {
    int m1, cm1, m2, cm2, mSum, cmSum, getInt();
    printf("Enter first length: ");
    m1 = getInt();
    cm1 = getInt();
    printf("Enter second length: ");
    m2 = getInt();
    cm2 = getInt();

    mSum = m1 + m2; //add the meters
    cmSum = cm1 + cm2; //add the centimeters
    if (cmSum >= 100) {
        cmSum = cmSum - 100;
        mSum = mSum + 1;
    }
    printf("\nSum is %dm %dcm\n", mSum, cmSum);
} //end main

int getInt() {
    char ch = getchar();
    // as long as the character is not a digit, keep reading
    while (!isdigit(ch)) ch = getchar() ;
    // at this point, ch contains the first digit of the number
    int num = 0;
    while (isdigit(ch)) { // as long as we get a digit
        num = num * 10 + ch - '0'; // update num
        ch = getchar();
    }
    return num;
} //end getInt
```

A sample run is as follows:

```
Enter first length: 7m 77cm
Enter second length: 5m 50cm

Sum is 9m 25cm
```

You are encouraged to do the following:

- Modify getInt so that it works for negative integers.

- Write a function getDouble, which returns the next floating-point number in the input. It should work even if the next number does not contain a decimal point.

EXERCISES 7

1. Explain why functions are important in writing a program.

2. Given the function header

   ```
   void test(int n)
   ```

   explain carefully what happens when the call test(5) is made.

3. Given the function header

   ```
   double fun(int n)
   ```

   explain carefully what happens when the following statement is executed:

   ```
   printf("The answer is %f\n", fun(9));
   ```

4. Given the function header

   ```
   void test(int m, int n, double x)
   ```

   say whether each of the following calls is valid or invalid. If invalid, state why.

   ```
   test(1, 2, 3);
   test(-1, 0.0, 3.5);
   test(7, 2);
   test(14, '7', 3.14);
   ```

5. Write a function sqr, which given an integer n, returns n2.

6. Write a function isEven, which given an integer n, returns 1 if n is even and 0 if n is odd.

7. Write a function isOdd, which given an integer n, returns 1 if n is odd and 0 if n is even.

8. Write a function `isPerfectSquare,` which given an integer n, returns 1 if n is a perfect square (e.g., 25, 81) and 0 if it is not. Use only elementary arithmetic operations. *Hint:* Try numbers starting at 1. Compare the number times itself with n.

9. Write a function `isVowel,` which given a character c, returns 1 if c is a vowel and 0 if it is not.

10. Write a function, which given an integer n, returns the sum

    $1 + 2 + \ldots + n$

11. Write a function, which given an integer n, returns the sum

    $1^2 + 2^2 + \ldots + n^2$

12. Write a function, which given three integer values representing the sides of a triangle, returns:

    - 0 if the values cannot be the sides of any triangle. This is so if any value is negative or zero, or if the length of any side is greater than or equal to the sum of the other two.

    - 1 if the triangle is scalene (all sides different).

    - 2 if the triangle is isosceles (two sides equal).

    - 3 if the triangle is equilateral (three sides equal).

13. Write a function, which given three integer values representing the sides of a triangle, returns 1 if the triangle is right angled and 0 if it is not.

14. Write a function `power,` which given a double value x and an integer n, returns x^n.

15. Using the algorithm of problem 10, Exercises 4, write a function, which given a year between 1900 and 2099, returns an integer value indicating the day on which Easter Sunday falls in that year. If d is the day of the month, return d if the month is March and -d if the month is April. For example, if the year is 1999, return -4 since Easter Sunday fell on April 4 in 1999. Assume that the given year is valid.

    Write a program, which reads two years, y1 and y2, and, using the function above, prints the day on which Easter Sunday falls for each year between y1 and y2.

16. Given values for `month` and `year,` write a function to return the number of days in the month.

17. Write a function `numLength,` which given an integer n, returns the number of digits in the integer. For example, given 309, the function returns 3.

18. Write a function `max3,` which given 3 integers, returns the biggest.

19. Write a function `isPrime,` which given an integer n, returns 1 if n is a prime number and 0 if it is not. A prime number is an integer > 1, which is divisible only by 1 and itself.

20. Using isPrime, write a program to prompt for an even number n greater than 4 and print all pairs of prime numbers that add up to n. Print an appropriate message if n is not valid. For example, if n is 22, your program should print

    ```
    3    19
    5    17
    11   11
    ```

21. You are required to generate a sequence of integers from a given positive integer n, as follows. If n is even, divide it by 2. If n is odd, multiply it by 3 and add 1. Repeat this process with the new value of n, stopping when $n = 1$. For example, if n is 13, the following sequence will be generated:

    ```
    13   40   20   10   5   16   8   4   2   1
    ```

    Write a function, which given n, returns the length of the sequence generated, including n and 1. For $n = 13$, your function should return 10.

    Using the function, write a program to read two integers m and n $(m < n)$, and print the maximum sequence length for the numbers between m and n, inclusive. Also print the number that gives the maximum length. For example, if $m = 1$ and $n = 10$, your program should print

    ```
    9 generates the longest sequence of length 20
    ```

22. We can code the 52 playing cards using the numbers 1 to 52. We can assign 1 to the Ace of Spades, 2 to the Two of Spades, and so on, up to 13 to the King of Spades. We can then assign 14 to the Ace of Hearts, 15 to the Two of Hearts, and so on, up to 26 to the King of Hearts. Similarly, we can assign the numbers 27–39 to Diamonds and 40–52 to Clubs.

    Write a function, which given integers rank and suit, returns the code for that card. Assume rank is a number from 1 to 13 with 1 meaning Ace and 13 meaning King; suit is 1, 2, 3, or 4 representing Spades, Hearts, Diamonds, and Clubs, respectively.

CHAPTER 8

▓ ▓ ▓

Arrays

In this chapter, we will explain the following:

- What is an array and how to declare one
- How to store values in an array
- How to read a known number of values into an array using a for loop
- How to process elements of an array using a for loop
- How to read an unknown number of values into an array using a while loop
- How to extract a required element from an array with a subscript
- How to find the sum of numbers stored in an array
- How to find the average of numbers stored in an array
- How to use an array to keep several counts
- How to work with a string as an array of characters
- How to reverse the elements in an array
- How to write a function to tell if a phrase is a palindrome
- How to pass an array as an argument to a function
- How to find the largest and smallest values in an array

8.1 Simple vs Array Variable

The variables we have been using so far (such as ch, n, sum) are normally called *simple* variables. At any given time, a simple variable can be used to store one item of data: for instance, one number or one character. Of course, the value stored in the variable can be changed, if we wish. However, there are many situations in which we wish to store a group of related items and to be able to refer to them by a common name. The *array variable* allows us to do this.

For example, suppose we wish to store a list of 60 scores made by students in a test. We can do this by inventing 60 different int variables and storing one score in one variable. But it would be quite tedious, cumbersome, unwieldy, and timeconsuming to write code to manipulate these 60 variables. (Think of how you would assign values to these 60 variables.) And what if we needed to deal with 200 scores?

A better way is to use an *array* to store the 60 scores. We can think of this array as having 60 'locations'– we use one location to store one *element*, in this case, one score. To refer to a particular score, we use a *subscript*. For example, if score is the name of the array, then score[5] refers to the score in position 5 – here 5 is used as a subscript. It is written inside the square brackets, [and].

In general, an array can be used to store a list of values of the *same type*; for instance, we speak of an array of integers, an array of characters, an array of strings, or an array of floating-point numbers. As you will see, using an array allows us to work with a list in a simple, systematic way, regardless of its size. We can process all or some items using a simple loop. We can also do things like search for an item in the list or sort the list in ascending or descending order.

8.2 Array Declaration

Before an array is used, it must be *declared*. For example, consider the statement:

```
int score[60];
```

This declares that score is an 'integer array' or an 'array of ints' with subscripts ranging from 0 to 59. An array declaration consists of

- The type (int, in this example)

- The name of the array (score, in this example)

- A left square bracket, [

- The size of the array (60, in this example)

- A right square bracket,]

In C, array subscripts start at 0 and go up to n-1, if n is the size of the array.

We can think of the declaration as creating 60 int variables that can be referred to collectively by the *array variable* score. To refer to a specific one of these scores, we use a *subscript* written in square brackets after the array name. In this example,

score[0] refers to the 1st score
score[1] refers to the 2nd score
score[2] refers to the 3rd score

.

.

score[58] refers to the 59th score
score[59] refers to the 60th score

As you can see, array subscripting is a bit awkward in C; it would be much nicer (and logical) if score[i] were to refer to the ith score. We will see how to get around this shortly.

It is an error to try to refer to an element that is outside the range of subscripts allowed. If you do, you will get an "array subscript" error. For example, you cannot refer to score[60], score[-1] and score[99] since they do not exist.

A subscript can be written using a constant (like 25), a variable (like n), or an expression (like i+1). The *value* of the subscript determines which element is being referred to.

In our example, *each element* of the array is an int and can be used in any way that an ordinary int variable can. In particular, a value can be stored in it, its value can be printed, and it ~~can be compared with another int.~~

We could picture score as in Figure 8-1.

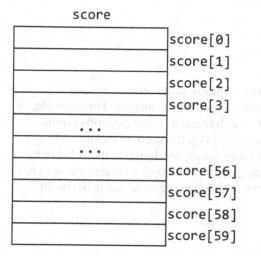

Figure 8-1. *Declaration of int score[60]*

Like a simple variable, when an array is declared, the values of its elements remain *undefined* until we execute statements that store values in them. This is discussed in Section 8.3, next.

To give another example, suppose we need to store the item numbers (integers) and prices (floating-point numbers) of 100 items. We can use one array (item, say) to hold the item numbers and another array (price, say) to hold the prices. These can be declared with this:

```
int item[100];
double price[100];
```

The elements of item range from item[0] to item[99] and the elements of price range from price[0] to price[99]. When we store values in these arrays (see next), we will ensure that

price[0] holds the price of item[0];
price[1] holds the price of item[1];

and, in general,

price[i] holds the price of item[i].

8.3 Store Values in an Array

Consider the array score. If we wish, we could set selected elements to specific values, as follows:

```
score[3] = 56;
score[7] = 81;
```

But what if we wish to set the 60 locations to 60 scores? Would we have to write 60 statements as in the following?

```
score[0] = 45;
score[1] = 63;
score[2] = 39;
.
.
.
score[59] = 78;
```

This is certainly one way of doing the job, but it is very tedious, timeconsuming, and inflexible. A neater way is to let the subscript be a *variable* rather than a *constant*. For example, score[h] can be used to refer to the score in location h; which score is meant depends on the value of h. If the value of h is 47, then score[h] refers to score[47], the score in location 47.

Note that score[h] can be used to refer to another score simply by changing the value of h, but, at any one time, score[h] refers to one specific score, determined by the current value of h.

Suppose the 60 scores are stored in a file scores.txt. The following code will read the 60 scores and store them in the array score:

```
FILE * in = fopen("scores.txt", "r");
for (int h = 0; h < 60; h++)
    fscanf(in, "%d", &score[h]);
```

Suppose the file scores.txt begins with the following data:

```
45 63 39 ...
```

The for loop is executed with the value of h ranging from 0 to 59:

- When h is 0, the first score, 45, is read and stored in score[0];

- When h is 1, the second score, 63, is read and stored in score[1];

- When h is 2, the third score, 39, is read and stored in score[2];

and so on, up to

- When h is 59, the 60th score is read and stored in score[59].

Note that this method is much more concise than writing 60 assignment statements. We are using one statement

```
fscanf(in, "%d", &score[h]);
```

to store the scores in 60 different locations. This is achieved by varying the value of the subscript, h. This method is also more flexible. If we had to deal with 200 scores, say, we only need to change 60 to 200 in the declaration of score and in the for statement (and supply the 200 scores in the data file). The previous method would require us to write 200 assignment statements.

If we wish to print the scores as they are read, we could write the for loop like this:

```
for (int h = 0; h < 60; h++) {
    scanf("%d", &score[h]);
    printf("%d\n", score[h]);
}
```

On the other hand, if we wish to print the scores *after* they are read and stored in the array, we could write *another* for loop:

```
for (h = 0; h < 60; h++)
    printf("%d\n", score[h]);
```

We have used the same loop variable h that was used to read the scores. But it is not required that we do so. Any other loop variable would have the same effect. For instance, we could have written:

```
for (int x = 0; x < 60; x++)
    printf("%d\n", score[x]);
```

What is important is the *value* of the subscript, *not the variable* that is used as the subscript.

We often need to set all elements of a numeric array to 0. This may be necessary, for instance, if we are going to use them to hold totals, or as counters. For example, to set the 60 elements of score to 0, we could write:

```
for (int h = 0; h < 60; h++)
    score[h] = 0;
```

The for loop is executed 60 times, with h taking on the values 0 to 59:

- The first time through the loop, h is 0, so score[0] is set to 0.

- The second time through the loop, h is 1, so score[1] is set to 0.

and so on, until

- The 60th time through the loop, h is 59, so score[59] is set to 0.

If we want to set the elements to a different value (-1, say), we could write:

```
for (int h = 0; h < 60; h++)
    score[h] = -1;
```

It should be noted that even though we have declared score to be of size 60, it is not required that we use all the elements. For example, suppose we want to set just the first 20 elements of score to 0, we could do this with the following:

```
for (int h = 0; h < 20; h++)
    score[h] = 0;
```

This sets elements score[0], score[1], score[2], up to score[19] to 0. Elements score[20] to score[59] remain undefined.

C provides another way of initializing an array – in its declaration. Consider this:

```
int score[5] = {75, 43, 81, 52, 68};
```

This declares score to be an array of size 5 *and* sets score[0] to 75, score[1] to 43, score[2] to 81, score[3] to 52 and score[4] to 68.

The initial values are enclosed in braces and separated by commas. No comma is necessary after the last value, but it is not an error to put one.

If *fewer than* 5 values are supplied, then 0s would be used to fill out the array. For example, the declaration

```
int score[5] = {75, 43};
```

sets score[0] to 75, score[1] to 43, score[2] to 0, score[3] to 0 and score[4] to 0.

If *more than* 5 values are supplied, you would get a warning or an error, depending on your compiler setting. For example, the following will generate a warning or error since there are 8 values:

```
int score[5] = {75, 43, 81, 52, 68, 49, 66, 37};
```

It is possible to omit the size of the array and write, for example, this:

```
int score[] = {75, 43, 81, 52, 68, 49, 66, 37};
```

In this case, the compiler counts the number of values to determine the size of the array. Here, the number of values is 8, so it is the same as if we had written this declaration:

```
int score[8] = {75, 43, 81, 52, 68, 49, 66, 37};
```

As another example, suppose we wanted to store the number of days in a month in a leap year. We could use this:

```
int month[] = {31,29,31,30,31,30,31,31,30,31,30,31};
```

This would set month[0] to 31, month[2] to 29, etc., and we would have to remember that month[0] refers to January, month[1] refers to February, and so on. We can get around this by using the following:

```
int month[] = {0,31,29,31,30,31,30,31,31,30,31,30,31};
```

Now, month[1] is 31and refers to January, month[2] is 29, and refers to February, and so on—this is more natural than the previous declaration. The element month[0] is 0 but we ignore it (see next).

8.3.1 About Not Using Element 0

As we have seen, starting from element 0 can be a bit awkward and unnatural when we have to say things like "the third element is stored in location 2"; the subscript is "out of sync" with the position of the element. It would be much more sensible and logical to say "the first element is stored in location 1" or "the fifth element is stored in location 5."

For situations like these, it is better to ignore element 0 and pretend that the subscripts start from 1. However, you will have to declare the size of your array to be one more than you actually need. For instance, if we want to cater for 60 scores, we will have to declare score as

```
int score[61];
```

This creates elements score[0] to score[60]. We can ignore score[0] and use only score[1] to score[60]. Having to declare an extra element is a small price to pay for being able to work with our problem in a more natural and logical manner.

There are times when it is better to work with an array from position 0. But, for those times when it is not, we will declare our array size to be one more than required and ignore the element in position 0. It is better programming practice to use the language to suit your purpose rather than constrain yourself to the idiosyncrasies of the language.

Suppose we want to cater for 60 scores. A good way to do this is as follows:

```
#define MaxScores 60
...
int score[MaxScores + 1];
```

We can now work with elements score[1] to score[MaxScores].

8.4 Average and Differences from Average

Consider the problem of finding the average of a set of numbers (integers) and the amount by which each number differs from the average. In order to find the average, we need to know all the numbers. In Section 5.3.1, we saw how to find the average by reading and storing one number at a time. Each new number read replaced the previous one. At the end, we could calculate the average but we've lost all the numbers.

Now, if we also want to know how much each number differs from the average, we would need to store the original numbers so that they are available after the average is calculated. We will store them in an array. The program will be based on the following assumptions:

- No more than 100 numbers will be supplied; this information is needed to declare the size of the array;

- The numbers will be terminated by 0; it is assumed that 0 is not one of the numbers.

The following shows how we want the program to work:

```
Enter up to 100 numbers (end with 0)
2 7 5 3 0

Numbers entered: 4
Sum of numbers: 17

The average is 4.25

Numbers and differences from average
   2   -2.25
   7    2.75
   5    0.75
   3   -1.25
```

Program P8.1 shows how to write the program to work like this.

Program P8.1

```c
//find average and difference from average
#include <stdio.h>
#define MaxNum 100
int main() {
    int a, num[MaxNum];
    int n = 0;
    double sum = 0;
    printf("Enter up to %d numbers (end with 0)\n", MaxNum);
    scanf("%d", &a);

    while (a != 0) {
        sum += a;
        num[n++] = a;   //store in location n, then add 1 to n
        scanf("%d", &a);
    }

    if (n == 0) printf("No numbers entered\n");
    else {
        printf("\nNumbers entered: %d\n", n);
        printf("Sum of numbers: %1.0f\n\n", sum);
        double average = sum / n;
        printf("The average is %3.2f\n", average);
        printf("\nNumbers and differences from average\n");
        for (int h = 0; h < n; h++)
            printf("%4d %6.2f\n", num[h], num[h] - average);
    }
}
```

Points to note about Program P8.1:

- Using #define, we set the symbolic constant MaxNum to 100, ... the array and in the prompt for numbers. This makes the program easy to modify if we change our mind and wish to cater for a different amount of numbers.

- We enter the while loop when the number read is not 0. Inside the loop, we add it to the sum, store it in the array, and count it. Each time we reach the end of the loop, the value of n is the amount of numbers stored in the array so far.

- On exit from the while loop, we test n. If it is still 0, then no numbers were supplied and there's nothing else to do. The program does not make the mistake of trying to divide by n if it is 0. If n is positive, we confidently divide the sum by it to find the average.

- The for loop 'steps through' the array, printing the numbers and their differences from the average. Here, n is the number of elements of the array that were actually used, not necessarily the entire array. The elements used are num[0] to num[n-1].

- The program works out the sum of the numbers as they are read. If we need to find the sum of the first n elements *after* they have been stored in the array, we can do this with the following:

```
sum = 0;
for(int h = 0; h < n; h++) sum += num[h];
```

Program P8.1 does the basics. But what if the user entered more than 100 numbers? Recall that, as declared, the elements of num range from num[0] to num[99].

Now suppose that n is 100, meaning that 100 numbers have already been stored in the array. If another one is entered, and it is not 0, the program will enter the while loop and attempt to execute the statement

```
num[n++] = a;
```

Since n is 100, this is now the same as

```
num[100] = a;
```

But there is no element num[100] – you will get an "array subscript" error. When you start working with arrays, you must be very careful that your program logic does not take you outside the range of subscripts. If it does, your program will crash.

To cater for this possibility, we could write the while condition as

```
while (a != 0 && n < MaxNum) { ...
```

If n is equal to MaxNum (100), it means we have already stored 100 values in the array and there is no room for any more. In this case, the loop condition will be false, the loop will not be entered, and the program will not try to store another value in the array.

This is another example of *defensive programming*: of trying to make our programs immune to outside forces. Now, there is no way for a user action to cause our program to crash by exceeding the bounds of the array.

8.5 Letter Frequency Count

Let us write a program that counts the frequency of each letter in the input. The program will treat an uppercase letter and its lowercase equivalent as the same letter; for example, E and e increment the same counter.

In Program P7.10, we wrote a function, `position`, which, given a character, returns 0 if the character is not a letter; if it is a letter, it returns its position in the alphabet. We will use `position` to solve this problem. However, we will rewrite it using the predefined character functions `isupper` and `islower`.

To solve this problem, we need to keep 26 counters, one for each letter of the alphabet. We need a counter for a's and A's, one for b's and B's, one for c's and C's, and so on. We could declare 26 variables called a, b, c, ..., up to z; a holds the count for a's and A's, b holds the count for b's and B's, and so on. And, in our program, we could write statements of the following form (assuming ch contains the next character):

```
if (ch == 'a' || ch == 'A') a++;
else if (ch == 'b' || ch == 'B') b++;
else if (ch == 'c' || ch == 'C') c++;
else if ...
```

This gets tiresome very quickly. And we will have similar problems when we have to print the results. Having to work with 26 variables for such a small problem is neither suitable nor convenient. As we will see, an array lets us solve this problem much more easily.

We will need an `int` array with 26 elements to hold the count for each letter of the alphabet. Since it is more natural to use element 1 (rather than element 0) to hold the count for a's and A's, element 2 (rather than element 1) to hold the count for b's and B's, and so on, we will declare the array `letterCount` as

```
int letterCount[27];
```

We will ignore `letterCount[0]` and use the following:

- `letterCount[1]` to hold the count for a's and A's

- `letterCount[2]` to hold the count for b's and B's

- `letterCount[3]` to hold the count for c's and C's

- etc.

- `letterCount[26]` to hold the count for z's and Z's

The complete program is shown as Program P8.2. It reads data from the file passage.txt and sends output to the file output.txt.

Program P8.2

```c
#include <stdio.h>
#include <ctype.h>
int main() {
    char ch;
    int n, letterCount[27], position(char);
    FILE * in = fopen("passage.txt", "r");
    FILE * out = fopen("output.txt", "w");

    for (n = 1; n <= 26; n++) letterCount[n] = 0;  //set counts to 0

    while ((ch = getc(in)) != EOF) {
        n = position(ch);
        if (n > 0) ++letterCount[n];
    }

    //print the results
    fprintf(out, "Letter  Frequency\n\n");
    for (n = 1; n <= 26; n++)
        fprintf(out, "%4c %8d\n", 'a' + n - 1, letterCount[n]);
    fclose(in);
    fclose(out);
} //end main

int position(char ch) {
    if (isupper(ch)) return ch - 'A' + 1;
    if (islower(ch)) return ch - 'a' + 1;
    return 0;
} //end position
```

Suppose passage.txt contains the following:

The quick brown fox jumps over the lazy dog.
If the quick brown fox jumped over the lazy dog then
Why did the quick brown fox jump over the lazy dog?

Program P8.2 sends the following output to the file output.txt:

Letter	Frequency
a	3
b	3
c	3
d	6
e	11
f	4
g	3
h	8
i	5
j	3
k	3
l	3
m	3
n	4
o	12
p	3
q	3
r	6
s	1
t	7
u	6
v	3
w	4
x	3
y	4
z	3

When a character ch is read, we call the function position, like this:

```
n = position(ch);
```

If n is greater than 0, we know that ch contains a letter and n is the position in the alphabet of that letter. For example, if ch contains Y, then n is 25, since Y is the 25th letter of the alphabet. If we add 1 to letterCount[n], we are adding 1 to the count for the letter that ch contains. Here, if we add 1 to letterCount[25], we are adding 1 to the count for Y. The following statement does the job:

```
if (n > 0) ++letterCount[n];
```

Take a look at the fprintf statement that prints one line of the output:

```
fprintf(out, "%4c %8d\n", 'a' + n - 1, letterCount[n]);
```

This prints a letter (in lowercase) followed by its count. Let us see how. The code for 'a' is 97. When n is 1,

```
'a' + n - 1
```

is evaluated as 97+1-1, which is 97; when 97 is printed with %c, it is interpreted as a character, so the letter a is printed. When n is 2,

```
'a' + n - 1
```

is evaluated as 97+2-1, which is 98; when 98 is printed with %c, it is interpreted as a character, so b is printed. When n is 3,

```
'a' + n - 1
```

is evaluated as 97+3-1, which is 99; when 99 is printed with %c, it is interpreted as a character, so c is printed. And so on. As n takes on the values from 1 to 26,

```
'a' + n - 1
```

will take on the codes for the letters from 'a' to 'z'.

As a matter of interest, we could have used the following special form of the for statement described earlier to achieve the same result. Here it is:

```
for (ch = 'a', n = 1; n <= 26; ch++, n++)
    fprintf(out, "%4c %8d\n", ch, letterCount[n]);
```

The loop is still executed with n going from 1 to 26. But, in sync with n, it is also executed with ch going from 'a' to 'z'. Note the use of ch++ to move on to the next character.

8.6 Making Better Use of fopen

Consider the statement:

```
FILE * in = fopen("passage.txt", "r");
```

This says to "open the file passage.txt for reading." It assumes that the file has been created and the appropriate data stored in it. But what if the user forgot to create the file or has put it in the wrong place (the wrong folder, for instance)? We can use fopen to check for this. If fopen cannot find the file, it returns the predefined value NULL (defined in stdio.h). We can test for this as follows:

```
FILE * in = fopen("passage.txt", "r");
if (in == NULL) {
    printf("File cannot be found\n");
    exit(1);
}
```

If in is NULL, the program prints a message and stops. If in is not NULL, the program proceeds as before.

The predefined function exit is used to terminate execution of a program and return control to the operating system. It is conventional to use exit(0) to indicate normal termination; other arguments are used to indicate some sort of error.

To use exit, we must write the directive

```
#include <stdlib.h>
```

at the head of our program, since exit is defined in the "standard library," stdlib.h. Among other things, this library contains functions for working with random numbers, functions for searching, and functions for sorting.

As usual, we can assign a value to in and test it for NULL, using the following:

```
FILE * in;
if ((in = fopen("passage.txt", "r")) == NULL) {
    printf("File cannot be found\n");
    exit(1);
}
```

Note that we cannot use FILE * in in the if condition, since a declaration is not permitted there.

Similarly, when we write

```
FILE * out = fopen("output.txt", "w");
```

we are assuming that the file output.txt exists or can be created. If it does not exist and cannot be created (the disk may be write protected or full, for instance), fopen will return NULL. We can test for this as follows:

```
FILE * out;
if ((out = fopen("output.txt", "w")) == NULL) {
    printf("File cannot be found or created\n");
    exit(1);
}
```

So far, we have written the name of our file in the fopen statement. To use a different file, we would have to change the name in the statement, and we would have to re-compile the program. Our program would be more flexible if we let the user tell us the name of the file when the program is run.

We can declare dataFile (say) to hold the name of the file with

```
char dataFile[40];
```

You can change 40 to any size you wish. If in has been declared as FILE *, we can prompt the user for the file name and test if everything is okay with this:

```
printf("Enter name of file: ");
scanf("%s", dataFile);
if ((in = fopen(dataFile, "r")) == NULL) {
    printf("File cannot be found\n");
    exit(1);
}
```

Since we are using %s to read the name of the file, the name may not contain a space. If your file name may contain a space, you can use gets.

8.7 Array as Argument to a Function

In Chapter 7, we saw how arguments are passed to functions. In C, arguments are passed "by value." When an argument is passed "by value," a temporary location is created with the value of the argument, and this temporary location is passed to the function. The function never has access to the original argument.

We also saw that when, for instance, we use gets(item) to read a string into the character array item, the function is able to put the string into the argument item. This implies that the function has access to the actual argument – no copy is involved.

In C, *an array name denotes the address of its first element*. When we use an array name as an argument to a function, the address of the first element is passed to the function that, therefore, has access to the array.

We now take a closer look at some issues involved in writing functions with array arguments.

We will write a function, sumList, which returns the sum of the integers in an array passed to the function. For example, if the array contains the following:

3	8	1	5	7
0	1	2	3	4

the function should return 24.

We *could* write the function header like this:

```
int sumList(int num[])
```

The array argument is written just like an array declaration but with no size specified. However, the square brackets must be present to distinguish it from a simple argument. For instance, if we had written int num, this would mean that num is an ordinary int variable.

You *can* specify a size, if you wish, using a constant, a symbolic constant, or any integer expression that can be evaluated at the time the program is compiled. (C99 and later versions of C allow *variable-length arrays* in which an array subscript can be specified at runtime. We will see an example in Section 9.4.1.) However, your program will be more flexible if you do not.

Now, suppose score is declared in main as

```
int score[10];
```

and we make the call

```
sumList(score);
```

We can simply think that, in the function, score is known by the name num; any reference to num is a reference to the original argument score.

The more precise explanation is this: since the name score denotes the address of score[0], *this* address is passed to the function where it becomes the address of the first element of num, num[0]. In fact, any address can be passed to the function where it will be taken to be the address of num[0].

The function is free to assume any size it wishes for num. Obviously, this could land us in trouble if we attempt to process array elements that do not exist. For this reason, it is good programming practice to 'tell' the function how many elements to process. We do this using another argument, as in:

```
int sumList(int num[], int n)
```

Now the calling function can tell sumList how many elements to process by supplying a value for n. Using the declaration of score, above, the call

```
sumList(score, 10);
```

tells the function to process the first 10 elements of score (the whole array). But, and herein lies the advantage of this approach: we could also make a call such as

```
sumList(score, 5);
```

to get the function to process the first 5 elements of score.

Using *this* function header, we write sumList as follows:

```
int sumList(int num[], int n) {
    int sum = 0;
    for (int h = 0; h < n; h++) sum += num[h];
    return sum;
}
```

The function 'steps through' the array, from num[0] to num[n-1], using a for loop. Each time through the loop, it adds one element to sum. On exit from the loop, the value of sum is returned as the value of the function.

The construct

```
for (h = 0; h < n; h++)
```

is typical for processing the first n elements of an array.

To use the function, consider the following code in `main`:

```
int sumList(int[], int), score[10];
for (int h = 0; h < 5; h++) scanf("%d", &score[h]);
printf("Sum of scores is %d\n", sumList(score, 5));
```

As usual, any function that wants to use `sumList` must declare it using a function prototype. Note the use of `int[]` to indicate that the first argument is an integer array. If we wish, we could use an identifier in declaring the prototype, as in:

```
int sumList(int list[], int);
```

The actual identifier used is not important. We could replace `list` by any valid identifier.

The `for` loop reads 5 values into the array. Note that since an array element is just like an ordinary variable, we must write `&score[h]` in `scanf` to read a value into `score[h]`.

Suppose the values read into `score` are as follows:

3	8	1	5	7
0	1	2	3	4

In `printf`, the call

```
sumList(score, 5)
```

will get the function to return the sum of the first 5 elements of `score`: that is, 24. You should gather by now that, to find the sum of the first 3 elements, say, we can write

```
sumList(score, 3)
```

8.8 String – Array of Characters

In Section 2.7 we showed you how to store a string in a "character array." Now that we know a bit about arrays, we can explain how strings are actually stored.

In C, a string is stored in an array of characters. Each character in the string is stored in one position in the array, starting at position 0. The null character, \ 0, is put after the last character. This is done so that programs can tell when the end of a string has been reached. For example, the string

```
"Enter rate:"
```

is stored as follows (◊ denotes a space):

E	n	t	e	r	◊	R	a	t	e	:	\0
0	1	2	3	4	5	6	7	8	9	10	11

(Of course, inside the computer, each character is represented by its numeric code, in binary.)

The *null string*, a string with no characters, is written as "" (two consecutive double quotes) and stored like this:

The *string* constant "a" is stored as follows:

This should not be confused with the *character* constant 'a', which has a numeric value (its integer code value) associated with it and can be used in arithmetic expressions. There is no numeric value associated with the *string* "a."

We can compare two *characters* using the relational operators ==, !=, <, <=, > and >=, but we *cannot* compare two strings, even single-character strings like "a" and "h," this way. To compare two strings, we can use the standard *string* function strcmp.

Suppose we intend to store a name in the variable name declared as

```
char name[25];
```

If we read a string into name using

```
gets(name);
```

or

```
scanf("%s", name);
```

C will put \0 after the last character stored. (This is called *properly terminating* the string with \0.) We must ensure that there is enough room in the array to store \0. So if we declare an array of size 25, we can store a string of at most 24 characters in it since we must reserve one location for \0.

For example, suppose Alice Wonder is typed in response to gets(name). The array name will look like this (only the used positions are shown):

A	l	i	c	e	◊	W	o	n	d	e	r	\0
0	1	2	3	4	5	6	7	8	9	10	11	12

Since name *is* an array, we can work with individual characters, if we so desire. For instance, name[0] refers to the first character, name[1] refers to the second, and so on. In general, we can use name[i] to refer to the character in position i. And, as we have seen, we can use name, by itself, to refer to the string stored in the array.

The *length* of a string is defined as the number of characters in it, not counting \0. The predefined string function strlen takes an array of characters as its argument and returns the length of the string stored in it. In this example, strlen(name) would return 12, the number of characters in "Alice Wonder." As a matter of interest, strlen starts counting characters from the beginning of the array until it finds \0; \0 is not counted.

In fact, all the standard string functions (like strlen, strcpy, strcat, and strcmp) assume that the strings we give them are properly terminated with \0. If they are not, unpredictable results will occur. Imagine what will happen, for instance, if we give strlen an array of characters but there was no \0 to indicate the end of the string. It will go on forever looking for \0.

When we write statements like the following:

```
char name[25] = "Alice Wonder";
```

or

```
strcpy(name, "Alice Wonder");
```

C *will* store \0 after the last character so we do not have to worry about it.

However, if we store characters in an array *ourselves*, we must be careful and add \0 at the end. This is very important if we intend to use any of the standard string functions with the string or if we intend to print it with %s. For example, consider this code:

```
char word[10];
int n = 0;
char ch = getchar();
while (!isalpha(ch)) ch = getchar(); //read and ignore non-letters
while (isalpha(ch)) {
    word[n++] = ch;
    ch = getchar();
}
word[n] = '\0';
```

The code reads characters from the input and stores the first word found in the array word. Here, a word is defined as any consecutive string of alphabetic characters. The first while loop reads over any nonalphabetic characters. It exits when it finds the first alphabetic character. The second while loop is executed as long as the character read *is* alphabetic. It uses n to step through the positions in the array, starting at position 0. On exit from this loop, \0 is stored in position n, since, at this time, n indicates the position *after* which the last letter was stored.

To illustrate, suppose the data was:

```
123$#%&First Caribbean7890
```

The first while loop will read characters until it reaches F, since F is the first alphabetic character in the data. The second loop will store

```
F in word[0]
i in word[1]
r in word[2]
s in word[3]
t in word[4]
```

Since n is incremented after each character is stored, the value of n at this stage is 5. When the space after t is read, the while loop exits and \0 is stored in word[5], properly terminating the string. The array word will look like this:

F	i	r	s	t	\0	
0	1	2	3	4	5	6

We can now use word with any of the standard string functions and can print it using %s, as in:

```
printf("%s", word);
```

%s will stop printing characters when it reaches \0.

The above code is not perfect – we used it mainly for illustrative purposes. Since word is of size 10, we can store a maximum of 9 letters (plus \0) in it. If the next word is longer than 9 letters (for example, serendipity), the code will attempt to access word[10], which does not exist, giving an "array subscript" error.

As an exercise, consider how you would handle words that are longer than what you have catered for. (*Hint*: check that n is valid before storing anything in word[n].)

To illustrate how we can work with individual characters in a string, we write a function, numSpaces, to count and return the number of spaces in a string str:

```
int numSpaces(char str[]) {
    int h = 0, spaces = 0;
    while (str[h] != '\0') {
        if (str[h] == ' ') spaces++;
        h++;
    }
    return spaces;
} //end numSpaces
```

Consider the code:

```
char phrase[] = "How we live and how we die";
printf("Number of spaces is %d\n", numSpaces(phrase));
```

The first statement creates an array of just the right size to hold the characters of the string plus \0. Since the phrase contains 26 characters (letters and spaces), the array phrase will be of size 27, with phrase[0] containing H, phrase[25] containing e and phrase[26] containing \0.

In printf, the call numSpaces(phrase) will transfer control to the function, where phrase will be known as str. In the function, the while loop will step through the array until it reaches \0. For each character, it will check if it is a space. If it is, 1 is added to spaces. On exit from the loop, the value of spaces is returned as the value of the function. For the sample phrase, the value returned will be 6.

As a matter of interest, the body of the while loop could be written as:

```
if (str[h++] == ' ') spaces++;
```

Here, h is incremented *after* we test if str[h] contains a space.

Exercises

1. Write a function to return the number of digits in a string str.

2. Write a function to return how many vowels there are in a string str. *Hint*: it would be useful to write a function isVowel that, given a character ch, returns 1 if ch is a vowel and 0 if it is not.

8.8.1 Reverse the Characters in a String

As another example, we write code to reverse the characters in a string str. For example, if str contains lived, we must change it to devil. To illustrate how the code will work, we picture str as follows:

l	i	v	e	d	\0	
0	1	2	3	4	5	6

We will first exchange str[0], l, and str[4], d, giving this:

d	i	v	e	l	\0	
0	1	2	3	4	5	6

Next, we will exchange str[1], i, and str[3], e, giving this:

d	e	v	i	l	\0	
0	1	2	3	4	5	6

str[2] is already in place (the middle letter does not move), so there is nothing more to do and the method ends with str reversed.

It appears that we will need two variables: one will take on subscript values starting from 0 and increasing, while the other will take on subscript values starting from length(str)-1 and decreasing. We will call them lo and hi. Initially, we will set lo to 0 and hi to length(str)-1.

The basic idea of the algorithm is as follows:

```
1. set lo to 0
2. set hi to length(str)-1
3. exchange the characters in positions lo and hi
4. add 1 to lo
5. subtract 1 from hi
6. repeat from step 3
```

When do we stop? Well, we can stop when there are no more characters to exchange. This will happen when lo becomes greater than or equal to hi. Or, put another way, we must keep exchanging characters as long as lo is less than hi. We can now write the algorithm as follows:

```
set lo to 0
set hi to length(str) - 1
while lo < hi do
    exchange the characters in positions lo and hi
    add 1 to lo
    subtract 1 from hi
endwhile
```

In this form, it is easily converted to C as follows (assume c is char):

```
lo = 0;
hi = strlen(str) - 1;
while (lo < hi) {
    c = str[lo];
    str[lo] = str[hi];
    str[hi] = c;
    lo++; hi--;
}
```

However, we can use the expressive power of the for statement to write this more concisely and, perhaps, more readable, as follows:

```
for (lo = 0, hi = strlen(str) - 1; lo < hi; lo++, hi--) {
    c = str[lo];
    str[lo] = str[hi];
    str[hi] = c;
}
```

Swapping two characters in a string is something we may want to do from time to time. It would be convenient to write a function (swap, say) to do this task. When we call swap, we will give it the string and the subscripts of the characters we want to exchange. For example, if word is a char array, the call

```
swap(word, i, j);
```

will exchange characters word[i] and word[j]. Since word *is* an array, the original array (not a copy) is passed to swap. When the function swaps two characters, it is swapping them in the actual argument, word.

The function can be written as follows:

```
void swap(char str[], int i, int j) {
    char c = str[i];
    str[i] = str[j];
    str[j] = c;
} //end swap
```

In the function, the actual argument (word, say) is known by the name str.

Using swap, we can reverse the characters with another function, reverse, written as follows:

```
void reverse(char str[]) {
    void swap(char [], int, int);
    int lo, hi;
    for (lo = 0, hi = strlen(str) - 1; lo < hi; lo++, hi--)
        swap(str, lo, hi);
} //end reverse
```

Since reverse uses swap, we must declare the prototype for swap in reverse. Note, again, that the prototype is similar to the function header, except that we omit the variable names. However, if you wish, you may include the names – any names will do.

Using these functions, we write Program P8.3, which reads a string, reverses it, and prints it.

Program P8.3

```
#include <stdio.h>
#include <string.h>
int main() {
    char sample[100];
    void reverse(char s[]);
    printf("Type some data and I will reverse it\n");
    gets(sample);
    reverse(sample);
    printf("%s\n", sample);
} //end main
```

```
void reverse(char str[]) {
    void swap(char [], int, int);
    int lo, hi;
    for (lo = 0, hi = strlen(str) - 1; lo < hi; lo++, hi--)
        swap(str, lo, hi);
} //end reverse

void swap(char str[], int i, int j) {
    char c = str[i];
    str[i] = str[j];
    str[j] = c;
} //end swap
```

The following is a sample run of P8.3:

```
Type some data and I will reverse it
Once upon a time
emit a nopu ecnO
```

Reversing a string may not seem too important in its own right, but there are times when we need to reverse the elements of an array. For example, we may have a list of student marks stored in an array and sorted in ascending order, like this:

32	45	59	67	81
0	1	2	3	4

If we want the marks in descending order, all we have to do is reverse the array, like this:

81	67	59	45	32
0	1	2	3	4

8.9 Palindrome

Consider the problem of determining if a given string is a palindrome (the same when spelt forwards or backwards). Examples of palindromes (ignoring case, punctuation and spaces) are:

```
civic
Race car
Madam, I'm Adam.
A man, a plan, a canal, Panama.
```

If all the letters were of the same case (upper or lower) and the string (word, say) contained no spaces or punctuation marks, we could solve the problem as follows:

```
assign word to another string, temp
reverse the letters in temp
if temp = word then word is a palindrome
else word is not a palindrome
```

In other words, if the reverse of a word is the same as the word, it is a palindrome. Sounds logical and correct. However, it is not efficient. Let us see why.

Suppose the word was thermostat. This method would reverse thermostat to get tatsomreht. Comparing the two tells us that thermostat is not a palindrome. But we can get the answer more quickly as follows:

```
compare the first and last letters, t and t
they are the same, so
compare the second and second to last letters, h and a
these are different so the word is not a palindrome
```

We will write a function called palindrome, which, given a string word, returns 1 if word is a palindrome and 0 if it is not. For the moment, we will assume that word is all uppercase or all lowercase and does not contain spaces or punctuation. The function will be based on the following idea:

```
compare the first and last letters
if they are different, the string is not a palindrome
if they are the same, compare the second and second to last letters
if they are different, the string is not a palindrome
if they are the same, compare the third and third to last letters
```

and so on; we continue until we find a non-matching pair (and it's not a palindrome) or there are no more pairs to compare (and it is a palindrome). We can express this logic in pseudocode as follows:

```
set lo to 0
set hi to length(word) - 1
while lo < hi do //while there are more pairs to compare
    if word[lo] != word[hi] then return 0 // not a palindrome
    //the letters match, move on to the next pair
    lo = lo + 1
    hi = hi - 1
endwhile
return 1 // all pairs match, it is a palindrome
```

The while loop compares pairs of letters; if it finds a non-matching pair, it immediately returns 0. If all pairs match, it will exit in the normal way when lo is no longer less than hi. In this case, it returns 1.

The function palindrome is shown in Program P8.4, which tests it by reading several words and printing whether or not each is a palindrome.

Program P8.4

```
#include <stdio.h>
#include <string.h>
int main() {
   char aWord[100];
   int palindrome(char str[]);
   printf("Type a word. (To stop, press 'Enter' only): ");
   gets(aWord);
   while (strcmp(aWord, "") != 0) {
      if (palindrome(aWord)) printf("is a palindrome\n");
      else printf("is not a palindrome\n");
      printf("Type a word. (To stop, press 'Enter' only): ");
      gets(aWord);
   }
} //end main

int palindrome(char word[]) {
   int lo = 0;
   int hi = strlen(word) - 1;
   while (lo < hi)
      if (word[lo++] != word[hi--]) return 0;
   return 1;
} //end palindrome
```

In the function, we use the single statement

```
if (word[lo++] != word[hi--]) return 0;
```

to express all the logic of the body of the while loop in the above algorithm. Since we use ++ and -- as suffixes, lo and hi are changed *after* word[lo] is compared with word[hi].

We could, of course, have expressed it as:

```
if (word[lo] != word[hi]) return 0;
lo++;
hi--;
```

The program prompts the user to type a word and tells her if it is a palindrome. It then prompts for another word. To stop, the user must press the "Enter" or "Return" key only. When she does this, the empty string is stored in aWord. The while condition checks for this by comparing aWord with "" (two consecutive double quotes denote the empty string). The following is a sample run of Program P8.1.

```
Type a word. (To stop, press "Enter" only): racecar
is a palindrome
Type a word. (To stop, press "Enter" only): race car
is not a palindrome
Type a word. (To stop, press "Enter" only): Racecar
is not a palindrome
Type a word. (To stop, press "Enter" only): DEIFIED
is a palindrome
Type a word. (To stop, press "Enter" only):
```

Note that race car is not a palindrome because 'e' is not the same as ' ' and Racecar is not a palindrome because 'R' is not the same as 'r'. We will fix this shortly.

8.9.1 A Better Palindrome Function

The function we wrote works for one-word palindromes with all uppercase or all lowercase letters. We now tackle the more difficult problem of checking words or phrases that may contain uppercase letters, lowercase letters, spaces, and punctuation marks. To illustrate our approach, consider the phrase:

Madam, I'm Adam

We will convert all the letters to one case (lower, say) and remove all spaces and non-letters, giving

madamimadam

We can now use the function we wrote in Program P8.4 to test if *this* is a palindrome.

Let us write a function lettersOnlyLower that, given a string phrase, converts all letters to lowercase and removes all spaces and non-letters. The function stores the converted string in the second argument. Here it is:

```c
void lettersOnlyLower(char phrase[], char word[]) {
   int i = 0, n = 0;
   char c;
   while ((c = phrase[i++]) != '\0')
      if (isalpha(c)) word[n++] = tolower(c);
   word[n] = '\0';
}
```

Comments on the function letters0nlyLower

- i is used to index the given phrase, stored in phrase.

- n is used to index the converted phrase, stored in word.

- The while loop looks at each character of phrase, in turn. If it is a letter, it is converted to lowercase using the predefined function tolower and stored in the next position in word; to use tolower, your program must be preceded by the directive

  #include <ctype.h>

- On exit from the while, word is properly terminated with \0.

Putting everything together, we get Program P8.5, which tests our new function, letterOnlyLower.

Program P8.5

```
#include <stdio.h>
#include <string.h>
#include <ctype.h>
int main() {
    char aPhrase[100], aWord[100];
    void lettersOnlyLower(char p[], char w[]);
    int palindrome(char str[]);
    printf("Type a phrase. (To stop, press 'Enter' only): ");
    gets(aPhrase);

    while (strcmp(aPhrase, "") != 0) {
        lettersOnlyLower(aPhrase, aWord);
        printf("Converted to: %s\n", aWord);
        if (palindrome(aWord)) printf("is a palindrome\n");
        else printf("is not a palindrome\n");
        printf("Type a word. (To stop, press 'Enter' only): ");
        gets(aPhrase);
    } //end while
} //end main

void lettersOnlyLower(char phrase[], char word[]) {
    int j = 0, n = 0;
    char c;
    while ((c = phrase[j++]) != '\0')
        if (isalpha(c))  word[n++] = tolower(c);
    word[n] = '\0';
```

```
} //end lettersOnlyLower

int palindrome(char word[]) {
    int lo = 0;
    int hi = strlen(word) - 1;
    while (lo < hi)
        if (word[lo++] != word[hi--]) return 0;
    return 1;
} //end palindrome
```

The program prompts the user for a phrase and tells her whether or not it is a palindrome. We also print the converted phrase to show you how the function works.

A sample run is shown here:

```
Type a phrase. (To stop, press "Enter" only): Madam I'm Adam
Converted to: madamimadam
is a palindrome
Type a phrase. (To stop, press "Enter" only): Flo, gin is a sin. I golf.
Converted to: floginisasinigolf
is a palindrome
Type a phrase. (To stop, press "Enter" only): Never odd or even.
Converted to: neveroddoreven
is a palindrome
Type a phrase. (To stop, press "Enter" only): Thermostat
Converted to: thermostat
is not a palindrome
Type a phrase. (To stop, press "Enter" only): Pull up if I pull up.
Converted to: pullupifipullup
is a palindrome
Type a phrase. (To stop, press "Enter" only):
```

8.10 Array of Strings – Name of Day Revisited

In Program P7.4, we wrote a function printDay, which printed the name of a day, given the number of the day. We will now write a function nameOfDay that will be given two arguments: the first is the number of a day and the second is a character array. The function will store, in the array, the *name* of the day corresponding to the number of the day. For example, the call

```
nameOfDay(6, dayName);
```

will store Friday in dayName, assuming dayName is a character array.

We show how to write nameOfDay using an array to store the names of the days. Suppose we have an array day as shown in Figure 8-2 (day[0] is not used and is not shown).

day

Sunday	day[1]
Monday	day[2]
Tuesday	day[3]
Wednesday	day[4]
Thursday	day[5]
Friday	day[6]
Saturday	day[7]

Figure 8-2. *The array day*

If d contains a value from 1 to 7, then day[d] contains the name of the day corresponding to d. For instance, if d is 3, day[d] contains Tuesday. But how can we store the names of the days in an array? What kind of array would we need?

We will need an array where each element can hold a string – an array of strings. But a string itself is stored in an array of characters. So we need an array of "array of characters" – we need a *two-dimensional* array. Consider the declaration

```
char day[8][10];
```

We can think of day as having 8 rows and 10 columns. If we store the name of a day in each row, then we can store 8 names. *Each* name is stored in an array of 10 characters. The rows are numbered from 0 to 7 and the columns are numbered from 0 to 9. As hinted in the above diagram, we will not use row 0. We will store the names in rows 1 to 7. If we store the names of the days in this array, it will look like this (we put the null string "" in day[0]):

C lets us to refer to the ith row with day[i]. If we need to, we can use day[i][k] to refer to the character in row i and column k. For example, day[3][2] is e and day[7][4] is r.

We can declare the array day and initialize it with the names of the days using this:

```
char day[8][10] = {"", "Sunday", "Monday", "Tuesday",
   "Wednesday", "Thursday", "Friday", "Saturday"};
```

This declaration will create the array shown in Figure 8-3. The strings to be placed in the array are enclosed by { and } and separated by commas with no comma after the last one. The first string, the null string, is placed in day[0], the second in day[1], the third in day[2], and so on.

	0	1	2	3	4	5	6	7	8	9
0	\0									
1	S	u	n	d	a	y	\0			
2	M	o	n	d	a	y	\0			
3	T	u	e	s	d	a	y	\0		
4	W	e	d	n	e	s	d	a	y	\0
5	T	h	u	r	s	d	a	y	\0	
6	F	r	i	d	a	y	\0			
7	S	a	t	u	r	d	a	y	\0	

Figure 8-3. *The 2-dimensional array day*

The complete function, nameOfDay, is shown in Program P8.6 in which main is used just to test the function.

Program P8.6

```
#include <stdio.h>
#include <string.h>
int main() {
    void nameOfDay(int, char[]);
    int n;
    char dayName[12];
    printf("Enter a day from 1 to 7: ");
    scanf("%d", &n);
    nameOfDay(n, dayName);
    printf("%s\n", dayName);
} //end main

void nameOfDay(int n, char name[]) {
    char day[8][10] = {"", "Sunday", "Monday", "Tuesday", "Wednesday",
            "Thursday", "Friday", "Saturday"};
    if (n < 1 || n > 7) strcpy(name, "Invalid day");
    else strcpy(name, day[n]);
} //end nameOfDay
```

In the function, the following statement checks the value of n.

```
if (n < 1 || n > 7) strcpy(name, "Invalid day");
else strcpy(name, day[n]);
```

227

If n is not a value from 1 to 7, the function stores Invalid day in name. If it *is* a valid day number, it stores the value of day[n] in name. For example, if n is 6, the function stores day[6], that is, Friday, in name.

In main, dayName is declared to be of size 12 since it needs to hold the string "Invalid day" if the day number is invalid.

8.11 A Flexible getString Function

So far, we have used the format specification %s to read a string containing no whitespace characters and the function gets to read a string up to the end-of-line. However, neither of these allows us to read a string delimited by double quotes, for instance. Suppose we had data as in the following format:

```
"Margaret Dwarika" "Clerical Assistant"
```

We would not be able to use %s or gets to read this data easily.

We will write a function, getString, which lets us read a string enclosed within 'delimiter' characters. For example, we could specify a string as $John Smith$ or "John Smith." This is a very flexible way of specifying a string. Each string can be specified with its own delimiters which could be different for the next string. It is particularly useful for specifying strings which may include special characters such as the double quotes without having to use an escape sequence like\".

For instance, in order to specify the following string in C:

```
"Don't move!" he commanded.
```

we must write:

```
"\"Don't move!\" he commanded."
```

With getString, this string could be supplied as

```
$"Don't move!" he commanded.$
```

or

```
%"Don't move!" he commanded.%
```

or using any other character as a delimiter, provided it is not one of the characters in the string. We could even use something like this:

```
7"Don't move!" he commanded."7
```

but would normally use special characters like ", $, % or # as delimiters.

We will write getString with two parameters: a file designated by in and a character array str. The function will read the next string from in and store it in str.

The function assumes that the first non-whitespace character met (delim, say) is the delimiter. Characters are read and stored until delim is met again, indicating the end of the string. The delimiter characters are not stored since they are not part of the string.

Suppose we have the following declarations in main:

```
FILE * input = fopen("quizdata.txt", "r");
char country[50];
```

and the file quizdata.txt contains strings delimited as described above. We would be able to read the next string from the file and store it in country with this:

```
getString(input, country);
```

It is up to us to ensure that country is big enough to hold the next string. If not, the program may crash or nonsense results will occur.

Here is getString:

```
void getString(FILE * in, char str[]) {
//stores, in str, the next string within delimiters
// the first non-whitespace character is the delimiter
// the string is read from the file 'in'

    char ch, delim;
    int n = 0;
    str[0] = '\0';
    // read over white space
    while (isspace(ch = getc(in))) ; //empty while body
    if (ch == EOF) return;

    delim = ch;
    while (((ch = getc(in)) != delim) && (ch != EOF))
        str[n++] = ch;
    str[n] = '\0';
} // end getString
```

Comments on getString

- The predefined function isspace returns 1 (true) if its char argument is a space, tab, or newline character and 0 (false), otherwise.
- If getString encounters end-of-file before finding a non-whitespace character (the delimiter), the empty string is returned in str. Otherwise, it builds the string by reading one character at a time; the string is terminated by the next occurrence of the delimiter, or end-of-file, whichever comes first.
- We can read a string from the standard input (the keyboard) by calling getString with stdin as the first argument.

8.12 A Geography Quiz Program

Let us write a program that quizzes a user on countries and their capitals. The program will illustrate some useful programming concepts such as reading from the keyboard *and* a file and being very flexible in terms of user input. The following is a sample run of the program, indicating how we want the finished program to work. The user is given two tries at a question. If she gets it wrong both times, the program tells her the correct answer.

```
What is the capital of Trinidad? Tobago
Wrong. Try again.
What is the capital of Trinidad? Port of Spain
Correct!
What is the capital of Jamaica? Kingston
Correct!
What is the capital of Grenada? Georgetown
Wrong. Try again.
What is the capital of Grenada? Castries
Wrong. Answer is St. George's
```

We will store the names of the countries and their capitals in a file (quizdata.txt, say). For each country, we will store its name, its capital, and a special string consisting only of the letters in the capital, all converted to uppercase. This last string will be used to enable users to type their answers with a lot of flexibility, and it will enable us to write a more efficient program. It is not absolutely necessary to provide this last string since we can get the program to create it for us (see note after Program P8.7). The string "*" is used to indicate the end of the data. The following shows some sample data:

```
"Trinidad" "Port of Spain" "PORTOFSPAIN"
"Jamaica" "Kingston" "KINGSTON"
"Grenada" "St. George's" "STGEORGES"
"*"
```

We show 3 strings per line but this is not necessary. The only requirement is that they are supplied in the right *order*. If you wish, you can have 1 string per line or 6 strings per line or different numbers of strings per line. Also, you can use any character to delimit a string, provided it is not a character in the string. And you can use different delimiters for different strings. It is perfectly okay to supply the above data as follows:

```
"Trinidad" $Port of Spain$ *PORTOFSPAIN*
%Jamaica% "Kingston" &KINGSTON&
$Grenada$ %St. George's% ^STGEORGES^
#*#
```

We can do this because of the flexibility of getString. We will use getString to read strings from the file and gets to get the user's answers typed at the keyboard.

Suppose a country's data are read into the variables country, capital and CAPITAL, respectively. (Remember that, in C, capital is a different variable from CAPITAL.) When the user types in an answer (answer, say), it must be compared with capital. If we use a straightforward comparison like

```
if (strcmp(answer, capital) == 0) ...
```

to check if answer is the same as capital, then answers such as "Portof Spain,""port of spain,"" Port ofSpain," and "st georges" would all be considered wrong. If we want these answers to be correct (and we probably should) we must convert all user answers to a common format before comparing.

We take the view that as long as all the letters are there, in the correct order, regardless of case, the answer is considered correct. When the user types an answer, we ignore spaces and punctuation and convert *the letters only* to uppercase. This is then compared with CAPITAL. For example, the answers above would be converted to "PORTOFSPAIN" and "STGEORGES" and would elicit a "Correct!" response.

In the palindrome program (P8.5), we wrote a function lettersOnlyLower that kept the letters only from a string and converted them to lowercase. Here, we want the same function but we convert to uppercase instead. We name the function lettersOnlyUpper. The code is identical to lettersOnlyLower except that tolower is replaced by toupper. Our test for correctness now becomes this:

```
lettersOnlyUpper(answer, ANSWER);
if (strcmp(ANSWER, CAPITAL) == 0) printf("Correct!\n");
```

All the details are captured in Program P8.7.

Program P8.7

```c
#include <stdio.h>
#include <string.h>
#include <ctype.h>
#include <stdlib.h>
#define MaxLength 50

int main() {
   void getString(FILE *, char[]);
   void askOneQuestion(char[], char[], char[]);
   char EndOfData[] = "*", country[MaxLength+1] ;
   char capital[MaxLength+1], CAPITAL[MaxLength+1];
   FILE * in = fopen("quizdata.txt", "r");
   if (in == NULL){
      printf("Cannot find file\n");
      exit(1);
   }
```

```
    getString(in, country);
    while (strcmp(country, EndOfData) != 0) {
        getString(in, capital);
        getString(in, CAPITAL);
        askOneQuestion(country, capital, CAPITAL);
        getString(in, country);
    }
} // end main

void askOneQuestion(char country[], char capital[], char CAPITAL[]) {
    void lettersOnlyUpper(char [], char[]);
    char answer[MaxLength+1], ANSWER[MaxLength+1];

    printf("\nWhat is the capital of %s?", country);
    gets(answer);
    lettersOnlyUpper(answer, ANSWER);
    if (strcmp(ANSWER, CAPITAL) == 0) printf("Correct!\n");
    else {
        printf("Wrong. Try again\n");
        printf("\nWhat is the capital of %s?", country);
        gets(answer);
        lettersOnlyUpper(answer, ANSWER);
        if (strcmp(ANSWER, CAPITAL) == 0) printf("Correct!\n");
        else printf("Wrong. Answer is %s\n", capital);
    }
} // end askOneQuestion

void lettersOnlyUpper(char word[], char WORD[]) {
    // stores the letters in word (converted to uppercase) in WORD
    int i = 0, n = 0;
    char c;

    while ((c = word[i++]) != '\0')
        if (isalpha(c)) WORD[n++] = toupper(c);
    WORD[n] = '\0';
} // end lettersOnlyUpper

void getString(FILE * in, char str[]) {
//stores, in str, the next string within delimiters
// the first non-whitespace character is the delimiter
// the string is read from the file 'in'
    char ch, delim;
    int n = 0;
    str[0] = '\0';
    // read over white space
    while (isspace(ch = getc(in))) ; //empty while body
    if (ch == EOF) return;
```

```
    delim = ch;
    while (((ch = getc(in)) != delim) && (ch != EOF))
        str[n++] = ch;
    str[n] = '\0';
} // end getString
```

As mentioned earlier, it is not absolutely necessary to store CAPITAL in the file. We can store country and capital only, and when these are read, convert capital with

```
lettersOnlyUpper(capital, CAPITAL);
```

You can use the idea of this program to write many similar ones. On the Geography theme, you can ask about mountains and heights, rivers and lengths, countries and population, countries and prime ministers, and so on. For a different application, you can use it to drill a user in English-Spanish (or any other combination of languages) vocabulary. Your questions could take the form:

```
What is the Spanish word for water?
```

or, if you prefer,

```
What is the English word for agua?
```

Better yet, let the user choose whether she is given English or Spanish words.

You can ask about books and authors, songs and singers, movies and stars. As an exercise, think of five other areas in which the idea of this program can be used to quiz a user.

8.13 Find the Largest Number

Let us consider the problem of finding the largest of a set of values stored in an array. The *principle* of finding the largest is the same as we discussed in Section 5.6. Suppose the integer array num contains the following values:

num

25	72	17	43	84	14	61
0	1	2	3	4	5	6

We can easily see that the largest number is 84 and that it is in location 4. But how does a program determine this? One approach is as follows:

- Assume that the first element (the one in position 0) is the largest; we do this by setting big to 0. As we step through the array, we will use big to hold the *position* of the largest number encountered so far; num[big] will refer to the actual number.

- Next, starting at position 1, we look at the number in each successive position, up to 6, and compare the number with the one in position big.

- The first time, we compare num[1] with num[0]; since num[1], 72, is larger than num[0], 25, we update big to 1. This means that the largest number so far is in position 1.

- Next, we compare num[2], 17, with num[big] (that is, num[1]), 72; since num[2] is smaller than num[1], we go on to the next number, leaving big at 1.

- Next, we compare num[3], 43, with num[big] (that is, num[1]), 72; since num[3] is smaller than num[1], we go on to the next number, leaving big at 1.

- Next, we compare num[4], 84, with num[big] (that is, num[1]), 72; since num[4] is larger than num[1], we update big to 4. This means that the largest number so far is in position 4.

- Next, we compare num[5], 14, with num[big] (that is, num[4]), 84; since num[5] is smaller than num[4], we go on to the next number, leaving big at 4.

- Next, we compare num[6], 61, with num[big] (that is, num[4]), 84; since num[6] is smaller than num[4], we go on to the next number, leaving big at 4.

- Since there is no next number, the process ends with the value of big being 4, the position of the largest number. The actual number is denoted by num[big]; since big is 4, this is num[4], which is 84.

We can express the process just described by the following pseudocode:

```
big = 0
for h = 1 to 6
   if num[h] > num[big] then big = h
endfor
print "Largest is ", num[big], " in position ", big
```

We will now write a function, getLargest, to find the largest value in an array. To be general, we will specify which portion of the array to search for the value. This is important since, most times, we declare an array to be of some maximum size (100, say) but do not always put 100 values in the array.

When we *declare* the array to be of size 100, we are *catering* for 100 values. But, at any time, the array may have less than this amount. We use another variable (n, say) to tell us how many values are currently stored in the array. For example, if n is 36, it means that values are stored in elements 0 to 35 of the array.

So when we are finding the largest, we must specify which elements of the array to search. We will write the function such that it takes three arguments – the array num, and two integers lo and hi—and returns the position of the largest number from num[lo] to num[hi], inclusive. It is up to the caller to ensure that lo and hi are within the range of subscripts declared for the array. For instance, the call

- getLargest(score, 0, 6) will return the position of the largest number from score[0] to score[6]; and the call

- getLargest(mark, 10, 20) will return the position of the largest number from mark[10] to mark[20].

Here is the function, getLargest:

```
int getLargest(int num[], int lo, int hi) {
   int big = lo;
   for (int h = lo + 1; h <= hi; h++)
      if (num[h] > num[big]) big = h;
   return big;
} //end getLargest
```

The function assumes the largest number is in position lo, the first one, by setting big to lo. In turn, it compares the numbers in locations lo+1 up to hi with the one in location big. If a bigger one is found, big is updated to the location of the bigger number.

8.14 Find the Smallest Number

The function, getLargest, could be easily modified to find the *smallest* value in an array. Simply change big to small, say, and replace > by <, giving this:

```
int getSmallest(int num[], int lo, int hi) {
   int small = lo;
   for (int h = lo + 1; h <= hi; h++)
      if (num[h] < num[small]) small = h;
   return small;
} //end getSmallest
```

This function returns the location of the smallest element from num[lo] to num[hi], inclusive. Later, we will show you how to use this function to arrange a set of numbers in ascending order.

We have shown how to find the largest and smallest values in an integer array. The procedure is exactly the same for arrays of other types such as double, char, or float. The only change that has to be made is in the declaration of the arrays. Keep in mind that when we compare two characters, the 'larger' one is the one with the higher numeric code.

8.15 A Voting Problem

We now illustrate how to use some of the ideas just discussed to solve the following problem.

In an election, there are seven candidates. Each voter is allowed one vote for the candidate of his/her choice. The vote is recorded as a number from 1 to 7. The number of voters is unknown beforehand but the votes are terminated by a vote of 0. Any vote that is not a number from 1 to 7 is an invalid (spoilt) vote.

A file, votes.txt, contains the names of the candidates. The first name is considered as candidate 1, the second as candidate 2, and so on. The names are followed by the votes. Write a program to read the data and evaluate the results of the election. Print all output to the file, results.txt.

Your output should specify the total number of votes, the number of valid votes, and the number of spoilt votes. This is followed by the votes obtained by each candidate and the winner(s) of the election.

Suppose you are given the following data in the file, votes.txt:

```
Victor Taylor
Denise Duncan
Kamal Ramdhan
Michael Ali
Anisa Sawh
Carol Khan
Gary Olliverie
3 1 2 5 4 3 5 3 5 3 2 8 1 6 7 7 3 5
6 9 3 4 7 1 2 4 5 5 1 4 0
```

Your program should send the following output to the file, results.txt:

```
Invalid vote: 8
Invalid vote: 9

Number of voters: 30
Number of valid votes: 28
Number of spoilt votes: 2

Candidate        Score

Victor Taylor      4
Denise Duncan      3
Kamal Ramdhan      6
Michael Ali        4
Anisa Sawh         6
Carol Khan         2
Gary Olliverie     3

The winner(s):
Kamal Ramdhan
Anisa Sawh
```

We need to store the names of the 7 candidates and the votes obtained by each. We will use an int array for the votes. In order to work naturally with candidates 1 to 7, we will write the declaration

```
int vote[8];
```

and use vote[1] to vote[7] for counting the votes for the candidates; vote[c] will hold the count for candidate c. We will not use vote[0].

But what kind of array can we use for the names, since a name itself is stored in a char array? We will need an "array of arrays" – a two-dimensional array. Consider the declaration

```
char name[8][15];
```

We can think of name as having 8 rows and 15 columns. If we store one name in each row, then we can store 8 names. *Each* name is stored in an array of 15 characters. The rows are numbered from 0 to 7 and the columns are numbered from 0 to 14. In our program, we will not use row 0. We will store the names in rows 1 to 7. If we store the sample names in this array, it will look like this:

	0	1	2	3	4	5	6	7	8	9	10	11	12	13	14
0	\0														
1	V	i	c	t	o	r		T	a	y	l	o	r	\0	
2	D	e	n	i	s	e		D	u	n	c	a	n	\0	
3	K	a	m	a	l		R	a	m	d	h	a	n	\0	
4	M	i	c	h	a	e	l		A	l	i	\0			
5	A	n	i	s	a		S	a	w	h	\0				
6	C	a	r	o	l		K	h	a	n	\0				
7	G	a	r	y		O	l	l	i	v	e	r	i	e	\0

To cater for longer names, we will use the following declaration to store the names of the candidates:

```
char name[8][31];
```

We will store the name of candidate c in name[c]; name[0] will not be used.

To make the program flexible, we will define the following symbolic constants:

```
#define MaxCandidates 7
#define MaxNameLength 30
```

and, in main, use these declarations:

```
char name[MaxCandidates + 1][MaxNameLength + 1];
int vote[MaxCandidates + 1];
```

The #define directives will be placed at the top of the program, before main. When we do this, the symbolic constants will be available to any function that needs to use them.

In general, variables and identifiers declared *outside* of any function are said to be external and are available to any function that comes after it in the same file. (The rules are a bit more complicated than this, but this will suffice for our purposes.) So if the declarations are placed at the top of the program, the variables and identifiers would be available to all functions in the program, assuming the entire program is stored in one file (as is the case with our programs).

One of the first things the program must do is read the names and set the vote counts to 0. We will write a function `initialize` to do this. This will also let us show you how to pass a 2-dimensional array to a function.

As explained previously, we will read a candidate's name in two parts (first name and last name) and then join them together to create a single name that we will store in `name[c]`. Here is the function:

```
void initialize(char name[][MaxNameLength + 1], int vote[]) {
   char lastName[MaxNameLength];
   for (int c = 1; c <= MaxCandidates; c++) {
      fscanf(in, "%s %s", name[c], lastName);
      strcat(name[c], " ");
      strcat(name[c], lastName);
      vote[c] = 0;
   }
} //end initialize
```

As we see in the case of the parameter vote, we just need the square brackets to signify that vote is a one-dimensional array. However, in the case of the two-dimensional array name, we *must* specify the size of the *second* dimension and we *must* use a constant or an expression whose value can be determined when the program is compiled. (C99 and later versions of C allow variable-length arrays in which an array subscript can be specified at runtime. We will see an example in Section 9.4.1.) The size of the *first* dimension may remain unspecified as indicated by empty square brackets. This holds for any two-dimensional array used as a parameter.

Next, we must read and process the votes. Processing vote v involves checking that it is valid. If it is, we want to add 1 to the score for candidate v. We will read and process the votes with the following:

```
fscanf(in, "%d", &v);
while (v != 0) {
   if (v < 1 || v > MaxCandidates) {
      fprintf(out, "Invalid vote: %d\n", v);
      ++spoiltVotes;
   }
   else {
      ++vote[v];
      ++validVotes;
   }
   fscanf(in, "%d", &v);
}
```

The key statement here is

```
++vote[v];
```

This is a clever way of using the vote v as a subscript to add 1 for the right candidate. For example, if v is 3, we have a vote for candidate 3, Kamal Ramdhan. We wish to add 1 to the vote count for candidate 3. This count is stored in vote[3]. When v is 3, the statement becomes

```
++vote[3];
```

This adds 1 to vote[3]. The beauty is that the same statement will add 1 for any of the candidates, depending on the value of v. This illustrates some of the power of using arrays. It does not matter whether there are 7 candidates or 700; the one statement will work for all.

Now that we know how to read and process the votes, it remains only to determine the winner(s) and print the results. We will delegate this task to the function printResults.

Using the sample data, the array vote will contain the following values after all the votes have been tallied (remember we are not using vote[0]).

vote

4	3	6	4	6	2	3
1	2	3	4	5	6	7

To find the winner, we must first find the largest value in the array. To do this, we will call getLargest (Section 8.13) with

```
int win = getLargest(vote, 1, MaxCandidates);
```

This will set win to the *subscript* of the largest value from vote[1] to vote[7] (since MaxCandidates is 7). In our example, win will be set to 3 since the largest value, 6, is in position 3. (6 is also in position 5 but the way the code is written, it will return the *first* position that contains the largest, if there is more than one.)

Now that we know the largest value is in vote[win], we can 'step through' the array, looking for those candidates with that value. This way, we will find *all* the candidates (one or more) with the highest vote and declare them as winners.

The details are given in the function printResults shown as part of Program P8.8, our solution to the voting problem posed at the beginning of this section.

Program P8.8

```
#include <stdio.h>
#include <string.h>
#define MaxCandidates 7
#define MaxNameLength 30
FILE *in, *out;

int main() {
   char name[MaxCandidates + 1][MaxNameLength + 1];
   int vote[MaxCandidates + 1];
   int v, validVotes = 0, spoiltVotes = 0;
   void initialize(char [][MaxNameLength + 1], int []);
   void printResults(char [][MaxNameLength + 1], int [], int, int);
```

239

```
    in = fopen("votes.txt", "r");
    out = fopen("results.txt", "w");
    initialize(name, vote);

    fscanf(in, "%d", &v);
    while (v != 0) {
        if (v < 1 || v > MaxCandidates) {
            fprintf(out, "Invalid vote: %d\n", v);
            ++spoiltVotes;
        }
        else {
            ++vote[v];
            ++validVotes;
        }
        fscanf(in, "%d", &v);
    }
    printResults(name, vote, validVotes, spoiltVotes);
    fclose(in);
    fclose(out);
} // end main

void initialize(char name[][MaxNameLength + 1], int vote[]) {
    char lastName[MaxNameLength];
    for (int c = 1; c <= MaxCandidates; c++) {
        fscanf(in, "%s %s", name[c], lastName);
        strcat(name[c], " ");
        strcat(name[c], lastName);
        vote[c] = 0;
    }
} // end initialize

int getLargest(int num[], int lo, int hi) {
    int big = lo;
    for (int h = lo + 1; h <= hi; h++)
        if (num[h] > num[big]) big = h;
    return big;
} //end getLargest

void printResults(char name[][MaxNameLength + 1], int vote[],
            int valid, int spoilt) {
    int getLargest(int v[], int, int);
    fprintf(out, "\nNumber of voters: %d\n", valid + spoilt);
    fprintf(out, "Number of valid votes: %d\n", valid);
    fprintf(out, "Number of spoilt votes: %d\n", spoilt);
    fprintf(out, "\nCandidate       Score\n\n");

    for (int c = 1; c <= MaxCandidates; c++)
        fprintf(out, "%-15s %3d\n", name[c], vote[c]);
```

```
    fprintf(out, "\nThe winner(s)\n");
    int win = getLargest(vote, 1, MaxCandidates);
    int winningVote = vote[win];
    for (int c = 1; c <= MaxCandidates; c++)
        if (vote[c] == winningVote) fprintf(out, "%s\n", name[c]);
} //end printResults
```

EXERCISES 8

1. Explain the difference between a simple variable and an array variable.

2. Write array declarations for each of the following: (a) a floating-point array of size 25 (b) an integer array of size 50 (c) a character array of size 32.

3. What is a subscript? Name three ways in which we can write a subscript.

4. What values are stored in an array when it is first declared?

5. Name two ways in which we can store a value in an array element.

6. Write a function which, given a number from 1 to 12 and a character array, stores the name of the month in the array. For example, given 8, it stores August in the array. Store the empty string if the number given is not valid.

7. You declare an array of size 500. Must you store values in all elements of the array?

8. Write code to read 200 names from a file and store them in an array.

9. An array num is of size 100. You are given two values i and k, with $0 \le i < k \le 99$. Write code to find the average of the numbers from num[i] to num[k], inclusive.

10. Write a function, which, given a string of arbitrary characters, returns the number of consonants in the string.

11. Modify the letter frequency count program (Program P8.2) to count the number of non-letters as well. Make sure you do not count the end-of-line characters.

12. Write a function that, given an array of integers and an integer n, reverses the first n elements of the array.

13. Write a program to read names and phone numbers into two arrays. Request a name and print the person's phone number. Use at least one function.

14. Write a function indexOf that, given a string s and a character c, returns the *position* of the first occurrence of c in s. If c is not in s, return -1. For example, indexOf("brother", 'h') returns 4 but indexOf("brother", 'a') returns -1.

15. Write a function substring that, given two strings s1 and s2, returns the starting position of the first occurrence of s1 in s2. If s1 is not in s2, return -1. For example, substring("mom","thermometer") returns 4 but substring("dad","thermometer") returns -1.

16. Write a function `remove` that, given a string `str` and a character `c`, removes all occurrences of `c` from `str`. For example, if `str` contains "brother," `remove(str,'r')` should change `str` to "bothe."

17. Write a program to read English words and their equivalent Spanish words into two arrays. Request the user to type several English words. For each, print the equivalent Spanish word. Choose a suitable end-of-data marker. Modify the program so that the user types Spanish words instead.

18. The number `27472` is said to be *palindromic* since it reads the same forwards or backwards. Write a function that, given an integer n, returns 1 if n is palindromic and 0 if it is not.

19. Write a program to find out, for a class of students, the number of families with 1, 2, 3, ... up to 8 or more children. The data consists of the number of children in each pupil's family, terminated by 0. (Why is 0 a good value to use?)

20. A survey of 10 pop artists is made. Each person votes for an artist by specifying the number of the artist (a value from 1 to 10). Write a program to read the names of the artists, followed by the votes, and find out which artist is the most popular. Choose a suitable end-of-data marker.

21. The children's game of 'count-out' is played as follows. *n* children (numbered 1 to *n*) are arranged in a circle. A sentence consisting of *m* words is used to eliminate one child at a time until one child is left. Starting at child 1, the children are counted from 1 to *m* and the *m*th child is eliminated. Starting with the child after the one just eliminated, the children are again counted from 1 to *m* and the *m*th child eliminated. This is repeated until one child is left. Counting is done circularly and eliminated children are not counted. Write a program to read values for *n* (assumed <= 100) and *m* (> 0) and print the number of the last remaining child.

22. The prime numbers from 1 to 2500 can be obtained as follows. From a list of the numbers 1 to 2500, cross out all multiples of 2 (but not 2 itself). Then, find the next number (n, say) that is not crossed out and cross out all multiples of n (but not n). Repeat this last step provided that n has not exceeded 50 (the square root of 2500). The numbers remaining in the list (except 1) are prime. Write a program that uses this method to print all primes from 1 to 2500. Store your output in a file called `primes.out`. This method is called the Sieve of Eratosthenes, named after the Greek mathematician, geographer, and philosopher.

23. There are 500 light bulbs (numbered 1 to 500) arranged in a row. Initially, they are all OFF. Starting with bulb 2, all even numbered bulbs are turned ON. Next, starting with bulb 3, and visiting every third bulb, it is turned ON if it is OFF, and it is turned OFF if it is ON. This procedure is repeated for every 4th bulb, then every 5h bulb, and so on up to the 500th bulb. Write a program to determine which bulbs are OFF at the end of the above exercise.

    There is something special about the bulbs that are OFF. What is it? Can you explain why it is so?

CHAPTER 9

▓ ▓ ▓

Searching, Sorting, and Merging

In this chapter, we will explain the following:

- How to search a list using sequential search
- How to sort a list using selection sort
- How to sort a list using insertion sort
- How to sort a list of strings
- How to sort parallel arrays
- How to search a sorted list using binary search
- How to merge two sorted lists

9.1 Sequential Search

In many cases, an array is used for storing a list of information. Having stored the information, it may be required to find a given item in the list. For example, an array may be used to store a list of the names of 50 people. It may then be required to find the position in the list at which a given name (Indira, say) is stored.

We need to develop a technique for searching the elements of an array for a given specific one. Since it is possible that the given item is not in the array, our technique must also be able to determine this. The *technique* for searching for an item is the same regardless of the *type* of elements in the array. However, the *implementation* of the technique may be different for different types of elements.

We will use an integer array to illustrate the technique called *sequential search*. Consider the array num of seven integers:

num

35	17	48	25	61	12	42
0	1	2	3	4	5	6

We wish to determine if the number 61 is stored. In search terminology, 61 is called the *search key* or, simply, the *key*. The search proceeds as follows:

- Compare 61 with the 1st number, num[0], which is 35; they do not match so we move on to the next number.

- Compare 61 with the 2nd number, num[1], which is 17; they do not match so we move on to the next number.

- Compare 61 with the 3rd number, num[2], which is 48; they do not match so we move on to the next number.

- Compare 61 with the 4th number, num[3], which is 25; they do not match so we move on to the next number.

- Compare 61 with the 5th number, num[4], which is 61; they match, so the search stops and we conclude that the key is in position 4.

But what if we were looking for 32? In this case, we will compare 32 with all the numbers in the array and none of them will match. We conclude that 32 is not in the array.

Assuming the array contains n numbers, we can express the above logic as follows:

```
for h = 0 to n - 1
    if (key == num[h]) then key found, exit the loop
endfor
if h < n then key found in position h
else key not found
```

This is a situation where we *may* want to exit the loop before we have looked at all elements in the array. On the other hand, we may have to look at all the elements before we can conclude that the key is not there.

If we find the key, we exit the loop and h will be less than n. If we exit the loop because h becomes n, then the key is not in the array.

Let us express this technique in a function search that, given an int array num, an integer key, and two integers lo and hi, searches for key from num[lo] to num[hi]. If found, the function returns the position in the array. If not found, it returns -1. For example, consider the statement:

```
n = search(num, 61, 0, 6);
```

This will search num[0] to num[6] for 61. It will find it in position 4 and return 4, which is then stored in n. The call

```
search(num, 32, 0, 6)
```

will return -1 since 32 is not stored in the array. Here is the function, search:

```
int search(int num[], int key, int lo, int hi) {
//search for key from num[lo] to num[hi]
    for (int h = lo; h <= hi; h++)
        if (key == num[h]) return h;
    return -1;
} //end search
```

We first set h to lo to start the search from that position. The for loop 'steps through' the elements of the array until it finds the key or h passes hi.

To give an example of how a search may be used, consider the voting problem of the last chapter. After the votes have been tallied, our arrays name and vote look like this (remember we did not use name[0] and vote[0]):

1	Victor Taylor	4
2	Denise Duncan	3
3	Kamal Ramdhan	6
4	Michael Ali	4
5	Anisa Sawh	6
6	Carol Khan	2
7	Gary Olliverie	3

Suppose we want to know how many votes Carol Khan received. We would have to search for her name in the name array. When we find it (in position 6), we can retrieve her votes from vote[6]. In general, if a name is in position n, the number of votes received will be vote[n].

We modify our search function to look for a name in the name array:

```
//search for key from name[lo] to name[hi]
int search(char name[][MaxNameLength+1], char key[], int lo, int hi) {
    for (int h = lo; h <= hi; h++)
        if (strcmp(key, name[h]) == 0) return h;
    return -1;
}
```

Recall that we compare two strings using strcmp. And in order to use any predefined string function, we must use the directive

#include <string.h>

at the head of our program.

We can use this function as follows:

```
n = search(name, "Carol Khan", 1, 7);
if (n > 0) printf("%s received %d vote(s)\n", name[n], vote[n]);
else printf("Name not found\n");
```

Using our sample data, search will return 6, which will be stored in n. Since 6 > 0, the code will print

```
Carol Khan received 2 vote(s)
```

9.2 Selection Sort

Consider the voting program of Section 8.15. In Program P8.8, we printed the results in the order in which the names were given. But suppose we want to print the results in alphabetical order by name or in order by votes received, with the winner(s) first. We would have to rearrange the names or the votes in the order we want. We say we would have to *sort* the names in *ascending* order or *sort* the votes in *descending* order.

Sorting is the process by which a set of values are arranged in ascending or descending order. There are many reasons to sort. Sometimes we sort in order to produce more readable output (for example, to produce an alphabetical listing). A teacher may need to sort her students in order by name or by average score. If we have a large set of values and we want to identify duplicates, we can do so by sorting; the repeated values will come together in the sorted list. There are many ways to sort. We will discuss a method known as *selection sort*.

Consider the following array:

num

57	48	79	65	15	33	52
0	1	2	3	4	5	6

Sorting num in ascending order using selection sort proceeds as follows:

1st pass

- Find the smallest number in positions 0 to 6; the smallest is 15, found in position 4.

- Interchange the numbers in positions 0 and 4. We get this:

num

15	48	79	65	57	33	52
0	1	2	3	4	5	6

2nd pass

- Find the smallest number in positions 1 to 6; the smallest is 33, found in position 5.

- Interchange the numbers in positions 1 and 5. We get this:

num

15	33	79	65	57	48	52
0	1	2	3	4	5	6

3rd pass

- Find the smallest number in positions 2 to 6; the smallest is 48, found in position 5.

- Interchange the numbers in positions 2 and 5. We get this:

num

15	33	48	65	57	79	52
0	1	2	3	4	5	6

4th pass

- Find the smallest number in positions 3 to 6; the smallest is 52, found in position 6.

- Interchange the numbers in positions 3 and 6. We get this:

num

15	33	48	52	57	79	65
0	1	2	3	4	5	6

5th pass

- Find the smallest number in positions 4 to 6; the smallest is 57, found in position 4.

- Interchange the numbers in positions 4 and 4. We get this:

num

15	33	48	52	57	79	65
0	1	2	3	4	5	6

6th pass

- Find the smallest number in positions 5 to 6; the smallest is 65, found in position 6.

- Interchange the numbers in positions 5 and 6. We get this:

num

15	33	48	52	57	65	79
0	1	2	3	4	5	6

and the array is now completely sorted.

If we let h go from 0 to 5, on each pass:

- We find the smallest number from positions h to 6.

- If the smallest number is in position s, we interchange the numbers in positions h and s.

- For an array of size n, we make n-1 passes. In our example, we sorted seven numbers in six passes.

The following is an outline of the algorithm:

```
for h = 0 to n - 2
    s = position of smallest number from num[h] to num[n-1]
    swap num[h] and num[s]
endfor
```

In Section 8.14, we wrote a function to return the position of the smallest number in an integer array. Here it is for easy reference:

```
//find position of smallest from num[lo] to num[hi]
int getSmallest(int num[], int lo, int hi) {
    int small = lo;
    for (int h = lo + 1; h <= hi; h++)
        if (num[h] < num[small]) small = h;
    return small;
} //end getSmallest
```

We also wrote a function swap that swapped two elements in a *character* array. We now rewrite swap to swap two elements in an *integer* array:

```
//swap elements num[i] and num[j]
void swap(int num[], int i, int j) {
    int hold = num[i];
    num[i] = num[j];
    num[j] = hold;
} //end swap
```

With getSmallest and swap, we can code the algorithm, above, as a function selectionSort. To emphasize that we can use any names for our parameters, we write the function to sort an integer array called list. To make it general, we also tell the function which portion of the array to sort by specifying subscripts lo and hi. Instead of the loop going from 0 to n-2 as in the algorithm, it now goes from lo to hi-1 – just a minor change for greater flexibility.

```
//sort list[lo] to list[hi] in ascending order
void selectionSort(int list[], int lo, int hi) {
    int getSmallest(int [], int, int);
    void swap(int [], int, int);
    for (int h = lo; h < hi; h++) {
        int s = getSmallest(list, h, hi);
        swap(list, h, s);
    }
} //end selectionSort
```

We now write Program P9.1 to test whether selectionSort works properly. The program requests up to 10 numbers (since the array is declared to be of size 10), stores them in the array num, calls selectionSort, then prints the sorted list.

Program P9.1

```
#include <stdio.h>
int main() {
    void selectionSort(int [], int, int);
    int v, num[10];
    printf("Type up to 10 numbers followed by 0\n");
    int n = 0;
    scanf("%d", &v);
    while (v != 0) {
        num[n++] = v;
        scanf("%d", &v);
    }
    //n numbers are stored from num[0] to num[n-1]
    selectionSort(num, 0, n-1);
    printf("\nThe sorted numbers are\n");
    for (int h = 0; h < n; h++) printf("%d ", num[h]);
    printf("\n");
} //end main

void selectionSort(int list[], int lo, int hi) {
//sort list[lo] to list[hi] in ascending order
    int getSmallest(int [], int, int);
```

```
    void swap(int [], int, int);
    for (int h = lo; h < hi; h++) {
        int s = getSmallest(list, h, hi);
        swap(list, h, s);
    }
} //end selectionSort

int getSmallest(int num[], int lo, int hi) {
//find position of smallest from num[lo] to num[hi]
    int small = lo;
    for (int h = lo + 1; h <= hi; h++)
        if (num[h] < num[small]) small = h;
        return small;
} //end getSmallest

void swap(int num[], int i, int j) {
//swap elements num[i] and num[j]
    int hold = num[i];
    num[i] = num[j];
    num[j] = hold;
} //end swap
```

The following is a sample run of the program:

```
Type up to 10 numbers followed by 0
57 48 79 65 15 33 52 0

The sorted numbers are
15 33 48 52 57 65 79
```

Comments on Program P9.1

The program illustrates how to read and store an unknown amount of values in an array. The program caters for up to 10 numbers but must work if fewer numbers are supplied. We use n to subscript the array and to count the numbers. Initially, n is 0. The following describes what happens with the sample data:

- The 1st number, 57, is read; it is not 0 so we enter the while loop. We store 57 in num[0] then add 1 to n, making it 1; one number has been read and n is 1.

- The 2nd number, 48, is read; it is not 0 so we enter the while loop. We store 48 in num[1] then add 1 to n, making it 2; two numbers have been read and n is 2.

- The 3rd number, 79, is read; it is not 0 so we enter the while loop. We store 79 in num[2] then add 1 to n, making it 3; three numbers have been read and n is 3.

- The 4th number, 65, is read; it is not 0 so we enter the while loop. We store 65 in num[3] then add 1 to n, making it 4; four numbers have been read and n is 4.

- The 5th number, 15, is read; it is not 0 so we enter the while loop. We store 15 in num[4] then add 1 to n, making it 5; five numbers have been read and n is 5.

- The 6th number, 33, is read; it is not 0 so we enter the while loop. We store 33 in num[5] then add 1 to n, making it 6; six numbers have been read and n is 6.

- The 7th number, 52, is read; it is not 0 so we enter the while loop. We store 52 in num[6] then add 1 to n, making it 7; seven numbers have been read and n is 7.

- The 8th number, 0, is read; it *is* 0 so we exit the while loop and the array looks like this:

num

57	48	79	65	15	33	52
0	1	2	3	4	5	6

At any stage, the value of n indicates how many numbers have been stored up to that point. At the end, n is 7 and seven numbers have been stored in the array. The rest of the program can assume that n gives the number of values actually stored in the array; the values are stored from num[0] to num[n-1].

For example, the call

```
selectionSort(num, 0, n-1);
```

is a request to sort num[0] to num[n-1] but, since n is 7, it is a request to sort num[0] to num[6].

As written, the program will crash if the user enters more than 10 numbers before typing 0. When the 11th number is read, an attempt will be made to store it in num[10], which does not exist, giving an "array subscript" error.
We can handle this by changing the while condition to this:

```
while (v != 0 && n < 10)
```

Now, if n reaches 10, the loop is not entered (since 10 is not less than 10) and no attempt will be made to store the 11th number. Indeed, all numbers after the 10th one will be ignored.

As usual, it is best to use a symbolic constant (MaxNum, say) set to 10, and use MaxNum, rather than the constant 10, throughout the program.
We have sorted an array in *ascending* order. We can sort num[0] to num[n-1] in *descending* order with the following algorithm:

```
for h = 0 to n - 2
    b = position of biggest number from num[h] to num[n-1]
    swap num[h] and num[b]
endfor
```

We urge you to try Exercises 1 and 2 to print the results of the voting problem in ascending order by name and descending order by votes received.

9.2.1 Analysis of Selection Sort

To find the smallest of k items, we make k-1 comparisons. On the first pass, we make n-1 comparisons to find the smallest of n items. On the second pass, we make n-2 comparisons to find the smallest of n-1 items. And so on, until the last pass where we make one comparison to find the smaller of two items. In general, on the ith pass, we make n-i comparisons to find the smallest of n-i+1 items. Hence:

Total number of comparisons = $1 + 2 + ... + n{-}1 = \frac{1}{2}\,n(n{-}1) \approx \frac{1}{2}\,n^2$

We say selection sort is of order $O(n^2)$ ("big O n squared"). The constant ½ is not important in "big O" notation since, as n gets very big, the constant becomes insignificant.

On each pass, we swap two items using three assignments. We make n-1 passes so we make $3(n{-}1)$ assignments in all. Using "big O" notation, we say that the number of assignments is $O(n)$. The constants 3 and 1 are not important as n gets large.

Does selection sort perform any better if there is order in the data? No. One way to find out is to give it a sorted list and see what it does. If you work through the algorithm, you will see that the method is oblivious to order in the data. It will make the same number of comparisons every time, regardless of the data.

As an exercise, modify the programming code so that it counts the number of comparisons and assignments made in sorting a list using selection sort.

9.3 Insertion Sort

Consider the same array as before:

num

57	48	79	65	15	33	52
0	1	2	3	4	5	6

Think of the numbers as cards on a table and picked up one at a time in the order in which they appear in the array. Thus, we first pick up 57, then 48, then 79, and so on, until we pick up 52. However, as we pick up each new number, we add it to our hand in such a way that the numbers in our hand are all sorted.

When we pick up 57, we have just one number in our hand. We consider one number to be sorted. When we pick up 48, we add it in front of 57 so our hand contains

48 57

When we pick up 79, we place it after 57 so our hand contains

48 57 79

When we pick up 65, we place it after 57 so our hand contains

48 57 65 70

At this stage, four numbers have been picked up and our hand contains them in sorted order. When we pick up 15, we place it before 48 so our hand contains

15 48 57 65 79

When we pick up 33, we place it after 15 so our hand contains

15 33 48 57 65 79

Finally, when we pick up 52, we place it after 48 so our hand contains

15 33 48 52 57 65 79

The numbers have been sorted in ascending order.

The method described illustrates the idea behind *insertion* sort. The numbers in the array will be processed one at a time, from left to right. This is equivalent to picking up the numbers from the table, one at a time. Since the first number, by itself, is sorted, we will process the numbers in the array starting from the second.

When we come to process num[h], we can assume that num[0] to num[h-1] are sorted. We then attempt to insert num[h] among num[0] to num[h-1] so that num[0] to num[h] are sorted. We will then go on to process num[h+1]. When we do so, our assumption that elements num[0] to num[h] are sorted will be true.

Sorting num in ascending order using insertion sort proceeds as follows:

1st pass

- Process num[1], that is, 48. This involves placing 48 so that the first two numbers are sorted; num[0] and num[1] now contain the following:

num

48	57	79	65	15	33	52
0	1	2	3	4	5	6

The rest of the array remains unchanged.

2nd pass

- Process num[2], that is, 79. This involves placing 79 so that the first three numbers are sorted; num[0] to num[2] now contain the following:

num

48	57	79	65	15	33	52
0	1	2	3	4	5	6

The rest of the array remains unchanged.

3rd pass

- Process num[3], that is, 65. This involves placing 65 so that the first four numbers are sorted; num[0] to num[3] now contain the following:

num

48	57	65	79	15	33	52
0	1	2	3	4	5	6

The rest of the array remains unchanged.

4th pass

- Process num[4], that is, 15. This involves placing 15 so that the first five numbers are sorted. To simplify the explanation, think of 15 as being taken out and stored in a simple variable (key, say) leaving a "hole" in num[4]. We can picture this as follows:

key

15

num

48	57	65	79		33	52
0	1	2	3	4	5	6

The insertion of 15 in its correct position proceeds as follows:

- Compare 15 with 79; it is smaller, so move 79 to location 4, leaving location 3 free. This gives the following:

key

15

num

48	57	65		79	33	52
0	1	2	3	4	5	6

- Compare 15 with 65; it is smaller, so move 65 to location 3, leaving location 2 free. This gives the following:

key

15

num

48	57		65	79	33	52
0	1	2	3	4	5	6

- Compare 15 with 57; it is smaller, so move 57 to location 2, leaving location 1 free. This gives the following:

key

15

num

48		57	65	79	33	52
0	1	2	3	4	5	6

- Compare 15 with 48; it is smaller, so move 48 to location 1, leaving location 0 free. This gives the following:

key

| 15 |

num

	48	57	65	79	33	52
0	1	2	3	4	5	6

- There are no more numbers to compare with 15, so it is inserted in location 0, giving the following:

key

| 15 |

num

15	48	57	65	79	33	52
0	1	2	3	4	5	6

- We can express the logic of placing 15 (key) by comparing it with the numbers to its left, starting with the nearest one. As long as key is less than num[k], for some k, we move num[k] to position num[k+1] and move on to consider num[k-1], providing it exists. It won't exist when k is actually 0. In this case, the process stops, and key is inserted in position 0.

5th pass

- Process num[5], that is, 33. This involves placing 33 so that the first six numbers are sorted. This is done as follows:

  - Store 33 in key, leaving location 5 free.

  - Compare 33 with 79; it is smaller, so move 79 to location 5, leaving location 4 free.

  - Compare 33 with 65; it is smaller, so move 65 to location 4, leaving location 3 free.

  - Compare 33 with 57; it is smaller, so move 57 to location 3, leaving location 2 free.

  - Compare 33 with 48; it is smaller, so move 48 to location 2, leaving location 1 free.

- Compare 33 with 15; it is bigger, so insert 33 in location 1. This gives the following:

key

| 33 |

num

15	33	48	57	65	79	52
0	1	2	3	4	5	6

- We can express the logic of placing 33 by comparing it with the numbers to its left, starting with the nearest one. As long as key is less than num[k], for some k, we move num[k] to position num[k+1] and move on to consider num[k-1], providing it exists. If key is greater than or equal to num[k] for some k, then key is inserted in position k+1. Here, 33 is greater than num[0] and so is inserted into num[1].

6th pass

- Process num[6], that is, 52. This involves placing 52 so that the first seven (all) numbers are sorted. This is done as follows:

  - Store 52 in key, leaving location 6 free.

  - Compare 52 with 79; it is smaller, so move 79 to location 6, leaving location 5 free.

  - Compare 52 with 65; it is smaller, so move 65 to location 5, leaving location 4 free.

  - Compare 52 with 57; it is smaller, so move 57 to location 4, leaving location 3 free.

- Compare 52 with 48; it is bigger, so insert 52 in location 3. This gives the following:

key   num

52		15	33	48	52	57	65	79
		0	1	2	3	4	5	6

The array is now completely sorted.
The following is an outline to sort the first n elements of an array, num, using insertion sort:

```
for h = 1 to n - 1 do
    insert num[h] among num[0] to num[h-1] so that
    num[0] to num[h] are sorted
endfor
```

Using this outline, we write the function insertionSort using the parameter list.

```
void insertionSort(int list[], int n) {
//sort list[0] to list[n-1] in ascending order
    for (int h = 1; h < n; h++) {
        int key = list[h];
        int k = h - 1; //start comparing with previous item
        while (k >= 0 && key < list[k]) {
            list[k + 1] = list[k];
            --k;
        }
```

```
        list[k + 1] = key;
    } //end for
} //end insertionSort
```

The while statement is at the heart of the sort. It states that as long as we are within the array (k >= 0) and the current number (key) is less than the one in the array (key < list[k]), we move list[k] to the right (list[k+1] = list[k]) and move on to the next number on the left (--k).

We exit the while loop if k is equal to -1 or if key is greater than or equal to list[k], for some k. In either case, key is inserted into list[k+1]. If k is -1, it means that the current number is smaller than all the previous numbers in the list and must be inserted in list[0]. But list[k+1] *is* list[0] when k is -1, so key is inserted correctly in this case.

The function sorts in ascending order. To sort in descending order, all we have to do is change < to > in the while condition, thus:

```
while (k >= 0 && key > list[k])
```

Now, a key moves to the left if it is *bigger*.

We write Program P9.2 to test whether insertionSort works correctly.

Program P9.2

```
#include <stdio.h>
int main() {
    void insertionSort(int [], int);
    int v, num[10];
    printf("Type up to 10 numbers followed by 0\n");
    int n = 0;
    scanf("%d", &v);
    while (v != 0) {
        num[n++] = v;
        scanf("%d", &v);
    }
    //n numbers are stored from num[0] to num[n-1]
    insertionSort(num, n);
    printf("\nThe sorted numbers are\n");
    for (int h = 0; h < n; h++) printf("%d ", num[h]);
    printf("\n");
} //end main

void insertionSort(int list[], int n) {
//sort list[0] to list[n-1] in ascending order
    for (int h = 1; h < n; h++) {
        int key = list[h];
        int k = h - 1; //start comparing with previous item
```

257

```
        while (k >= 0 && key < list[k]) {
            list[k + 1] = list[k];
            --k;
        }
        list[k + 1] = key;
    } //end for
} //end insertionSort
```

The program requests up to 10 numbers (since the array is declared to be of size 10), stores them in the array num, calls insertionSort, then prints the sorted list. The following is a sample run of P9.2:

```
Type up to 10 numbers followed by 0
57 48 79 65 15 33 52 0

The sorted numbers are
15 33 48 52 57 65 79
```

9.3.1 Analysis of Insertion Sort

In processing item *j*, we can make as few as one comparison (if num[j] is bigger than num[j-1]) or as many as *j-1* comparisons (if num[j] is smaller than all the previous items). For random data, it is expected that we would make ½(j-1) comparisons, on average. Hence, the average total number of comparisons to sort *n* items is as follows:

$$\sum_{j=2}^{n} \frac{1}{2}(j-1) = \frac{1}{2}\{1+2+\cdots+n-1\} = \frac{1}{4}n(n-1) \approx \frac{1}{4}n^2$$

We say insertion sort is of order $O(n^2)$ ("big O *n* squared"). The constant ¼ is not important as n gets large.

Each time we make a comparison, we also make an assignment. Hence, the total number of assignments is also ¼ $n(n-1) \approx$ ¼ n^2.

We emphasize that this is an average for random data. Unlike selection sort, the actual performance of insertion sort depends on the data supplied. If the given array is already sorted, insertion sort will quickly determine this by making *n-1* comparisons. In this case, it runs in $O(n)$ time. One would expect that insertion sort will perform better the more order there is in the data.

If the given data is in descending order, insertion sort performs at its worst since each new number has to travel all the way to the beginning of the list. In this case, the number of comparisons is ½ $n(n-1) \approx$ ½ n^2. The number of assignments is also ½ $n(n-1) \approx$ ½ n^2.

Thus, the number of comparisons made by insertion sort ranges from *n-1* (best) to ¼ n^2 (average) to ½ n^2 (worst). The number of assignments is always the same as the number of comparisons.

As an exercise, modify the programming code so that it counts the number of comparisons and assignments made in sorting a list using insertion sort.

9.3.2 Insert an Element in Place

Insertion sort uses the idea of adding a new element to an already sorted list so that the list remains sorted. We can treat this as a problem in its own right (nothing to do with insertion sort). Specifically, given a sorted list of items from list[m] to list[n], we want to add a new item (newItem, say) to the list so that list[m] to list[n+1] are sorted.

Adding a new item increases the size of the list by 1. We assume that the array has room to hold the new item. We write the function insertInPlace to solve this problem.

```
void insertInPlace(int newItem, int list[], int m, int n) {
//list[m] to list[n] are sorted
//insert newItem so that list[m] to list[n+1] are sorted
    int k = n;
    while (k >= m && newItem < list[k]) {
        list[k + 1] = list[k];
        --k;
    }
    list[k + 1] = newItem;
} //end insertInPlace
```

Now that we have insertInPlace, we can rewrite insertionSort (calling it insertionSort2) as follows:

```
void insertionSort2(int list[], int lo, int hi) {
//sort list[lo] to list[hi] in ascending order
    void insertInPlace(int, int [], int, int);
    for (int h = lo + 1; h <= hi; h++)
        insertInPlace(list[h], list, lo, h - 1);
} //end insertionSort2
```

Note that the prototype for insertionSort2 is now this:

```
void insertionSort2(int [], int, int);
```

and to sort an array num of n items, we must call it like this:

```
insertionSort2(num, 0, n-1);
```

9.4 Sort an Array of Strings

Consider the problem of sorting a list of names in alphabetical order. We have seen that, in C, each name is stored in a character array. To store several names, we need a two-dimensional character array. For example, consider the following list of names.

	0	1	2	3	4	5	6	7	8	9	10	11	12	13	14
0	S	a	m	l	a	l	,		R	a	w	l	E	\0	
1	W	i	l	l	i	a	m	s	,		M	a	r	k	\0
2	D	e	l	w	i	n	,		M	a	c	\0			
3	T	a	y	l	o	r	,		V	i	c	t	o	r	\0
4	M	o	h	a	m	e	d	,		A	b	u	\0		
5	S	i	n	g	h	,		K	R	i	s	h	n	a	\0
6	T	a	w	a	r	i	,		T	a	u	\0			
7	A	b	d	o	o	l	,		Z	a	i	d	\0		

To store this list, we will require a declaration such as the following:

```
char list[8][15];
```

To cater for longer names, we can increase 15, and to cater for more names, we can increase 8. The *process* of sorting list is essentially the same as sorting an array of integers. The major difference is that whereas we use < to compare two numbers, we must use strcmp to compare two names. In the function insertionSort shown earlier, the while condition changes from this:

```
while (k >= lo && key < list[k])
```

to the following, where key is now declared as char key[15]:

```
while (k >= lo && strcmp(key, list[k]) < 0)
```

Also, we must now use strcpy (since we can't use = for strings) to assign a name to another location. We will see the complete function in the next section.

9.4.1 Variable-Length Arrays

We will use this example to show how variable-length arrays (VLAs) may be used in C. This feature is available only in C versions from C99 and later. The idea is that the size of an array may be specified at runtime as opposed to compile time.

In the function below, note the declaration of list (char list[][max]) in the parameter list. The size of the first dimension is left unspecified, as for one-dimensional arrays. The size of the second dimension is specified using the parameter max; the value of max will be specified when the function is called. This gives us a bit more flexibility since we can specify the size of the second dimension at runtime.

```
void insertionSort3(int lo, int hi, int max, char list[][max]) {
//Sort the strings in list[lo] to list[hi] in alphabetical order.
//The maximum string size is max - 1 (one char taken up by \0).
    char key[max];
    for (int h = lo + 1; h <= hi; h++) {
        strcpy(key, list[h]);
        int k = h - 1; //start comparing with previous item
        while (k >= lo && strcmp(key, list[k]) < 0) {
            strcpy(list[k + 1], list[k]);
            --k;
        }
        strcpy(list[k + 1], key);
    } //end for
} // end insertionSort3
```

We write a simple main routine to test insertionSort3 as shown in Program P9.3.

Program P9.3

```
#include <stdio.h>
#include <string.h>
#define MaxNameSize 14
#define MaxNameBuffer MaxNameSize+1
#define MaxNames 8

int main() {
    void insertionSort3(int, int, int max, char [][max]);
    char name[MaxNames][MaxNameBuffer] =
            {"Samlal, Rawle", "Williams, Mark","Delwin, Mac",
            "Taylor, Victor", "Mohamed, Abu","Singh, Krishna",
            "Tawari, Tau", "Abdool, Zaid" };

    insertionSort3(0, MaxNames-1, MaxNameBuffer, name);
    printf("\nThe sorted names are\n\n");
    for (int h = 0; h < MaxNames; h++) printf("%s\n", name[h]);
} //end main

void insertionSort3(int lo, int hi, int max, char list[][max]) {
//Sort the strings in list[lo] to list[hi] in alphabetical order.
//The maximum string size is max - 1 (one char taken up by \0).
    char key[max];
    for (int h = lo + 1; h <= hi; h++) {
        strcpy(key, list[h]);
```

```
    int k = h - 1; //start comparing with previous item
    while (k >= lo && strcmp(key, list[k]) < 0) {
        strcpy(list[k + 1], list[k]);
        --k;
    }
    strcpy(list[k + 1], key);
    } //end for
} // end insertionSort3
```

The declaration of name initializes it with the eight names shown earlier. When run, the program produces the following output:

```
The sorted names are

Abdool, Zaid
Delwin, Mac
Mohamed, Abu
Samlal, Rawle
Singh, Krishna
Tawari, Tau
Taylor, Victor
Williams, Mark
```

9.5 Sort Parallel Arrays

It is quite common to have related information in different arrays. For example, suppose, in addition to name, we have an integer array id such that id[h] is an identification number associated with name[h], as shown here.

It is quite common to have related information in different arrays. For example, suppose, in addition to name, we have an integer array id such that id[h] is an identification number associated with name[h], as shown here.

	Name	id
0	Samlal, Rawle	8742
1	Williams, Mark	5418
2	Delwin, Mac	4833
3	Taylor, Victor	4230
4	Mohamed, Abu	8583
5	Singh, Krishna	2458
6	Tawari, Tau	5768
7	Abdool, Zaid	7746

Consider the problem of sorting the names in alphabetical order. At the end, we would want each name to have its correct ID number. So, for example, after the sorting is done, name[0] should contain A00001, Zaid and id[0] should contain 7746.

To achieve this, each time a name is moved during the sorting process, the corresponding ID number must also be moved. Since the name and ID number must be moved "in parallel," we say we are doing a *parallel sort* or we are sorting *parallel arrays*.

We rewrite insertionSort3 to illustrate how to sort parallel arrays. We simply add the code to move an ID whenever a name is moved. We call it parallelSort.

```
void parallelSort(int lo, int hi, int max, char list[][max], int id[]) {
//Sort the names in list[lo] to list[hi] in alphabetical order, ensuring
//that each name remains with its original id number.
//The maximum string size is max - 1 (one char taken up by \0).
    char key[max];
    for (int h = lo + 1; h <= hi; h++) {
        strcpy(key, list[h]);
        int m = id[h];  // extract the id number
        int k = h - 1; //start comparing with previous item
        while (k >= lo && strcmp(key, list[k]) < 0) {
            strcpy(list[k + 1], list[k]);
            id[k+ 1] = id[k];  // move up id when we move a name
            --k;
        }
        strcpy(list[k + 1], key);
        id[k + 1] = m; // store id in the same position as the name
    } //end for
} //end parallelSort
```

We test parallelSort by writing the following main routine:

```
#include <stdio.h>
#include <string.h>
#define MaxNameSize 14
#define MaxNameBuffer MaxNameSize+1
#define MaxNames 8
int main() {
    void parallelSort(int, int, int max, char [][max], int[]);
    char name[MaxNames][MaxNameBuffer] =
            {"Samlal, Rawle", "Williams, Mark","Delwin, Mac",
             "Taylor, Victor", "Mohamed, Abu","Singh, Krishna",
             "Tawari, Tau", "Abdool, Zaid" };
    int id[MaxNames] = {8742,5418,4833,4230,8583,2458,5768,3313};

    parallelSort(0, MaxNames-1, MaxNameBuffer, name, id);
    printf("\nThe sorted names and IDs are\n\n");
```

```
    for (int h = 0; h < MaxNames; h++)
        printf("%-18s %d\n", name[h], id[h]);
} //end main
```

When run, it produces the following output:

```
The sorted names and IDs are

Abdool, Zaid        3313
Delwin, Mac         4833
Mohamed, Abu        8583
Samlal, Rawle       8742
Singh, Krishna      2458
Tawari, Tau         5768
Taylor, Victor      4230
Williams, Mark      5418
```

We note, in passing, that "parallel arrays" can be more conveniently stored using *C structures*. We will discuss an example in Section 10.9 after we've learned a bit about structures.

9.6 Binary Search

Binary search is a very fast method for searching a list of items for a given one, *providing the list is sorted* (either ascending or descending). If the list is *not* in order, it can be sorted using any of the methods described earlier.

To illustrate the method, consider a list of 11 numbers, sorted in ascending order.

num

17	24	31	39	44	49	56	66	72	78	83
0	1	2	3	4	5	6	7	8	9	10

Suppose we wish to search for 56. The search proceeds as follows:

- First, we find the middle item in the list. This is 49 in position 5. We compare 56 with 49. Since 56 is bigger, we know that if 56 is in the list, it *must* be *after* position 5, since the numbers are in ascending order. In our next step, we confine our search to locations 6 to 10.

- Next, we find the middle item from locations 6 to 10. This is the item in location 8, that is, 72.

- We compare 56 with 72. Since 56 is smaller, we know that if 56 is in the list, it *must* be *before* position 8, since the numbers are in ascending order. In our next step, we confine our search to locations 6 to 7.

- Next, we find the middle item from locations 6 to 7. In this case, we can choose either item 6 or item 7. The algorithm we will write will choose item 6, that is, 56.

- We compare 56 with 56. Since they are the same, our search ends successfully, finding the required item in position 6.

Suppose we were searching for 60. The search will proceed as above until we compare 60 with 56 (in location 6).

- Since 60 is bigger, we know that if 60 is in the list, it must be *after* position 6, since the numbers are in ascending order. In our next step, we confine our search to locations 7 to 7. This is just one location.

- We compare 60 with item 7, that is, 66. Since 60 is smaller, we know that if 60 is in the list, it must be before position 7. Since it can't be after position 6 and before position 7, we conclude that it is not in the list.

At each stage of the search, we confine our search to some portion of the list. Let us use the variables lo and hi as the subscripts that define this portion. In other words, our search will be confined to the numbers from num[lo] to num[hi], inclusive.

Initially, we want to search the entire list so that we will set lo to 0 and hi to 10, in this example. How do we find the subscript of the middle item? We will use the calculation

mid = (lo + hi) / 2;

Since integer division will be performed, the fraction, if any, is discarded. For example when lo is 0 and hi is 10, mid becomes 5; when lo is 6 and hi is 10, mid becomes 8; and when lo is 6 and hi is 7, mid becomes 6.

As long as lo is less than or equal to hi, they define a nonempty portion of the list to be searched. When lo is equal to hi, they define a single item to be searched. If lo ever gets *bigger* than hi, it means we have searched the entire list and the item was not found.

Based on these ideas, we can now write a function binarySearch. To be more general, we will write it so that the calling routine can specify which portion of the array it wants the search to look for the item.

Thus, the function must be given the item to be searched for (key), the array (list), the start position of the search (lo), and the end position of the search (hi). For example, to search for the number 56 in the array num, above, we can issue the following call:

binarySearch(56, num, 0, 10)

The function must tell us the result of the search. If the item is found, the function will return its location. If not found, it will return -1.

```
int binarySearch(int key, int list[], int lo, int hi) {
//search for key from list[lo] to list[hi]
//if found, return its location; otherwise, return -1
    int mid;
    while (lo <= hi) {
        mid = (lo + hi) / 2;
        if (key == list[mid]) return mid; // found
        if (key < list[mid]) hi = mid - 1;
        else lo = mid + 1;
    }
    return -1; //lo and hi have crossed; key not found
} //end binarySearch
```

If item contains a number to be searched for, we can write the following code to call binarySearch and check the result of the search:

```
int ans = binarySearch(item, num, 0, 12);
if (ans == -1) printf("%d not found\n", item);
else printf("%d found in location %d\n", item, ans);
```

If we wish to search for item from locations i to j, we can write this:

```
int ans = binarySearch(item, num, i, j);
```

9.7 Word Frequency Count

Let's write a program to read an English passage and count the number of times each word appears. The output consists of an alphabetical listing of the words and their frequencies. We can use the following outline to develop our program:

```
while there is input
    get a word
    search for word
    if word is in the table
    add 1 to its count
    else
        add word to the table
        set its count to 1
    endif
endwhile
print table
```

This is a typical "search and insert" situation. We search for the next word among the words stored so far. If the search succeeds, we need only to increment its count. If the search fails, the word is put in the table, and its count set to 1.

A major design decision here is how to search the table, which, in turn, will depend on where and how a new word is inserted in the table. The following are two possibilities:

1. A new word is inserted in the next free position in the table. This implies that a sequential search must be used to look for an incoming word since the words would not be in any particular order. This method has the advantages of simplicity and easy insertion, but searching takes longer as more words are put in the table.

2. A new word is inserted in the table in such a way that the words are always in alphabetical order. This may entail moving words that have already been stored so that the new word may be slotted in the right place. However, since the table is in order, a binary search can be used to search for an incoming word.

For this method, searching is faster, but insertion is slower than in (1). Since, in general, searching is done more frequently than inserting, (2) might be preferable.

Another advantage of (2) is that, at the end, the words will already be in alphabetical order and no sorting will be required. If (1) is used, the words will need to be sorted to obtain the alphabetical order.

We will write our program using the approach in (2). The complete program is shown as Program P9.4.

Program P9.4

```
#include <stdio.h>
#include <string.h>
#include <ctype.h>
#include <stdlib.h>

#define MaxWords 50
#define MaxLength 10
#define MaxWordBuffer MaxLength+1

int main() {
    int getWord(FILE *, char[]);
    int binarySearch(int, int, char [], int max, char [][max]);
    void addToList(char[], int max, char [][max], int[], int, int);
    void printResults(FILE *, int max, char [][max], int[], int);
    char wordList[MaxWords][MaxWordBuffer], word[MaxWordBuffer];
    int frequency[MaxWords], numWords = 0;
    FILE * in = fopen("passage.txt", "r");
    if (in == NULL){
        printf("Cannot find file\n");
        exit(1);
    }
    FILE * out = fopen("output.txt", "w");
    if (out == NULL){
        printf("Cannot create output file\n");
        exit(2);
    }

    for (int h = 1; h <= MaxWords ; h++) frequency[h] = 0;

    while (getWord(in, word) != 0) {
        int loc = binarySearch (0, numWords-1, word, MaxWordBuffer,
            wordList);
        if (strcmp(word, wordList[loc]) == 0)
          ++frequency[loc]; //word found
    else //this is a new word
        if (numWords < MaxWords) { //if table is not full
            addToList(word, MaxWordBuffer, wordList, frequency, loc,
            numWords-1);
            ++numWords;
        }
```

```
        else fprintf(out, "'%s' not added to table\n", word);
    }
    printResults(out, MaxWordBuffer, wordList, frequency, numWords);
} // end main

int getWord(FILE * in, char str[]) {
// store the next word, if any, in str; convert word to lowercase
// return 1 if a word is found; 0, otherwise
    char ch;
    int n = 0;
    // read over white space
    while (!isalpha(ch = getc(in)) && ch != EOF) ; //empty while body
    if (ch == EOF) return 0;
    str[n++] = tolower(ch);
    while (isalpha(ch = getc(in)) && ch != EOF)
        if (n < MaxLength) str[n++] = tolower(ch);
    str[n] = '\0';
    return 1;
} // end getWord

int binarySearch(int lo, int hi, char key[], int max, char list[][max]) {
//search for key from list[lo] to list[hi]
//if found, return its location;
//if not found, return the location in which it should be inserted
//the calling program will check the location to determine if found
    while (lo <= hi) {
        int mid = (lo + hi) / 2;
        int cmp = strcmp(key, list[mid]);
        if (cmp == 0) return mid; // found
        if (cmp < 0) hi = mid - 1;
        else lo = mid + 1;
    }
    return lo; //not found; should be inserted in location lo
} //end binarySearch

void addToList(char item[], int max, char list[][max],
          int freq[], int p, int n) {
//adds item in position list[p]; sets freq[p] to 1
//shifts list[n] down to list[p] to the right
    for (int h = n; h >= p; h--) {
        strcpy(list[h+1], list[h]);
        freq[h+1] = freq[h];
    }

    strcpy(list[p], item);
    freq[p] = 1;
} //end addToList
```

```
void printResults(FILE *out, int max, char list[][max],
          int freq[], int n) {
    fprintf(out, "Words        Frequency\n\n");
    for (int h = 0; h < n; h++)
        fprintf(out, "%-15s %2d\n", list[h], freq[h]);
} //end printResults
```

Suppose the file passage.txt contains the following data (from *If* by *Rudyard Kipling*):

```
If you can dream—and not make dreams your master;
 If you can think—and not make thoughts your aim;
If you can meet with Triumph and Disaster
 And treat those two impostors just the same...
If you can fill the unforgiving minute
 With sixty seconds' worth of distance run,
Yours is the Earth...
```

When Program P9.4 was run with this data, it produced the following output:

Words	Frequency
aim	1
and	4
can	4
disaster	1
distance	1
dream	1
dreams	1
earth	1
fill	1
if	4
impostors	1
is	1
just	1
make	2
master	1
meet	1
minute	1
not	2
of	1
run	1
same	1
seconds	1
sixty	1
the	3
think	1

```
those        1
thoughts     1
treat        1
triumph      1
two          1
unforgivin   1
with         2
worth        1
you          4
your         2
yours        1
```

Comments on Program P9.4

- For our purposes, we assume that a word begins with a letter and consists of letters only. If you want to include other characters (such as a hyphen or apostrophe), you need change only the getWord function.

- MaxWords denotes the maximum number of distinct words catered for. For testing the program, we have used 50 for this value. If the number of distinct words in the passage exceeds MaxWords (50, say), any words after the 50th will be read but not stored, and a message to that effect will be printed. However, the count for a word already stored will be incremented if it is encountered again.

- MaxLength (we use 10 for testing) denotes the maximum length of a word. Strings are declared using MaxLength+1 (defined as MaxWordBuffer) to cater for \0, which must be added at the end of each string.

- main checks that the input file exists and that the output file can be created. Next, it initializes the frequency counts to 0. It then processes the words in the passage based on the outline shown at the beginning of this Section.

- getWord reads the input file and stores the next word found in its string argument. It returns 1 if a word is found and 0, otherwise. If a word is longer than MaxLength, only the first MaxLength letters are stored; the rest are read and discarded. For example, unforgiving is truncated to unforgivin using a word size of 10.

- All words are converted to lowercase so that, for instance, The and the are counted as the same word.

- We wrote binarySearch so that if the word is found, its location (loc, say) is returned. If not found, the location in which the word *should be inserted* is returned. The test

- `if (strcmp(word, wordList[loc]) == 0)`

- determines whether it was found. addToList is given the location in which to insert a new word. Words to the right of, and including, this location are ▪▪▪▪▪▪▪▪▪ ▪▪▪ ▪▪▪▪▪▪ ▪▪ ▪▪▪▪ for the new word.

- In declaring a function prototype, some compilers allow a two-dimensional array parameter to be declared as in char [][], with no size specified for either dimension. Others require that the size of the second dimension *must* be specified. Specifying the size of the second dimension should work on all compilers. In our program, we specify the second dimension using the parameter max, whose value will be supplied when the function is called.

9.8 Merge Sorted Lists

Merging is the process by which two or more ordered lists are combined into one ordered list. For example, given two lists of numbers, A and B, as follows:

A: 21 28 35 40 61 75
B: 16 25 47 54

They can be combined into one ordered list, C, as follows:

C: 16 21 25 28 35 40 47 54 61 75

The list C contains all the numbers from lists A and B. How can the merge be performed?

One way to think about it is to imagine that the numbers in the given lists are stored on cards, one per card, and the cards are placed face up on a table, with the smallest at the top. We can imagine the lists A and B as follows:

```
21      16
28      25
35      47
40      54
61
75
```

We look at the top two cards, 21 and 16. The smaller, 16, is removed and placed in C. This exposes the number 25. We have this:

```
21      25
28      47
35      54
40
61
75
```

The top two cards are now 21 and 25. The smaller, 21, is removed and added to C, which now contains 16 21. This exposes the number 28. We have this:

```
28     25
35     47
40     54
61
75
```

The top two cards are now 28 and 25. The smaller, 25, is removed and added to C, which now contains 16 21 25. This exposes the number 47. We have this:

```
28     47
35     54
40
61
75
```

The top two cards are now 28 and 47. The smaller, 28, is removed and added to C, which now contains 16 21 25 28. This exposes the number 35. We have this:

```
35     47
40     54
61
75
```

The top two cards are now 35 and 47. The smaller, 35, is removed and added to C, which now contains 16 21 25 28 35. This exposes the number 40. We have this:

```
40     47
61     54
75
```

The top two cards are now 40 and 47. The smaller, 40, is removed and added to C, which now contains 16 21 25 28 35 40. This exposes the number 61. We have this:

```
61     47
75     54
```

The top two cards are now 61 and 47. The smaller, 47, is removed and added to C, which now contains 16 21 25 28 35 40 47. This exposes the number 54. We have this:

```
61     54
75
```

The top two cards are now 61 and 54. The smaller, 54, is removed and added to C, which now contains 16 21 25 28 35 40 47 54. The list B has no more numbers.

We copy the remaining elements (61 75) of A to C, which now contains the following:

16 71 73 78 88 91 92 54 94 75

The merge is now completed.

At each step of the merge, we compare the smallest remaining number of A with the smallest remaining number of B. The smaller of these is added to C. If the smaller comes from A, we move on to the next number in A; if the smaller comes from B, we move on to the next number in B.

This is repeated until all the numbers in either A or B have been used. If all the numbers in A have been used, we add the remaining numbers from B to C. If all the numbers in B have been used, we add the remaining numbers from A to C.

We can express the logic of the merge as follows:

```
while (at least one number remains in both A and B) {
    if (smallest in A < smallest in B)
        add smallest in A to C
        move on to next number in A
    else
        add smallest in B to C
        move on to next number in B
    endif
}
if (A has ended) add remaining numbers in B to C
else add remaining numbers in A to C
```

9.8.1 Implement the Merge

Assume that an array A contains m numbers stored in A[0] to A[m-1], and an array B contains n numbers stored in B[0] to B[n-1]. Assume that the numbers are stored in ascending order. We want to merge the numbers in A and B into another array C such that C[0] to C[m+n-1] contains all the numbers in A and B sorted in ascending order.

We will use integer variables i, j, and k to subscript the arrays A, B, and C, respectively. "Moving on to the next position" in an array can be done by adding 1 to the subscript variable.

We can implement the merge with the following code:

```
i = 0; //i points to the first (smallest) number in A
j = 0; //j points to the first (smallest) number in B
k = -1; //k will be incremented before storing a number in C[k]
while (i < m && j < n) {
    if (A[i] < B[j]) C[++k] = A[i++];
    else C[++k] = B[j++];
}
if (i == m) //copy B[j] to B[n-1] to C
    for ( ; j < n; j++) C[++k] = B[j];
else // j == n, copy A[i] to A[m-1] to C
    for ( ; i < m; i++) C[++k] = A[i];
```

Program P9.5 shows a simple main function that tests the logic of our method. We write the merge as a function that, given the arguments A, m, B, n, and C, performs the merge and returns the number of elements, m+n, in C. When run, the program prints the contents of C, like this:

16 21 25 28 35 40 47 54 61 75

Program P9.5

```c
#include <stdio.h>
int main () {
    int merge(int[], int, int[], int, int[]);
    int A[] = {21, 28, 35, 40, 61, 75};
    int B[] = {16, 25, 47, 54};
    int C[20];
    int n = merge(A, 6 , B, 4, C);
    for (int h = 0; h < n; h++) printf("%d ", C[h]);
    printf("\n\n");
} //end main

int merge(int A[], int m, int B[], int n, int C[]) {
    int i = 0; //i points to the first (smallest) number in A
    int j = 0; //j points to the first (smallest) number in B
    int k = -1; //k will be incremented before storing a number in C[k]
    while (i < m && j < n) {
        if (A[i] < B[j]) C[++k] = A[i++];
        else C[++k] = B[j++];
    }
    if (i == m) ///copy B[j] to B[n-1] to C
        for ( ; j < n; j++) C[++k] = B[j];
    else // j == n, copy A[i] to A[m-1] to C
        for ( ; i < m; i++) C[++k] = A[i];
    return m + n;
} //end merge
```

As a matter of interest, we can also implement merge as follows:

```c
int merge(int A[], int m, int B[], int n, int C[]) {
    int i = 0; //i points to the first (smallest) number in A
    int j = 0; //j points to the first (smallest) number in B
    int k = -1; //k will be incremented before storing a number in C[k]
    while (i < m || j < n) {
        if (i == m) C[++k] = B[j++];
        else if (j == n) C[++k] = A[i++];
```

```
        else if (A[i] < B[j]) C[++k] = A[i++];
        else C[++k] = B[j++];
    }
    return m + n;
} //end merge
```

The while loop expresses the following logic: as long as there is at least one element to process in either A or B, we enter the loop. If we are finished with A (i == m), copy an element from B to C. If we are finished with B (j == n), copy an element from A to C. Otherwise, copy the smaller of A[i] and B[j] to C. Each time we copy an element from an array, we add 1 to the subscript for that array.

While the previous version implements the merge in a straightforward way, it seems reasonable to say that this version is a bit neater.

EXERCISES 9

1. In the voting problem of Section 8.15, print the results in alphabetical order by candidate name. Hint: in sorting the name array, when you move a name, make sure and move the corresponding item in the vote array.

2. In the voting problem of Section 8.15, print the results in descending order by candidate score.

3. Write a function to sort a double array in *ascending* order using selection sort. Do the sort by finding the *largest* number on each pass.

4. Write a program to find out, for a class of students, the number of families with 1, 2, 3, ... up to 8 or more children. The data consists of the number of children in each pupil's family, terminated by 0. Print the results in decreasing order by family-size popularity. That is, print the most popular family-size first and the least popular family-size last.

5. A survey of 10 pop artists is made. Each person votes for an artist by specifying the number of the artist (a value from 1 to 10). Write a program to read the names of the artists, followed by the votes, and find out which artist is the most popular. Choose a suitable end-of-data marker.

   Print a table of the results with the most popular artist first and the least popular last.

6. The *median* of a set of *n* numbers (not necessarily distinct) is obtained by arranging the numbers in order and taking the number in the middle. If *n* is odd, there is a unique middle number. If *n* is even, then the *average* of the two middle values is the median. Write a program to read a set of *n* positive integers (assume *n* < 100) and print their median; *n* is not given but 0 indicates the end of the data.

7. The *mode* of a set of *n* numbers is the number that appears most frequently. For example, the mode of 7 3 8 5 7 3 1 3 4 8 9 is 3.

Write a program to read a set of *n* arbitrary positive integers (assume *n* < 100) and print their mode; n is not given but 0 indicates the end of the data.

Write an efficient program to find the mode if it is known that the numbers all lie between 1 and 999, inclusive, with no restriction on the amount of numbers supplied; 0 ends the data.

8. An array num contains k numbers in num[0] to num[k-1], sorted in descending order. Write a function insertInPlace which, given num, k and another number x, inserts x in its proper position such that num[0] to num[k] are sorted in descending order. Assume the array has room for x.

9. A multiple-choice examination consists of 20 questions. Each question has 5 choices, labeled A, B, C, D, and E. The first line of data contains the correct answers to the 20 questions in the first 20 consecutive character positions, for example:

BECDCBAADEBACBAEDDBE

Each subsequent line contains the answers for a candidate. Data on a line consists of a candidate number (an integer), followed by 1 or more spaces, followed by the 20 answers given by the candidate in the next 20 *consecutive* character positions. An X is used if a candidate did not answer a particular question. You may assume all data are valid and stored in a file exam.dat. A sample line is:

4325   BECDCBAXDEBACCAEDXBE

There are at most 100 candidates. A line containing a "candidate number" 0 only indicates the end of the data.

Points for a question are awarded as follows:– correct answer: 4 points; wrong answer: -1 point; no answer: 0 points.

Write a program to process the data and print a report consisting of candidate number and the total points obtained by the candidate, *in ascending order by candidate number*. At the end, print the average number of points gained by the candidates.

10. An array A contains integers that first increase in value and then decrease in value, for example:

A

17	24	31	83	78	72	66	56	49	44	39
0	1	2	3	4	5	6	7	8	9	10

It is unknown at which point the numbers start to decrease. Write efficient code to copy the numbers from A to another array B so that B is sorted in ascending order. Your code must take advantage of the way the numbers are arranged in A. (*Hint*: perform a merge starting at both ends.)

11. You are given two integer arrays A and B each of maximum size 500. If A[0] contains m, say, then m numbers are stored in arbitrary order from A[1] to A[m]. If B[0] contains n, say, then n numbers are stored in arbitrary order from B[1] to B[n].

    Write code to merge the elements of A and B into another array C such that C[0] contains m+n and C[1] to C[m+n] contain the numbers in *ascending* order.

12. An anagram is a word or phrase formed by rearranging the letters of another word or phrase. Examples of one-word anagrams are: sister/resist and senator/treason. We can get more interesting anagrams if we ignore letter case and punctuation marks. Examples are: Time-table/Bet I'm Late, Clint Eastwood/Old West Action, and Astronomers/No More Stars.

    a. Write a function that, given two strings, returns 1 if the strings are anagrams of each other and 0 if they are not.

    b. An input file contains one word or phrase per line. Write a program to read the file and output all words/phrases (from the file) that are anagrams of each other. Print a blank line between each group of anagrams.

CHAPTER 10

■ ■ ■

Structures

In this chapter, we will explain the following:

- What a structure is

- How to declare a structure

- How to use typedef to work with structures more conveniently

- How to work with an array of structures

- How to search an array of structures

- How to sort an array of structures

- How to declare nested structures

- How to use structures to manipulate fractions

- How to use structures to store parallel arrays

- How structures can be passed to a function

10.1 The Need for Structures

In C, a structure is a collection of one or more variables, possibly of different types, grouped together under a single name for convenient handling.

There are many situations in which we want to process data about a certain entity or object but the data consists of items of various types. For example, the data for a student (the *student record*) may consist of several *fields* such as a name, address, and telephone number (all of type string); number of courses taken (integer); fees payable (floating-point); names of courses (string); grades obtained (character); and so on.

The data for a car may consist of manufacturer, model, and registration number (string); seating capacity and fuel capacity (integer); and mileage and price (floating-point). For a book, we may want to store author and title (string); price (floating-point); number of pages (integer); type of binding: hardcover, paperback, spiral (string); and number of copies in stock (integer).

Suppose we want to store data for 100 students in a program. One approach is to have a separate array for each field and use subscripts to link the fields together. Thus, name[i], address[i], fees[i], and so on, refer to the data for the ith student.

The problem with this approach is that if there are many fields, the handling of several parallel arrays becomes clumsy and unwieldy. For example, suppose we want to pass a student's data to a function via the parameter list. This will involve the passing of several arrays. Also, if we are sorting the students by name, say, each time two names are interchanged, we have to write statements to interchange the data in the other arrays as well. In such situations, C *structures* are convenient to use.

10.2 How to Declare a Structure

Consider the problem of storing a date in a program. A date consists of three parts: the day, the month, and the year. Each of these parts can be represented by an integer. For example, the date "September 14, 2006" can be represented by the day, 14; the month, 9; and the year, 2006. We say that a date consists of three *fields*, each of which is an integer.

If we want, we can also represent a date by using the *name* of the month, rather than its number. In this case, a date consists of three fields, one of which is a string and the other two are integers.

In C, we can declare a *date type* as a *structure* using the keyword struct. Consider this declaration:

```
struct date {int day, month, year;};
```

It consists of the keyword struct followed by some name we choose to give to the structure (date, in the example); this is followed by the declarations of the fields enclosed in left and right braces. Note the semicolon at the end of the declaration just before the right brace – this is the usual case of a semicolon ending a declaration. The right brace is followed by a semicolon, ending the struct declaration.

We could also have written the declaration as follows, where each field is declared individually:

```
struct date {
    int day;
    int month;
    int year;
};
```

This could be written as follows, but the style above is preferred for its readability:

```
struct date {int day; int month; int year;};
```

Given the struct declaration, we can declare variables of type struct date, as follows:

```
struct date dob; //to hold a "date of birth"
```

This declares dob as a "structure variable" of type date. It has three fields called day, month, and year. This can be pictured as follows:

We refer to the day field as dob.day, the month field as dob.month, and the year field as dob.year. In C, the period (.), as used here, is referred to as the *structure member operator*. To [illegible], a field is specified by the structure variable name, followed by a period, followed by the field name.

We could declare more than one variable at a time, as follows:

```
struct date borrowed, returned; //for a book in a library, say
```

Each of these variables has three fields: day, month, and year. The fields of borrowed are referred to by borrowed.day, borrowed.month, and borrowed.year. The fields of returned are referred to by returned.day, returned.month, and returned.year.

In this example, each field is an int and can be used in any context in which an int variable can be used. For example, to assign the date "November 14, 2015" to dob, we can use this:

```
dob.day = 14;
dob.month = 11;
dob.year = 2015;
```

This can be pictured as follows:

	day	month	year
dob	14	11	2015

We can also read values for day, month, and year with the following:

```
scanf("%d %d %d", &dob.day, &dob.month, &dob.year);
```

Suppose today was declared as follows:

```
struct date today;
```

Assuming we had stored a value in today, we could then assign all the fields of today to dob with the following:

```
dob = today;
```

This one statement is equivalent to the following:

```
dob.day = today.day;
dob.month = today.month;
dob.year = today.year;
```

We can print the "value" of dob with this:

```
printf("The party is on %d/%d/%d\n", dob.day, dob.month, dob.year);
```

For this example, the following will be printed:

```
The party is on 14/11/2015
```

Note that each field has to be printed individually. We *could* also write a function printDate, say, which prints a date given as an argument. The following program shows how printDate can be written and used.

```c
#include <stdio.h>

struct date {
   int day;
   int month;
   int year;
};

int main() {
   struct date dob;
   void printDate(struct date);

   dob.day = 14 ;
   dob.month = 11;
   dob.year = 2015;

   printDate(dob);
}

void printDate(struct date d) {
   printf("%d/%d/%d \n", d.day, d.month, d.year);
}
```

When run, the program prints

```
14/11/2015
```

We note, in passing, that C provides a date and time structure, tm, in the standard library. In addition to the date, it provides, among other things, the time to the nearest second. To use it, your program must be preceded by the following:

```c
#include <time.h>
```

The construct struct date is a bit cumbersome to use, compared to single word types such int or double. Fortunately, C provides us with typedef to make working with structures a little more convenient.

10.2.1 typedef

We can use `typedef` to give a name to Known variable, type, and data items can inform the given to declare variables of that type. We can also use `typedef` to construct shorter or more meaningful names for predefined C types or for user-declared types, such as structures. For example, the following statement declares a new type-name `Whole`, which is synonymous with the predefined type `int`:

```
typedef int Whole;
```

Note that `Whole` appears in the same position as a variable would, not right after the word `typedef`. We can then declare variables of type `Whole`, as follows:

```
Whole amount, numCopies;
```

This is exactly equivalent to

```
int amount, numCopies;
```

For those accustomed to the term `real` of languages like Pascal or FORTRAN, the following statement allows them to declare variables of type `Real`:

```
typedef float Real;
```

In this book, we use at least one uppercase letter to distinguish type names declared using `typedef`.

We could give a short, meaningful name, `Date`, to the date structure shown earlier with the following declaration:

```
typedef struct date {
    int day;
    int month;
    int year;
} Date;
```

Recall that C distinguishes between uppercase and lowercase letters so that `date` is different from `Date`. We could, if we wanted, have used any other identifier, such as `DateType`, instead of `Date`.

We could now declare "structure variables" of type `Date`, such as the following:

```
Date dob, borrowed, returned;
```

Notice how much shorter and neater this is compared to the following:

```
struct date dob, borrowed, returned;
```

Since there is hardly any reason to use this second form, we could omit date from the declaration above and write this:

```
typedef struct {
   int day;
   int month;
   int year;
} Date;
```

Thereafter, we can use Date whenever the struct is required. For example, we can rewrite printDate
as follows:

```
void printDate(Date d) {
   printf("%d/%d/%d \n", d.day, d.month, d.year);
}
```

To pursue the date example, suppose we want to store the "short" name – the first three letters, for example Aug – of the month. We will need to use a declaration such as this:

```
typedef struct {
   int day;
   char month[4]; //one position for \0 to end string
   int year;
} Date;
```

We can represent the date "November 14, 2015" in a Date variable dob with the following:

```
dob.day = 14;
strcpy(dob.month, "Nov");//remember to #include <string.h> to use strcpy
dob.year = 2015;
```

And we can write printDate as follows:

```
void printDate(Date d) {
   printf("%s %d, %d \n", d.month, d.day, d.year);
}
```

The call

```
printDate(dob);
```

will print this:

```
Nov 14, 2015
```

Suppose we want to store information about students. For each student, we want to store their name, age, and gender (male or female). Assuming that a name is no longer than 30 characters, we could use the following declaration:

```
typedef struct {
   char name[31];
   int age;
   char gender;
} Student;
```

We can now declare variables of type Student, as follows:

```
Student stud1, stud2;
```

Each of stud1 and stud2 will have its own fields – name, age, and gender. We can refer to these fields
as follows:

```
stud1.name stud1.age stud1.gender
stud2.name stud2.age stud2.gender
```

As usual, we can assign values to these fields or read values into them. And, if we want, we can assign all the fields of stud1 to stud2 with one statement:

```
stud2 = stud1;
```

10.3 Array of Structure

Suppose we want to store data on 100 students. We will need an array of size 100, and each element of the array will hold the data for one student. Thus, each element will have to be a structure – we need an "array of structures."

We can declare the array with the following, similar to how we say "int pupil[100]" to declare an integer array of size 100:

```
Student pupil[100];
```

This allocates storage for pupil[0], pupil[1], pupil[2], …, up to pupil[99]. Each element pupil[i] consists of three fields that can be referred to as follows:

```
pupil[i].name    pupil[i].age    pupil[i].gender
```

First we will need to store some data in the array. Assume we have data in the following format (name, age, gender):

```
"Jones, John" 24 M
"Mohammed, Lisa" 33 F
"Singh, Sandy" 29 F
"Layne, Dennis" 49 M
"END"
```

Suppose the data are stored in a file input.txt and in is declared as follows:

```
FILE * in = fopen("input.txt", "r");
```

If str is a character array, assume we can call the function

```
getString(in, str)
```

to store the next data string in quotes in str without the quotes. Also assume that readChar(in) will read the data and return the next non-whitespace character.

Exercise: Write the functions getString and readChar.

We can read the data into the array pupil with the following code:

```
int n = 0;
char temp[31];
getString(in, temp);
while (strcmp(temp, "END") != 0) {
   strcpy(pupil[n].name, temp);
   fscanf(in, "%d", &pupil[n].age);
   pupil[n].gender = readChar(in);
   n++;
   getString(in, temp);
}
```

At the end, n contains the number of students stored, and pupil[0] to pupil[n-1] contain the data for those students.

To ensure that we do not attempt to store more data than we have room for in the array, we should check that n is within the bounds of the array. Assuming that MaxItems has the value 100, this can be done by changing the while condition to the following:

```
while (n < MaxItems && strcmp(temp, "END") != 0)
```

or by inserting the following just after the statement n++; inside the loop:

```
if (n == MaxItems) break;
```

10.4 Search an Array of Structure

With the data stored in the array, we can manipulate it in various ways. For instance, we can write a function to search for a given name. Assuming the data is stored in no particular order, we can use a sequential search as follows:

```
int search(char key[], Student list[], int n) {
//search for key in list[0] to list[n-1]
//if found, return the location; if not found, return -1
   for (int h = 0; h < n; h++)
      if (strcmp(key, list[h].name) == 0) return h;
   return -1;
} //end search
```

Given the previous data, the call

```
search("Singh, Sandy", pupil, 4)
```

will return 2, and the following call will return -1:

```
search("Layne, Sandy", pupil, 4)
```

10.5 Sort an Array of Structure

Suppose we want the list of students in alphabetical order by name. It will be required to sort the array pupil. The following function uses an insertion sort to do the job. The process is identical to sorting an int array, say, except that the name field is used to govern the sorting.

```
void sort(Student list[], int n) {
//sort list[0] to list[n-1] by name using an insertion sort
   Student temp;
   int k;
   for (int h = 1; h < n; h++) {
      Student temp = list[h];
      k = h - 1;
      while (k >= 0 && strcmp(temp.name, list[k].name) < 0) {
         list[k + 1] = list[k];
         k = k - 1;
      }
   }
   list[k + 1] = temp;
} //end sort
```

Observe this statement:

```
list[k + 1] = list[k];
```

This assigns all the fields of list[k] to list[k+1].

If we want to sort the students in order by age, all we need to change is the while condition. To sort in ascending order, we write this:

```
while (k >= 0 && temp.age < list[k].age)
//move smaller numbers to the left
```

To sort in descending order, we write this:

```
while (k >= 0 && temp.age > list[k].age)
//move bigger numbers to the left
```

We could even separate the list into male and female students by sorting on the gender field. Since *F* comes before *M* in alphabetical order, we can put the females first by writing this:

```
while (k >= 0 && temp.gender < list[k].gender)
//move Fs to the left
```

And we can put the males first by writing this:

```
while (k >= 0 && temp.gender > list[k].gender)
//move Ms to the left
```

10.6 Read, Search, and Sort a Structure

We illustrate the ideas discussed earlier by writing Program P10.1. The program performs the following:

- Reads data for students from a file, input.txt, and stores them in an array of structures.

- Prints the data in the order stored in the array.

- Tests search by reading several names and looking for them in the array.

- Sorts the data in alphabetical order by name.

- Prints the sorted data.

The program also illustrates how the functions getString and readChar may be written. getString lets us read a string enclosed within *any* "delimiter" characters. For example, we could specify a string as $John Smith$ or "John Smith." This is a very flexible way of specifying a string. *Each* string can be specified with its own delimiters, which could be different for the next string. It is particularly useful for specifying strings that may include special characters such as the double quotes without having to use an escape sequence such as \".

Program P10.1

```
#include <stdio.h>
#include <stdlib.h>
#include <string.h>
#include <ctype.h>
#define MaxStudents 100
#define MaxNameLength 30
#define MaxNameBuffer MaxNameLength+1
typedef struct {
   char name[MaxNameBuffer];
   int age;
   char gender;
} Student;
```

```
int main() {
   Student pupil[MaxStudents];
   char aName[MaxNameBuffer];
   void getString(FILE *, char[]);
   int getData(FILE *, Student[]);
   int search(char[], Student[], int);
   void sort(Student[], int);
   void printStudent(Student);
   void getString(FILE *, char[]);

   FILE * in = fopen("input.txt", "r");
   if (in == NULL) {
      printf("Error opening input file.\n");
      exit(1);
   }

   int numStudents = getData(in, pupil);
   if (numStudents == 0) {
      printf("No data supplied for students");
      exit(1);
   }

   printf("\n");
   for (int h = 0; h < numStudents; h++) printStudent(pupil[h]);
   printf("\n");

   getString(in, aName);
   while (strcmp(aName, "END") != 0) {
      int ans = search(aName, pupil, numStudents);
      if (ans == -1) printf("%s not found\n", aName);
      else printf("%s found at location %d\n", aName, ans);
      getString(in, aName);
   }

   sort(pupil, numStudents);
   printf("\n");
   for (int h = 0; h < numStudents; h++) printStudent(pupil[h]);
} //end main

void printStudent(Student t) {
   printf("Name: %s Age: %d Gender: %c\n", t.name, t.age, t.gender);
} //end printStudent

int getData(FILE *in, Student list[]) {
   char temp[MaxNameBuffer];
   void getString(FILE *, char[]);
   char readChar(FILE *);
```

```
   int n = 0;
   getString(in, temp);
   while (n < MaxStudents && strcmp(temp, "END") != 0) {
      strcpy(list[n].name, temp);
      fscanf(in, "%d", &list[n].age);
      list[n].gender = readChar(in);
      n++;
      getString(in, temp);
   }
   return n;
} //end getData

int search(char key[], Student list[], int n) {
//search for key in list[0] to list[n-1]
//if found, return the location; if not found, return -1
   for (int h = 0; h < n; h++)
      if (strcmp(key, list[h].name) == 0) return h;
   return -1;
} //end search

void sort(Student list[], int n) {
//sort list[0] to list[n-1] by name using an insertion sort
   Student temp;
   int k;
   for (int h = 1; h < n; h++) {
      temp = list[h];
      k = h - 1;
      while (k >= 0 && strcmp(temp.name, list[k].name) < 0) {
         list[k + 1] = list[k];
         k = k - 1;
      }
      list[k + 1] = temp;
   } //end for
} //end sort

void getString(FILE * in, char str[]) {
// stores, in str, the next string within delimiters
// the first non-whitespace character is the delimiter
// the string is read from the file 'in'
   char ch, delim;
   int n = 0;
   str[0] = '\0';
   // read over white space
   while (isspace(ch = getc(in))) ; //empty while body
   if (ch == EOF) return;

   delim = ch;
   while (((ch = getc(in)) != delim) && (ch != EOF))
      str[n++] = ch;
```

```
        str[n] = '\0';
} // end getString
char readChar(FILE * in) {
    char ch;
    while (isspace(ch = getc(in))) ; //empty while body
    return ch;
} //end readChar
```

Suppose the file input.txt contains the following data:

```
"Jones, John" 24 M
"Mohammed, Lisa" 33 F
"Singh, Sandy" 29 F
"Layne, Dennis" 49 M
"Singh, Cindy" 16 F
"Ali, Imran" 39 M
"Kelly, Trudy" 30 F
"Cox, Kerry" 25 M
"END"
"Kelly, Trudy"
"Layne, Dennis"
"Layne, Cindy"
"END"
```

The program prints this:

```
Name: Jones, John Age: 24 Gender: M
Name: Mohammed, Lisa Age: 33 Gender: F
Name: Singh, Sandy Age: 29 Gender: F
Name: Layne, Dennis Age: 49 Gender: M
Name: Singh, Cindy Age: 16 Gender: F
Name: Ali, Imran Age: 39 Gender: M
Name: Kelly, Trudy Age: 30 Gender: F
Name: Cox, Kerry Age: 25 Gender: M

Kelly, Trudy found at location 6
Layne, Dennis found at location 3
Layne, Cindy not found

Name: Ali, Imran Age: 39 Gender: M
Name: Cox, Kerry Age: 25 Gender: M
Name: Jones, John Age: 24 Gender: M
Name: Kelly, Trudy Age: 30 Gender: F
Name: Layne, Dennis Age: 49 Gender: M
Name: Mohammed, Lisa Age: 33 Gender: F
Name: Singh, Cindy Age: 16 Gender: F
Name: Singh, Sandy Age: 29 Gender: F
```

10.7 Nested Structures

C allows us to use a structure as part of the definition of another structure – a structure within a structure, called a *nested* structure. Consider the Student structure. Suppose that, instead of age, we want to store the student's date of birth. This might be a better choice since a student's date of birth is fixed, whereas his age changes, and the field would have to be updated every year.

We could use the following declaration:

```
typedef struct {
   char name[31];
   Date dob;
   char gender;
} Student;
```

If mary is a variable of type Student, then mary.dob refers to her date of birth. But mary.dob is *itself* a Date structure. If necessary, we can refer to *its* fields with mary.dob.day, mary.dob.month, and mary.dob.year.

If we want to store a name in a more flexible way – for example, first name, middle initial, and last name, we could use a structure like this:

```
typedef struct {
   char first[21];
   char middle;
   char last[21];
} Name;
```

The Student structure now becomes the following, which contains two structures, Name and Date:

```
typedef struct {
   Name name; //assumes Name has already been declared
   Date dob; //assumes Date has already been declared
   char gender;
} Student;
```

If st is a variable of type Student,

st.name refers to a structure of the type Name;
st.name.first refers to the student's first name; and
st.name.last[0] refers to the first letter of her last name.

Now, if we want to sort the array pupil by last name, the while condition in the function sort becomes this:

```
while (k >= 0 && strcmp(temp.name.last, pupil[k].name.last) < 0)
```

A structure may be nested as deeply as you want. The dot (.) operator associates from left to right. If a, b, and c are structures, the construct

a.b.c.d

is interpreted as

((a.b).c).d

10.8 Work with Fractions

Consider the problem of working with fractions, where a fraction is represented by two integer values: one for the numerator and the other for the denominator. For example, 5/9 is represented by the two numbers 5 and 9.

We will use the following structure to represent a fraction:

```
typedef struct {
    int num;
    int den;
} Fraction;
```

If f is variable of type Fraction, we can store 5/9 in f with this:

```
f.num = 5;
f.den = 9;
```

This can be pictured as follows:

```
        num     den
   ┌───────┬───────┐
 f │   5   │   9   │
   └───────┴───────┘
```

We can also read two values representing a fraction and store them in f with a statement such as this:

```
scanf("%d %d", &f.num, &f.den);
```

We can write a function, printFraction, to print a fraction. It is shown in the following program.

```
#include <stdio.h>

typedef struct {
    int num;
    int den;
} Fraction;
```

```
int main() {
   void printFraction(Fraction);
   Fraction f;

   f.num = 5;
   f.den = 9;
   printFraction(f);
}

void printFraction(Fraction f) {
   printf("%d/%d", f.num, f.den);
}
```

When run, the program will print

5/9

10.8.1 Manipulate Fractions

We can write functions to perform various operations on fractions. For instance, since

$$\frac{a}{b} + \frac{c}{d} = \frac{ad + bc}{bd}$$

we can write a function to add two fractions as follows:

```
Fraction addFraction(Fraction a, Fraction b) {
   Fraction c;
   c.num = a.num * b.den + a.den * b.num;
   c.den = a.den * b.den;
   return c;
} //end addFraction
```

Similarly, we can write functions to subtract, multiply, and divide fractions.

```
Fraction subFraction(Fraction a, Fraction b) {
   Fraction c;
   c.num = a.num * b.den - a.den * b.num;
   c.den = a.den * b.den;
   return c;
} //end subFraction

Fraction mulFraction(Fraction a, Fraction b) {
   Fraction c;
   c.num = a.num * b.num;
   c.den = a.den * b.den;
   return c;
} //end mulFraction
```

```
Fraction divFraction(Fraction a, Fraction b) {
    Fraction c;
    c.num = a.num * b.den;
    c.den = a.den * b.num;
    return c;
} //end divFraction
```

To illustrate their use, suppose we want to find $\frac{2}{5}$ of $\{\frac{3}{7} + \frac{5}{8}\}$

We can do this with the following statements:

```
Fraction a, b, c, sum, ans;
a.num = 2; a.den = 5;
b.num = 3; b.den = 7;
c.num = 5; c.den = 8;
sum = addFraction(b, c);
ans = mulFraction(a, sum);
printFraction(ans);
```

Strictly speaking, the variables sum and ans are not necessary, but we've used them to simplify the explanation. Since an argument to a function can be an expression, we could get the same result with this:

```
printFraction(mulFraction(a, addFraction(b, c)));
```

When run, this code will print the following, which is the correct answer:

```
118/280
```

However, if you want, you can write a function to reduce a fraction to its lowest terms. This can be done by finding the highest common factor (HCF) of the numerator and denominator. You then divide the numerator and denominator by their HCF. For example, the HCF of 118 and 280 is 2 so 118/280 reduces to 59/140. Writing this function is left as an exercise.

10.9 A Voting Problem

This example will be used to illustrate several points concerning the passing of arguments to functions. It further highlights the differences between array arguments and simple-variable arguments. We will show how *a function can return more than one value to a calling function by using a structure*. To do so, we will write a program to solve the voting problem we met in Section 8.15. Here it is again:

> *Problem*: In an election, there are seven candidates. Each voter is allowed one vote for the candidate of their choice. The vote is recorded as a number from 1 to 7. The number of voters is unknown beforehand, but the votes are terminated by a vote of 0. Any vote that is not a number from 1 to 7 is an invalid (spoiled) vote.

A file, votes.txt, contains the names of the candidates. The first name is considered as candidate 1, the second as candidate 2, and so on. The names are followed by the votes. Write a program to read the data and evaluate the results of the election. Print all output to the file, results.txt.

Your output should specify the total number of votes, the number of valid votes, and the number of spoiled votes. This is followed by the votes obtained by each candidate and the winner(s) of the election.

Suppose the file votes.txt contains the following data:

```
Victor Taylor
Denise Duncan
Kamal Ramdhan
Michael Ali
Anisa Sawh
Carol Khan
Gary Olliverie

3 1 2 5 4 3 5 3 5 3 2 8 1 6 7 7 3 5
6 9 3 4 7 1 2 4 5 5 1 4 0
```

Your program should send the following output to results.txt:

```
Invalid vote: 8
Invalid vote: 9

Number of voters: 30
Number of valid votes: 28
Number of spoilt votes: 2

Candidate       Score
Victor Taylor     4
Denise Duncan     3
Kamal Ramdhan     6
Michael Ali       4
Anisa Sawh        6
Carol Khan        2
Gary Olliverie    3

The winner(s):
    Kamal Ramdhan
    Anisa Sawh
```

We now explain how we can solve this problem using C structures. Consider these declarations:

```c
typedef struct {
    char name[31];
    int numVotes;
} PersonData;
PersonData candidate[8];
```

Here, candidate is an array of structures. We will use candidate[1] to candidate[7] for the seven candidates; we will not use candidate[0]. This will allow us to work more naturally with the votes. For a vote v, say), candidate[v] will be updated. If we use candidate[0], we would have the awkward situation where for a vote v, candidate[v-1] would have to be updated.

An element candidate[h] is not just a single data item but a structure consisting of two fields. These fields can be referred to as follows:

candidate[h].name and candidate[h].numVotes

To make the program flexible, we will define the following symbolic constants:

```
#define MaxCandidates 7
#define MaxNameLength 30
#define MaxNameBuffer MaxNameLength+1
```

We also change the earlier declarations to the following:

```
typedef struct {
   char name[MaxNameBuffer];
   int numVotes;
} PersonData;
PersonData candidate[MaxCandidates+1];
```

The solution is based on the following outline:

```
initialize
process the votes
print the results
```

The function initialize will read the names from the file in and set the vote counts to 0. The file is passed as an argument to the function. We will read a candidate's name in two parts (first name and last name) and then join them together to create a single name that we will store in person[h].name. Data will be read for max persons. Here is the function:

```
void initialize(PersonData person[], int max, FILE *in) {
   char lastName[MaxNameBuffer];
   for (int h = 1; h <= max; h++) {
      fscanf(in, "%s %s", person[h].name, lastName);
      strcat(person[h].name, " ");
      strcat(person[h].name, lastName);
      person[h].numVotes = 0;
   }
} //end initialize
```

Processing the votes will be based on the following outline:

```
get a vote
while the vote is not 0
   if the vote is valid
      add 1 to validVotes
      add 1 to the score of the appropriate candidate
```

```
    else
       print invalid vote
       add 1 to spoiltVotes
    endif
    get a vote
endwhile
```

After all the votes are processed, this function will need to return the number of valid and spoiled votes. But how can a function return more than one value? It can, if the values are stored in a structure and the structure returned as the "value" of the function.

We will use the following declaration:

```
typedef struct {
   int valid, spoilt;
} VoteCount;
```

And we will write processVotes as follows:

```
VoteCount processVotes(PersonData person[], int max, FILE *in, FILE *out) {
   VoteCount temp;
   temp.valid = temp.spoilt = 0;

   int v;
   fscanf(in, "%d", &v);
   while (v != 0) {
      if (v < 1 || v > max) {
         fprintf(out, "Invalid vote: %d\n", v);
         ++temp.spoilt;
      }
      else {
         ++person[v].numVotes;
         ++temp.valid;
      }
      fscanf(in, "%d", &v);
   } //end while
   return temp;
} //end processVotes
```

Next, we write main, preceded by the compiler directives and the structure declarations.

```
#include <stdio.h>
#include <string.h>
#define MaxCandidates 7
#define MaxNameLength 30
#define MaxNameBuffer MaxNameLength+1

typedef struct {
   char name[MaxNameBuffer];
   int numVotes;
```

```
  } PersonData;
PersonData candidate[MaxCandidates];

typedef struct {
   int valid, spoilt;
} VoteCount;

int main() {
   void initialize(PersonData[], int, FILE *);
   VoteCount processVotes(PersonData[], int, FILE *, FILE *);
   void printResults(PersonData[], int, VoteCount, FILE *);

   PersonData candidate[MaxCandidates+1];
   VoteCount count;
   FILE *in = fopen("votes.txt", "r");
   FILE *out = fopen("results.txt", "w");

   initialize(candidate, MaxCandidates, in);
   count = processVotes(candidate, MaxCandidates, in, out);
   printResults(candidate, MaxCandidates, count, out);

   fclose(in);
   fclose(out);
} //end main
```

The declarations of PersonData and VoteCount come before main. This is done so that other functions can refer to them, without having to repeat the entire declarations. If they were declared in main, then the names PersonData and VoteCount would be known only in main, and other functions would have no access to them.

Now that we know how to read and process the votes, it remains only to determine the winner(s) and print the results. We will delegate this task to the function printResults.

Using the sample data, the array candidate will contain the values shown below after all the votes have been tallied (remember, we are not using candidate[0]).

	name	numVotes
1	Victor Taylor	4
2	Denise Duncan	3
3	Kamal Ramdhan	6
4	Michael Ali	4
5	Anisa Sawh	6
6	Carol Khan	2
7	Gary Olliverie	3

To find the winner, we must first find the largest value in the array. To do this, we will call a function getLargest as follows:

```
int win = getLargest(candidate, 1, MaxCandidates);
```

This will set win to the subscript of the largest value in the numVotes field from candidate[1] to candidate[7] (since MaxCandidates is 7):

In our example, win will be set to 3 since the largest value, 6, is in position 3. (6 is also in position 5, but we just need the largest value, which we can get from either position.)

Here is getLargest:

```
int getLargest(PersonData person[], int lo, int hi) {
//returns the index of the highest vote from person[lo] to person[hi]
   int big = lo;
   for (int h = lo + 1; h <= hi; h++)
      if (person[h].numVotes > person[big].numVotes) big = h;
   return big;
} //end getLargest
```

Now that we know the largest value is in candidate[win].numVotes, we can "step through" the array, looking for those candidates with that value. This way, we will find all the candidates, if there is more than one, with the highest vote and declare them as winners.

An outline of printResults is as follows:

```
printResults
   print the number of voters, valid votes and spoilt votes
   print the score of each candidate
   determine and print the winner(s)
```

The details are given in the function printResults:

```
void printResults(PersonData person[], int max, VoteCount c, FILE*out) {
   int getLargest(PersonData[], int, int);
   fprintf(out, "\nNumber of voters: %d\n", c.valid + c.spoilt);
   fprintf(out, "Number of valid votes: %d\n", c.valid);
   fprintf(out, "Number of spoilt votes: %d\n", c.spoilt);
   fprintf(out, "\nCandidate Score\n\n");

   for (int h = 1; h <= max; h++)
      fprintf(out, "%-15s %3d\n", person[h].name,
      person[h].numVotes);

   fprintf(out, "\nThe winner(s)\n");
   int win = getLargest(person, 1, max);
   int winningVote = person[win].numVotes;
   for (int h = 1; h <= max; h++)
      if (person[h].numVotes == winningVote) fprintf(out, "%s\n",
         person[h].name);
} //end printResults
```

Putting all the pieces together, we get Program P10.2, the program to solve the voting problem.

Program P10.2

```c
#include <stdio.h>
#include <string.h>
#define MaxCandidates 7
#define MaxNameLength 30
#define MaxNameBuffer MaxNameLength+1

typedef struct  {
   char name[MaxNameBuffer];
   int numVotes;
} PersonData;
PersonData candidate[MaxCandidates];

typedef struct {
   int valid, spoilt;
} VoteCount;

int main() {
   void initialize(PersonData[], int, FILE *);
   VoteCount processVotes(PersonData[], int, FILE *, FILE *);
   void printResults(PersonData[], int, VoteCount, FILE *);

   PersonData candidate[MaxCandidates+1];
   VoteCount count;
   FILE *in = fopen("votes.txt", "r");
   FILE *out = fopen("results.txt", "w");

   initialize(candidate, MaxCandidates, in);
   count = processVotes(candidate, MaxCandidates, in, out);
   printResults(candidate, MaxCandidates, count, out);

   fclose(in);
   fclose(out);
} //end main

void initialize(PersonData person[], int max, FILE *in) {
   char lastName[MaxNameBuffer];
   for (int h = 1; h <= max; h++) {
      fscanf(in, "%s %s", person[h].name, lastName);
      strcat(person[h].name, " ");
      strcat(person[h].name, lastName);
      person[h].numVotes = 0;
   }
} //end initialize
```

```
VoteCount processVotes(PersonData person[], int max, FILE *in, FILE *out) {
    VoteCount temp;
    temp.valid = temp.spoilt = 0;

    int v;
    fscanf(in, "%d", &v);
    while (v != 0) {
        if (v < 1 || v > max) {
            fprintf(out, "Invalid vote: %d\n", v);
            ++temp.spoilt;
        }
        else {
            ++person[v].numVotes;
            ++temp.valid;
        }
        fscanf(in, "%d", &v);
    } //end while
    return temp;
} //end processVotes

int getLargest(PersonData person[], int lo, int hi) {
//returns the index of the highest vote from person[lo] to person[hi]
    int big = lo;
    for (int h = lo + 1; h <= hi; h++)
        if (person[h].numVotes > person[big].numVotes) big = h;
    return big;
} //end getLargest

void printResults(PersonData person[], int max, VoteCount c, FILE *out) {
    int getLargest(PersonData[], int, int);
    fprintf(out, "\nNumber of voters: %d\n", c.valid + c.spoilt);
    fprintf(out, "Number of valid votes: %d\n", c.valid);
    fprintf(out, "Number of spoilt votes: %d\n", c.spoilt);
    fprintf(out, "\nCandidate Score\n\n");

    for (int h = 1; h <= max; h++)
        fprintf(out, "%-15s %3d\n", person[h].name, person[h].numVotes);

    fprintf(out, "\nThe winner(s)\n");
    int win = getLargest(person, 1, max);
    int winningVote = person[win].numVotes;
    for (int h = 1; h <= max; h++)
        if (person[h].numVotes == winningVote)
            fprintf(out, "%s\n", person[h].name);
} //end printResults
```

Suppose it was required to print the names of the candidates in *descending* order by numVotes. To do this, the structure array candidate must be sorted in descending order using the numVotes field to control the sorting. This could be done by the following function call:

```
sortByVote(candidate, 1, MaxCandidates);
```

sortByVote uses an insertion sort and is written using the formal parameter person (any name will do), as shown here:

```
void sortByVote(PersonData person[], int lo, int hi) {
//sort person[lo..hi] in descending order by numVotes
   PersonData insertItem;
  // process person[lo+1] to person[hi]
   for (int h = lo + 1; h <= hi; h++) {
      // insert person h in its proper position
      insertItem = person[h];
      int k = h -1;
      while (k >= lo && insertItem.numVotes > person[k].numVotes) {
         person[k + 1] = person[k];
         --k;
      }
      person[k + 1] = insertItem;
   }
} //end sortByVote
```

Observe that the structure of the function is pretty much the same as if we were sorting a simple integer array. The major difference is in the while condition where we must specify which field is used to determine the sorting order. (In this example, we also use >, rather than <, since we are sorting in descending order rather than ascending order.) When we are about to process person[h], we copy it to the temporary structure, insertItem. This frees person[h] so that person[h-1] may be shifted into position h, if necessary. To shift an array element to the right, we use the following simple assignment:

```
person[k + 1] = person[k];
```

This moves the entire structure (two fields, in this example).

If we need to sort the candidates in alphabetical order, we could use the function sortByName:

```
void sortByName(PersonData person[], int lo, int hi) {
//sort person[lo..hi] in alphabetical order by name
   PersonData insertItem;
  // process person[lo+1] to person[hi]
   for (int h = lo + 1; h <= hi; h++) {
      // insert person j in its proper position
      insertItem = person[h];
      int k = h -1;
```

```
    while (k > 0 && strcmp(insertItem.name, person[k].name) < 0) {
        person[k + 1] = person[k];
        --k;
    }
    person[k + 1] = insertItem;
  }
} //end sortByName
```

The function sortByName is identical with sortByVote except for the while condition, which specifies which field is used in comparisons and the use of < for sorting in ascending order. Note the use of the standard string function, strcmp, for comparing two names. If strcmp(s1, s2) is negative, it means that the string s1 comes before the string s2 in alphabetical order.

As an exercise, rewrite the program for solving the voting problem so that it prints the results in descending order by votes and in alphabetical order.

10.10 Pass Structures to Functions

In the voting problem, we saw examples where candidate, an array of structures, was passed to various functions. We now discuss some other issues that arise in passing a structure to a function.

Consider a structure for a "book type" with the following fields:

```
typedef struct {
   char author[31];
   char title[51];
   char binding;   //paperback, hardcover, spiral, etc.
   double price;
   int quantity;   //quantity in stock
} Book;
Book text;
```

This declares a new type called Book, and text is declared as a variable of type Book.

We could pass individual fields to functions in the usual way; for a simple variable, its value is passed, but, for an array variable, its address is passed. Thus:

```
fun1(text.quantity); // value of text.quantity is passed
fun2(text.binding);  // value of text.binding is passed
fun3(text.price);    // value of text.price is passed
```

but,

```
fun4(text.title); // address of array text.title is passed
```

We could even pass the first letter of the title, as follows:

```
fun5(text.title[0]); // value of first letter of title is passed
```

To pass the entire structure, we use this:

```
fun6(text);
```

Of course, the header for each of these functions must be written with the appropriate parameter type.

In the last example, the fields of text are copied to a temporary place (called the *run-time heap*), and the copy is passed to fun6; that is, the structure is passed "by value." If a structure is complicated or contains arrays, the copying operation could be time consuming. In addition, when the function returns, the values of the structure elements must be removed from the heap; this adds to the overhead – the extra processing required to perform a function call.

To avoid this overhead, the *address* of the structure could be passed. This can be done with the following statement:

```
fun6(&text);
```

However, further discussion involves a deeper knowledge of pointers that is beyond the scope of this book.

EXERCISES 10

1. Write a program to read names and phone numbers into a structure array. Request a name and print the person's phone number. Use binary search to look up the name.

2. Write a function that, given two date structures, d1 and d2, returns -1 if d1 comes before d2, 0 if d1 is the same as d2, and 1 if d1 comes after d2.

3. Write a function that, given two date structures, d1 and d2, returns the number of days that d2 is ahead of d1. If d2 comes before d1, return a negative value.

4. A time in 24-hour clock format is represented by two numbers; for example, 16 45 means the time 16:45: that is, 4:45 p.m.

   a. Using a structure to represent a time, write a function that, given two time structures, t1 and t2, returns the number of minutes from t1 to t2. For example, if the two given times are 16 45 and 23 25, your function should return 400.

   b. Modify the function so that it works as follows: if t2 is less than t1, take it to mean a time for the next day. For example, given the times 20:30 and 6:15, take this to mean 8.30 p.m. to 6.15 a.m. of the next day. Your function should return 585.

5. A length, specified in meters and centimeters, is represented by two integers. For example, the length 3m 75cm is represented by 3 75. Using a structure to represent a length, write functions to compare, add, and subtract two lengths.

6. A file contains the names and distances jumped by athletes in a long-jump competition. Using a structure to hold a name and distance (which is itself a structure as in Exercise 5), write a program to read the data and print a list of names and distance jumped in order of merit (best jumper first).

7. A data file contains registration information for six courses – CS20A, CS21A, CS29A, CS30A, CS35A, and CS36A. Each line of data consists of a seven-digit student registration number followed by six (ordered) values, each of which is 0 or 1. A value of 1 indicates that the student is registered for the corresponding course; 0 means the student is not. Thus, 1 0 1 0 1 1 means that the student is registered for CS20A, CS29A, CS35A, and CS36A, but not for CS21A and CS30A.

   You may assume that there are no more than 100 students and a registration number 0 ends the data.

   Write a program to read the data and produce a class list for each course. Each list consists of the registration numbers of those students taking the course.

8. At a school's bazaar, activities were divided into stalls. At the close of the bazaar, the manager of each stall submitted information to the principal consisting of the name of the stall, the income earned, and its expenses. Here are some sample data:

   ```
   Games 2300.00 1000.00
   Sweets 900.00 1000.00
   ```

   a. Create a structure to hold a stall's data

   b. Write a program to read the data and print a report consisting of the stall name and net income (income – expenses), in order of decreasing net income (that is, with the most profitable stall first and the least profitable stall last). In addition, print the number of stalls, the total profit or loss of the bazaar, and the stall(s) that made the most profit. Assume that a line containing xxxxxx only ends the data.

Index

Get the eBook for only $5!

Why limit yourself?

Now you can take the weightless companion with you wherever you go and access your content on your PC, phone, tablet, or reader.

Since you've purchased this print book, we're happy to offer you the eBook in all 3 formats for just $5.

Convenient and fully searchable, the PDF version enables you to easily find and copy code—or perform examples by quickly toggling between instructions and applications. The MOBI format is ideal for your Kindle, while the ePUB can be utilized on a variety of mobile devices.

To learn more, go to www.apress.com/companion or contact support@apress.com.

Printed in the United States
By Bookmasters